ALSO BY MELISSA WELLER

A Good Bake

Very Good Bread

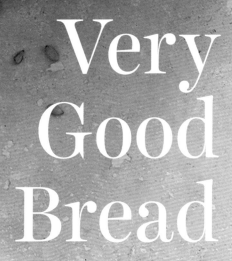

Very Good Bread

The Science of Dough and
the Art of Making Bread at Home

Melissa Weller

Photographs by Dana Gallagher

ALFRED A. KNOPF   NEW YORK   2024

THIS IS A BORZOI BOOK PUBLISHED BY ALFRED A. KNOPF

www.aaknopf.com

Knopf, Borzoi Books, and the colophon are registered
trademarks of Penguin Random House LLC.

LIBRARY OF CONGRESS CATALOGING-IN-PUBLICATION DATA
Names: Weller, Melissa, author. | Gallagher, Dana, photographer.
Title: Very good bread : the science of dough and the art of making
    bread at home / Melissa Weller ; photographs by Dana Gallagher.
Description: First edition. | New York : Alfred A. Knopf, 2024. |
    Includes index.
Identifiers: LCCN 2023048484 | ISBN 9780593320402 (hardcover) |
    ISBN 9780593320419 (ebook)
Subjects: LCSH: Cooking (Bread) | Bread. | LCGFT: Cookbooks.
Classification: LCC TX769 .W388 2024 | DDC 641.81/5—dc23/
    eng/20231205
LC record available at https://lccn.loc.gov/2023048484

Jacket photograph by Dana Gallagher
Jacket design by Kelly Blair

Manufactured in China
First Edition

For my son, Wyatt

Contents

Introduction

When I am asked what I do, I say, "I am a baker." I bake things. I am not a pastry chef. I bake things. In my career as a baker, I have primarily focused on baking bread. Bread is my passion. And bread is about science and chemistry. It ties my former career as a chemical engineer together with my current career as a baker. It is something that I do not get tired of and always continue to learn more about.

I have always been attracted to all things European. Growing up in central Pennsylvania, I dreamed of traveling throughout Europe. My parents couldn't afford a European vacation, though, and instead, summers were spent camping at the seashore. My academic goals were no different. Though I wanted to study French, I entered college as a chemical engineering major with a course load full of science and math classes and very few, if any, free electives. During my freshman year, I was fortunate to place out of the required English class, and I signed up for a French class in its place. I was one of the worst in the class. I was shy to speak, and my diction skills were horrible. My French professor continuously told me not to translate the words in my head, but to just understand them. What did that mean? I hired a tutor and gradually improved. I was determined to study French with the hope that someday I could study in France.

By the end of my freshman year and without my parents' permission, I enrolled in a dual degree program. I continued to study chemical engineering, but this way, I could also continue to learn French. When the time came to study in France my junior year, I was ecstatic. Through my university, I lived with a French family in Tours, in the center of the Loire Valley. My time in France changed me, and all the new foods around me rocked my world. Everything tasted better—the bread, the butter, the pastries, even the Granny Smith apples. I quickly became obsessed with the baguettes and the brioche I tried; I wanted to know how to make them myself. That summer, when I returned home to central Pennsylvania, I began making brioche à tête at home. They were dense and tasted like yeast. They were a far cry from what I had tasted in France, and I wanted to know how to make them better!

After college I began working as a chemical engineer in Allentown, Pennsylvania, and in my free time I continued to read cookbooks, devouring anything related to bread and pastry. When many of my friends and peers were starting business school, I decided to move to San Francisco and work in restaurants. My time in San Francisco was inspirational. I was immersed in an industry I was passionate about. I went to almost every top restaurant to taste their desserts, and I sought out all the good bakeries. I bought enough cookbooks to fill a room, and I continued to bake at home. I learned how to make puff pastry from Dorie Greenspan's *Baking with Julia* and I learned about sourdough from *Nancy Silverton's Breads from the La Brea Bakery*. I still wanted to learn how to make baguettes like those I had tried in France, so I moved to New York and enrolled at the French Culinary Institute in New York City.

After culinary school, I still had a lot to learn, and I focused on getting experience. It was easier twenty years ago to work in a restaurant under an esteemed pastry chef than it was to find a bakery to learn to make the bread I craved. My first job was under Gina DePalma, the extremely talented pastry chef at Babbo Ristorante. From her I learned more than just Italian pastries and desserts. I learned how to set up an efficient production. She became my mentor, and she helped me get my first bread baking job at Bread Alone in the Catskills.

My job at Bread Alone during the summer of 2007 was intense. It was unlike the delicate pastry work at Babbo. I worked as a mixer and was responsible for over four thousand pounds of dough daily. This was a manual job, and it required strength. There were two large mixers, each working through hundreds of pounds of dough at one time. It was my job to get all of the mixes done in an efficient and timely manner. If one mixer was busy mixing the dough, I needed to be scaling the ingredients for the second mixer. Once the second mixer was going, I needed to quickly empty the dough from the first mixer into the fermentation tubs. This required an incredible amount of strength and stamina. It forced me to focus on how to improve my speed in ways that did not require strength, like memorizing the formulas for all the doughs.

I took this skill set with me to Sullivan Street Bakery. Determined to become a strong baker, I focused on perfecting all the different positions at the bakery. I began as a mixer and moved up to scaling the dough. We used a balance scale, and you needed to cut and scale the dough quickly enough so that none of the shapers were waiting while you scaled pieces for them. What this meant was that I needed to know the weight of a certain amount of dough just by feeling it. I scaled dough for what seemed like months before I was "permitted" to begin shaping. Shaping came quickly to me and then came baking. I learned about the efficiency of maintaining a full oven, about oven hot spots and oven repair. I made beautiful Italian loaves of bread, and I began to get an intuitive feel for proofing that bread.

After working at Sullivan Street Bakery for one year, I left to work as the head baker at Thomas Keller's Per Se. To be offered the head baker position, I needed to prepare a tasting of five to six different breads that I prepared in the restaurant's kitchen. I was very nervous for the tasting and felt underqualified. I had just over one year of experience as a baker, and my skill set was focused on Italian breads. I did not know how to make a baguette, and this was part of the tasting! I decided to get very prepared. I took a baguette and bread making class in Minneapolis with the Bread Bakers Guild of America, and I made a very detailed step-by-step schedule of how I would prepare all the breads. There were five chefs present to taste my work, and even though I made many mistakes, everyone agreed that the breads tasted exceptionally good. And with my fine-dining experience and bakery experience, I was offered the head baker position. I was nervous and ecstatic at once.

At Per Se I learned how to perfect baguettes and other French breads. I must have scored thousands of baguettes and épis (those baguettes that are cut with scissors to resemble a wheat sheaf). We baked everything in a classic electric three-deck French oven. There were many times the oven would break or one of the glass front doors would break, and I learned a lot about oven repair!

I left Per Se when I was pregnant with my son. And after my son was born, I looked for something that would allow me time with him while continuing to pursue the craft of baking. Roberta's, a pizza restaurant, was a ten-minute commute from my apartment. It felt like the wild west, 180 degrees from the perfection of French bread at Per Se. There was an outdoor wood-fired oven, a space to work indoors, and a blank canvas on what I could create. I was drawn to the wood-fired oven, learning to bake at different temperatures and different heat sources, and I was smitten with the idea that I could create my own breads.

When I departed Roberta's and began making bagels at Sadelle's, I could not have anticipated that the bagels would receive the rave reviews that they did. I was simply happy to challenge myself with a new baking project. I wanted to learn how to make the best, most authentic bagels. To me that means learning about their history, understanding the science of the dough, and mastering their bake.

I believe that my greatest strength as a baker is my willingness to learn. I always want to know more. And thanks to my varied baking experiences, I have been fortunate enough to accumulate a wealth of recipes and techniques for all different types and styles of bread. Mastering bread baking is not just about mastering your skills making baguettes, it's about understanding and mastering bagels and pizza, which are bread, too. It's about understanding mixing and fermentation, shaping and baking. It takes patience and organization, lots of both, actually. Bread baking can be intimidating because you are working with yeast, a living thing. When I began baking bread, there were very few books that explained the science—the hows and the whys. Thankfully, there are so many more resources available today.

I hope this book becomes a resource for you. The first chapter is a bread primer, and it has two recipes that are building blocks for the more complicated recipes in later chapters. If you are patient and curious and follow the recipes carefully, you, too, will learn how to bake very good bread at home.

Setting Yourself Up for Success

Baking is all about precision and about chemistry. You put one thing into a hot oven, where it undergoes a transformation and emerges as another. Each step along the way, as well as many other factors, influences the final product. Because of this, I am very particular about how I execute even the most minute tasks. Below are some of the steps and considerations that I take throughout these recipes, and why.

Read the Recipe

Read the recipe through from start to finish before you do anything else. I'm sure you've heard this piece of advice before, but I can't stress how essential it is, and how much easier it will make your life in the end. This way you will understand the complete time frame and know how to plan ahead.

Write a Baking Schedule

After reading the recipe from beginning to end, go back through the recipe with a piece of paper and pen in hand, and write out a baking schedule. I write my schedule on a piece of paper, factoring in the parameters of my own day. Here is a sample of what your schedule might look like:

Day One

This day is about getting the starter ready and mixing the dough. At the end of the day, the dough is shaped and then retarded in the refrigerator overnight.

8:00 a.m. Mix the starter.

10:00 a.m. Autolyse the water and the flours for the dough.

12:00 p.m. Add the sourdough starter to the dough.

12:30 p.m. Add the salt to the dough.

1:00 p.m. First stretch and fold.

1:30 p.m. Second stretch and fold.

2:00 p.m. Third stretch and fold.

2:30 p.m. Fourth stretch and fold.

3:30 p.m. Final stretch and fold.

4:30 p.m. Shape and retard the loaf overnight.

Day Two

This is the baking day. The loaf can be baked at any time throughout the day. I like to bake it early in the morning.

8:00 a.m. Preheat the oven.
8:30 a.m. Bake the loaf.
9:20 a.m. Remove the loaf from the oven and let it cool.

Mise en Place

This is a French culinary term for "everything in place," and it refers to having all your ingredients in front of you and prepared. Get out all your ingredients, as well as the equipment and tools you are going to need for a recipe. Prep and measure your ingredients, and once you are done with them, put away the containers that those ingredients came in. Mise en place also includes making sure your sourdough starter is ready to use.

Work Clean

Before you begin, clear your work area of anything you don't need. And as you proceed with a recipe, clean up your work area as you go. Having a neat and clean work area is something that really separates the amateurs from the pros, and it is something I really stress when I am teaching. Working clean makes you proud of what you are doing. It also results in neater-looking breads.

Preheating the Oven and Checking Its Temperature

I am very specific about how I preheat my oven. First, I give ample time to preheat—usually 20 to 30 minutes. Keep an oven thermometer in your oven and confirm that it has reached the desired temperature before adding your bread to the oven. Before I got a new, better oven in my apartment, I used to keep a baking stone on the floor of my oven at all times. With a home oven, especially a weak apartment oven like the one I baked in for many years at home, the heat rushes out every time you open the oven door. But the heat penetrates the stone, so if you keep the stone in the oven, the oven better maintains its temperature when you open and close the oven door or introduce cold dough.

Weighing vs. Measuring

Professional bakers weigh ingredients—they do not measure. This may feel foreign to you at first because you've been using measuring cups all your life. But once you get used to weighing, you'll see that it is actually easier and much less messy than measuring by volume. It's actually quite simple: You put a bowl on a food scale; next, you tare the scale (zero it out) so you're not weighing the bowl. Then add the first ingredient you are going to weigh to the bowl. Once you've added it, tare (zero out) the scale again so it's back at zero and add the next ingredient. Continue until you've added all of the ingredients that are going into that bowl. Weighing ingredients is also much more accurate than measuring. Because there will always be variations in the density of ingredients, there will always be variations in volumetric measurements; weighed measurements, on the other hand, are always precise. I'm trained to be precise, so I always weigh my ingredients.

Metric is the system of measuring used throughout the world except in the United States. Metric weight is measured in terms of grams and kilograms. Bread bakers prefer to use metric measurements rather than ounces and pounds. The reason for this is that the metric system works in increments of 10, and it makes formulating recipes using baker's percentages easier. You base a recipe on 1 kilogram of flour. If you decide you want water at a 70% ratio, then you know to add 0.700 kilograms, or 700 grams, water. Salt is usually 2.2%, so you know to add 22 grams. So the math is easy. Because I am a bread baker, this book is in metric. I also give volumetric measures to be helpful.

Temperature of Ingredients

Temperature is an important factor when you're baking, especially when you're working with yeast and sourdough starter. The rate at which yeast grows and ferments is dictated by the temperature of both the ingredients and the environment. When I bake, I always consider the temperature, and throughout these recipes, you'll see me referring to temperatures often. So just be mindful of temperatures when you're baking. What's your room temperature? What's the temperature of the liquid in your recipe? What's the temperature of your flour?

Ingredients

I try to use the best ingredients I can find in whatever I am baking. At home, having the right ingredients requires some organization, particularly with breadmaking when a recipe calls for a special flour. I am by nature a planner and an organizer, so I try my best to plan out what I want to make in advance. But often, I get the urge to make something, and of course I don't have everything I need to make it. Though I usually source my specialty flours online, on these occasions I just run to the grocery store and get the best flour they have. As important as it is to use good ingredients—and I do believe it is—in the end, fresh homemade bread is special in and of itself, and whatever you make it with, you will enjoy it.

Butter

I use unsalted butter for baking and salted butter to spread on freshly baked bread or toast. Using unsalted butter for baking is common in professional kitchens, the idea being that if you start with unsalted butter, you can control how much salt you use. These recipes have been tested using Land O'Lakes butter, which is a very consistent product and also widely available. When I buy salted butter for spreading, I like to splurge: I seek out beurre de baratte, which is a French hand-churned salted butter from Normandy.

Eggs

I use large eggs because I can count on each one weighing about 50 grams.

Flour

Bread flour Bread flour is a white wheat flour and the base of the vast majority of these recipes. The bran (the outer coating) and the germ (the part that becomes a plant) of the wheat kernel have been removed and what is left is the endosperm, which is made up of starch (polymers amylose and amylopectin), gluten-forming proteins, and vitamins and minerals. Bread flour has more protein than all-purpose, pastry, and cake flours. The more protein in flour, the more gluten will form, and the stronger and more elastic your dough will be.

There are two gluten-forming proteins: glutenin and gliadin. When water is introduced to the flour, the two proteins combine to form gluten. Glutenin proteins are longer pieces that are strong and stretchy, whereas gliadin proteins are smaller and compact and give flow to the dough. Different bread flours may have similar protein content but can behave differently based on how much glutenin versus gliadin they have. At home, I use King Arthur Unbleached Bread Flour. It has a protein content of 12.7% and is a versatile bread flour.

Brown rice flour

Brown rice flour is gluten-free, with a coarse texture. I use it to dust proofing baskets and linens because it does not absorb into the dough and prevents it from sticking to its proofing liner. It can be used interchangeably with rye flour for this purpose.

Buckwheat flour

Buckwheat flour is gluten-free. Buckwheat has a distinct brownish-gray color (I think it's pretty) and an even more distinct earthy flavor. In France, buckwheat is grown in Brittany in the northwest, where it is commonly used in savory crepes called galettes. I was inspired by a trip to Paris to make buckwheat baguettes. Look for stone-ground flour, locally milled if possible. My go-to buckwheat flour comes from Anson Mills, where they grow a Japanese heirloom variety.

Dark-roasted malted barley flour

Dark-roasted malted barley flour is barley that has been sprouted, then roasted to a dark brown color and milled to a fine powder. It is commonly found in European bakeries. I purchase dark-roasted malted barley from beer brewing supply companies and then mill it at home. (I have used both a home flour mill and a burr mill coffee grinder with success.) I have also purchased the flour directly online.

Durum flour

Durum flour comes from durum wheat, a species of wheat that is high in protein and super hard (*durum* is Latin for "hard"). Because it is so solid, it requires a special mill to break it down, first into coarse semolina, and then more finely for durum flour. Durum flour has a yellow hue and a nutty, toasty flavor profile.

Einkorn flour

Einkorn flour comes from an ancient variety of wheat. It behaves similarly to spelt flour (see opposite) because it has a high protein content primarily from gliadin and does not contain much glutenin. The gliadin makes it very stretchable or extensible, but does not offer strength or elasticity.

High-gluten flour

High-gluten flour is what I use when I make bagels. The higher protein content contributes to their chewiness. I typically prefer a protein content of 13.5% or higher, but when I am pressed for time, I have also substituted bread flour with equally good results.

Rye flour

Rye flour is heartier than wheat. Hardy rye grains grow in harsher, colder climates. Rye flours are typically available as light, medium, and dark rye. Light rye flour comes from the endosperm of the rye kernel. It is low in protein and high in starch. Medium rye flour contains the germ and the endosperm; and dark rye flour contains not only the germ and endosperm, but also the outer layers of the rye kernel, where you find the bran and protein. The protein in dark rye flour can be high, but it is gliadin and does not have the ability to stretch and expand the way glutenin does. All the recipes here use rye in combination with bread flour so that there is gluten to give the loaves structure. At home I seek out whole-grain dark rye flour, like the organic whole dark rye flour from Central Milling.

Spelt flour   Spelt flour is from a strain of wheat native to Europe. Spelt flour is highly extensible because it is high in gliadin and low in glutenin. Extensibility is the ability of the dough to stretch and flow. Adding a small proportion of spelt flour to bread flour helps create a bread dough that can be stretched more easily without tearing. I like to use spelt flour in baguette and pizza dough for this reason.

Whole wheat bread flour   Whole wheat bread flour has a high protein content and contains the bran, germ, and endosperm of the wheat. I like to use finely milled whole wheat bread flour, where the entire wheat kernel is finely milled including the bran. The texture is not as coarse as the flour where the components are separated and the bran is added back in. At home I prefer Central Milling's organic whole wheat bread flour. When I am in a pinch, I buy whole wheat flour that's not labeled as bread flour. I find that many common brands of whole wheat flour have protein contents of at least 12%, which is perfect for breadmaking.

Nonstick Cooking Spray

Professional bakeries use nonstick cooking spray to grease baking pans and sheets. It is easy to use and efficient—it is easy to get a thin, even, and thorough coat that gets into the crevices of any shape of pan. I use Pam spray at home.

Salt

Fine sea salt   Fine sea salt is the type of salt I use exclusively in my baking. Professional bakeries use large quantities of salt typically purchased as fifty-pound bags of fine sea salt. To match the salt I use at bakeries, I like to use La Baleine fine sea salt at home. Sea salt can be used interchangeably with other types of salt, such as kosher salt, but only if you weigh it; the volumes of different types of salt vary considerably.

Flaky sea salt   Flaky sea salt is for when I want to add a pinch of large flaky, mineral-tasting salt on top of a baked good as a finishing touch. The easiest such salt to find is Maldon, which is from England. I also use a similar Nordic salt. Both have large thin shard-like flakes that add a wonderful crunchy element to foods.

Kosher salt   I use Diamond Crystal brand kosher salt for curing fish. Diamond Crystal contains no additives or anticaking agents, which means it is less dense and dissolves more easily.

Seeds and Spices

I look for high-quality seeds and spices. Most of my seeds for bagel making, like sesame and poppy, and my dehydrated garlic come from Nuts.com. I love the turmeric, nutmeg, and cardamom from Diaspora Co.; SOS Chefs in New York City supplies me with cumin, cinnamon, black peppercorns, and the bulk of my spices.

Sourdough Starter

A starter is a natural leavening (a mix of flour, water, and natural yeast) that is used to make bread rise. It is what gives sourdough bread its characteristic sour, or tangy, flavor. See Making a Sourdough Starter from Scratch (page xxviii) to make your own. In a pinch, you can also buy it from your local bakery, or order it online from King Arthur Flour.

Sweeteners

Granulated sugar

I stick with Domino's or, if I'm in California, C&H, because my priority when choosing a sugar to bake with is consistent texture. Both are pure cane sugars.

Malted barley syrup

Malted barley syrup is an unrefined sweetener made from malted (sprouted) barley. It is traditionally used to sweeten bagels. Honey can also be used to sweeten bagels, which is more typical of Montreal-style bagels.

Water

Water is one of the main ingredients in making bread. I live in New York City and use tap water. The New York City water supply is one of the largest unfiltered water supplies in the country. I do not use bottled or filtered water because my water tastes good. (In fact, many people insist that the composition of New York City water is responsible for the quality of its bagels, though there is much more to good bagel and bread making than that.) I have made excellent bread and bagels in many different cities using good tap water. If you prefer or need to filter the tap water you drink, then I recommend that you do the same with the water you use to make your bread.

Yeast

I love fresh yeast, and in my professional kitchens, I use fresh yeast more often than not. But when I bake at home, I use only instant yeast because it is so easy to get. You can buy instant yeast in the baking section of grocery stores in little packets, although I suggest you seek out one-pound bags from a baking supply store or online sources. The yeast I buy, both for home baking and in my professional kitchens, is SAF instant yeast, which comes in a one-pound red bag. You can find it easily from online sources and some specialty food stores. Store it in the freezer and dip into it as needed; you could bake every recipe in this book and never have to buy another packet of yeast. If you do buy the small packets, the most common brand you will see is Fleischmann's, which is labeled RapidRise Instant Yeast/Fast-Acting. It is the same thing as the SAF instant yeast.

Equipment and Tools

I don't like to tell anyone that they have to go out and spend a bunch of money just to make my recipes, but baking does require specific vessels—different sizes and shapes of pans are just tools of the trade. Here I list the equipment that I use in my day-to-day life, baking at home or in professional kitchens, that makes baking easy and more enjoyable.

Equipment

Aluminum Baking Sheets

I use 12-gauge commercial baking sheets that have a lip, or rim, around them, usually sold as "sheet pans." They conduct heat evenly and they don't buckle in the oven the way some baking sheets do. My home kitchen is stocked with half-sheet pans (18 × 13 inches), which is what I refer to in this book as a "baking sheet." Since this is a standardized product, they stack well, which means you can store a lot of them in your kitchen with no problem. It's a good idea to have at least four, but two will do the trick, sometimes with some juggling involved.

Baking Stone

I have a baking stone that I use when I load bread directly into the oven (i.e., not in or on a pan), like baguettes or pizza, and bagels and bialys. I recommend choosing a large rectangular stone, which may also be sold as a pizza stone. My stone measures 20 × 13½ inches, and it fits on a rack in my oven.

Bannetons

I use round wicker baskets called bannetons to proof my loaves. I purchase them from the San Francisco Baking Institute. They are 8 to 9 inches in diameter and come with an elastic linen liner. But you can also easily work with what you have in your own kitchen: just choose bowls that are about 3 quarts in volume and line them with lightweight kitchen towels.

Cooling Racks

I use cooling racks to place baking sheets on when they first come out of the oven. And then I transfer the baked goods directly onto the cooling racks to cool completely. Moving baked goods off the hot pan onto a cooling rack means they don't continue to cook from the residual heat of the pan and the rack allows the air to circulate around them. You can live without a cooling rack, but in the pursuit of perfect baked goods, one or two are worth the small investment.

Digital Scale

A scale is an essential in any baker's kitchen. I recommend using weight for all of the recipes in this book, but I have provided the volumetric measurements if that's your jam. Buy a sturdy, good-quality scale. I like the 1-gram increment scales, and particularly like the Escali scales. In addition to my 1-gram increment scale, I also use a pocket scale when I want to be more precise with salt or instant yeast measurements. This scale measures in 0.01-gram increments. Occasionally, when I need to weigh 0.5 grams of yeast, I use this scale. It is also called a jeweler's scale. Now I don't expect you to get one of these, and so rounding up or using a teaspoon measurement is fine.

Dutch Oven

I bake large, round loaves in a 5-quart Dutch oven. A 6- or 7-quart Dutch oven also works well. As the bread bakes and gives off steam, the lid on the Dutch oven traps the steam and helps the loaf to expand. Halfway through the bake, the lid is removed to help dry out the loaf. My personal favorite Dutch oven is a Lodge cast-iron 2-in-1 combo, which comprises a cast-iron Dutch oven with a skillet lid. The pair can be inverted so the skillet is on the bottom and the Dutch oven rests on top like a "cloche" or bell. Once the cloche is removed, the bread browns more evenly, resting on the skillet base without the interference of sides. Although I love my Dutch oven combo, all the recipes are written for a standard Dutch oven.

Enamelware Rectangular Roasting Pan Lid

This lightweight lid helps to retain moisture when I bake rolls and small loaves like the Sourdough Baguettes (page 233) directly on the hearth baking stone. I use it the same way I use the Dutch oven lid, removing it partway through the baking time. It's lightweight, which makes it easy to handle, and its dimensions fit exactly on top of my rectangular baking stone. I don't want you to go out and purchase something that you will use just once. But if you want to geek out on making baguettes at home like I do, I find it very beneficial. Its dimensions are 18 × 13½ × 4½ inches high.

Flipping Board

This simple narrow rectangular board helps bakers move baguettes onto the oven peel for baking. It's about 24 × 4 inches. It is essential in a bakery, but I do not always have one at home. I have cut pieces of cardboard box that work just as well. I recommend you make your own flipping board before going out and purchasing one.

Industrial Plastic Wrap

I love to buy professional-grade plastic wrap, which comes in an 18-inch roll and is so much more effective than what they sell in grocery stores. It actually sticks and seals, whereas the other stuff just falls off. You can buy it online or from restaurant supply stores. Buy one roll and it will last you almost forever.

Linen Couche

I use a thick linen fabric called a couche specifically for proofing baguettes. It is sturdy enough to support the baguettes, and it wicks away moisture from their surface, which helps the bread release from the fabric. I get the 26 × 36-inch linen couche from San Francisco Baking Institute. It can be substituted with thick linen or cotton cloth.

Loaf Pans

You will need Pullman loaf pans in two sizes: 9 × 4 inches and 13 × 4 inches. I love the straight sides of the Pullman loaf pan, particularly in breadmaking. The Pullman pan has a lid that slides on, which I use when I make some breads, such as the Caraway Rye Pullman (page 136); it gives the loaf square edges, which is nice for sandwiches. I leave the lid off for other loaves, such as the Whole Wheat Olive Oil Brioche (page 210), where I want a rounded, golden brown top. The lid doesn't just affect the shape of the loaf, it also makes for a tighter crumb because it is holding it in. By forgoing the lid, you get a lighter, airier loaf because you are not constricting the dough.

Muffin Tins

I suggest you keep two types: one regular tin that has 12 standard muffin cups, and two jumbo tins, each with 6 jumbo cups. I use the regular tin for Black Truffle Fantails (page 181), and I use the jumbo tins to make the Fondue Brioches à Tête (page 222).

Oven Peel

At home I use a metal peel, which is more slippery than a wooden peel, making it easier to shimmy pizza and bread into the oven. The peel should be 12 inches across, which is wide enough for a pizza.

Parchment Paper

Once you've baked in a professional kitchen, you wouldn't think of baking on a baking sheet that wasn't lined with parchment paper. Using parchment makes easy work of cleanup: You just lift off the paper and throw it away, no scrubbing involved. (If you want to conserve paper, you can do what is required in many professional kitchens, which is turn the parchment around and bake on the other side before throwing it out.) Sheets of parchment paper that fit perfectly in a half-sheet pan are available at baking supply stores and online. They are very convenient to use because you don't have to measure and cut, and they also don't curl up the way parchment cut from a roll does. At conventional grocery stores, you can also buy folded sheets of parchment, which are equally convenient.

Sieves
It's nice to have fine-mesh sieves in a few different sizes, for rinsing grains, draining anything you've soaked (such as dried fruit), or straining the pulp out of citrus juice.

Spice Grinder
I use a spice grinder, which looks exactly like a coffee grinder (and a coffee grinder can be used in its place) for grinding spices and seeds, such as the caraway seeds for the Marbled Rye (page 129).

Stand Mixer
A stand mixer is an essential in a baker's kitchen. There are some things, like creaming butter and sugar together, where handheld beaters could be substituted. But for making bread dough, which requires some strength, only a stand mixer will do. You can also walk away from a stand mixer while it's working, which means you can multitask: get ingredients ready or clean up, while the mixer is doing its work. I use a 6-quart KitchenAid mixer, but the 8-quart mixer is amazing, and if I were buying one again, that is the one I would buy. If all you have is a handheld mixer, that would work for making cookies and cakes, but it is not as effective for making bread.

Stainless Steel Bowls
Stainless steel bowls are really important in baking. They're more efficient than ceramic bowls because they're lightweight and they don't break. You need stainless steel bowls when you're setting up a double boiler. And when you're weighing ingredients into a bowl, a lightweight bowl is important, so the scale doesn't top out. Stainless steel bowls are also practical from a storage point of view because they nest. And, they are inexpensive; I suggest you buy a set of nesting bowls for everyday use. Save the beautiful ceramic bowls for serving purposes.

Tools

Bench Knife
A bench knife is a simple rectangular tool that bakers use to scrape the counter clean and to cut dough. If you buy a good one, it will have a sharp enough edge that it can function as a knife. In a professional bread bakery, it is an everyday tool that we use to cut hundreds of pieces of dough, which

we then throw on the scale, for even scaling. The important thing for me in choosing a bench knife is that it be tall enough that I can cut through a block of dough without the dough hitting the handle.

Digital Probe Thermometer

Throughout these recipes, you'll see I call for water at a specific temperature, and the way to measure the temperature is with this inexpensive gadget. I also use it to take the internal temperature of dough.

Kitchen Shears

Once you get used to using kitchen shears in the cooking and baking process, you won't know how you ever lived without them. I reach for them for everything from cutting parchment paper and opening packages to cutting focaccia. The key difference between kitchen shears and any other scissors is that the two sides come apart, so you can wash them thoroughly, which is important since they come in contact with food.

Lame

A lame is a blade with a handle used to score bread. There are a variety of different lames. Some lames come with the blade attached to the handle, but my preference is to have a separate handle and double-edged razor blade. Once one side of the razor blade dulls, I flip it around to use the other side, and I like to have at least a few double blades at home. Bread scores turn out more beautiful with a sharp blade, and I go through the blades frequently.

Offset Spatula

An offset spatula is a long metal spatula with a handle that juts out at an angle (offset), which gives you more control. I use both large and small offset spatulas, and I use them primarily for pastry work like evening out batter in a cake pan or for spreading fillings over sheets of dough. Often I grab one as a helpful tool in breadmaking.

Oven Thermometer

To make sure I'm baking at the correct temperature, I keep an oven thermometer in the oven at all times. I've tried different brands and they all seem to break—or the glass gets so fogged up you can't read them. So, yes, you have to replace them from time to time. But the good news is, they aren't expensive.

Paring Knife

My go-to small knife is a small serrated paring knife made by Victorinox. Because it is serrated, I don't have to worry about sharpening it. It has a plastic handle. It's really basic. And equally inexpensive. But it works perfectly. I use it for all small tasks like slicing garlic.

Plastic Bowl Scraper

This simple, inexpensive handheld tool is essential in bread baking. Bread dough tends to be very sticky. A bowl scraper is stiff but also flexible, and it's curved on one side to match the curve of a bowl so you can really scrape your bowl clean with it. It doesn't have a handle, so you hold it in your palm, and it feels like an extension of your hand. They cost about a dollar. Get one.

Rolling Pin

I use an 18-inch straight rolling pin (which bakers refer to as a French rolling pin) exclusively. This is a rolling pin without handles, which allows me to feel how much pressure I am putting on the dough. French rolling pins come with tapered ends or straight all the way across; I like the straight ones. Though I don't ever use a rolling pin with handles, I understand that a rolling pin with handles can be easier for the novice, and they are also more ergonomically correct. So if you want to use a rolling pin with handles, look for one with ball bearings, because they are gentle on your wrists.

Serrated Bread Knife

I have two serrated knives, one offset and one regular. I use the offset serrated knife for slicing bread. When you use an offset serrated knife and are slicing downward through the loaf, your hand doesn't hit the cutting board when it gets to the bottom, as the knife blade gets there first. I use a standard serrated knife to cut through cake layers. Having both is ideal, but if you were going out to buy just one, I would suggest the offset knife, which is more versatile.

Silicone Spatulas

Flexible silicone spatulas are essential for cleaning mixing bowls. I have a few shapes and sizes, all heatproof, that I reach for at different moments.

Spray Bottle

An inexpensive spray bottle is essential to create steam in your home oven. I fill it up with room-temperature water and liberally spray bread that bakes directly on my baking stone, like Sourdough Baguettes (page 233).

Straightedge

A straightedge, or ruler, is essential for measuring dough when you're rolling it, and to use as a guide for a pastry cutter when cutting dough for more precise breads, such as brioche feuilleté.

Yeast and Sourdough Starter Tutorial

Bread rises organically with yeast and/or sourdough starter. Both can be intimidating when you are starting out. Here is a basic understanding of how they work.

Yeast

Yeast is a leavener, like baking soda or baking powder, and it causes baked goods to rise. The difference is that baking soda and powder are chemical leaveners, whereas yeast is an organic leavener. (A third type of leavener is mechanical. An example of a mechanical leavener is whipped egg whites.) Whether you are working with dry yeast, fresh (cake) yeast, or natural yeast (sourdough starter), yeast eats the sugars and starches in your dough and produces carbon dioxide and alcohol. The carbon dioxide leavens the dough. Different types of yeast are used to leaven different baked goods. Some recipes are leavened with commercial yeast (such as the instant yeast I use in many of these recipes), some with sourdough starter, and some with a combination of the two. I often use a combination: the commercial yeast for reliability and consistency and the sourdough starter for the flavor it adds. (For more detail, see Sourdough Starter Tutorial, page xxvi.)

The two principal factors in activating yeast are temperature and time: the temperature of the dough and the amount of time you let it ferment and proof.

Below is a short glossary of terms related to yeast.

Crumb   The crumb refers to the texture inside a baked good. It is defined by the gelatinized starch and the holes that are produced during the leavening of the baked good. A sourdough loaf should have a nice big open-holed honeycomb structure. Brioche should have a tighter crumb, with a lot of small wide uniform holes and no big ones.

Preferment   A preferment is dough that is fermented before it is added to the main dough, which will also be fermented. The types of preferments used in this book are sourdough starter and poolish. All preferments add flavor to dough and ferment the dough.

Poolish   A poolish is a type of preferment. It is equal parts water and flour and a small amount of commercial yeast. It is mixed between 12 and 24 hours before mixing the dough into which it will be added. I use a poolish in making baguettes because it adds extensibility to the dough, which enables me to stretch out the baguettes into their beautiful shape.

Retard   To retard dough means to slow down the fermentation process. This is done by cooling the dough, which you do by putting it in the refrigerator. Yeast growth slows down in cooler temperatures, so by cooling the dough you slow down the fermentation process. Besides fermentation, the other thing that is happening is that the enzymes that exist in flour and yeast break down the starches (complex sugars) in the flour into simple sugars. Simple sugars contribute to the flavor of the dough and also cause it to brown in the oven. By retarding the dough, you give the enzymes the opportunity to break down the starches into sugars, which enhances the flavor of the dough. Also, the increased sugar in the dough means increased browning, so by waiting, you get that deep, burnished exterior on breads and pastries.

Sourdough Starter Tutorial

Sourdough starter is a natural leavening made from a culture of flour, water, and natural yeast found in the air; bacteria work in harmony with the yeast to create flavor in the culture, so each sourdough starter has a unique character. You can buy sourdough starter from an established bakery or online, or you can make yours from scratch.

To make sourdough starter from scratch, you start with flour, water, and a small amount of honey. Choosing the flour that you build your starter from is important. Many organic stone-ground flours contain a fair amount of yeast, because yeast spores attach themselves to grains, and in the case of organic stone-ground flours, that yeast remains attached to the grain during the process of milling it into flour. Rye flour in particular is known to have a very high natural yeast content, which is why I start with rye flour when building a starter from scratch. (You may have heard about people beginning a starter with grapes; that is because natural yeast is found on the skins of grapes. I believe there is more yeast found in stone-ground rye flour than grapes, so that's the strategy I use.) Yeast feeds off sugar, which is why I add honey to my starter; it acts like a vitamin boost, kick-starting the growth of the yeast. As the days progress and I am building my starter, I scale back the amount of rye flour and replace it with bread flour and whole wheat flour.

Yeast is like a pet. It needs food (flour), water, and a warm environment to thrive.

It takes six days for sourdough starter to ripen fully to a point where you can use it. When you are building your starter, you "feed" it twice a day. Yeast feeds off of flour, so "feeding" your starter means mixing a small amount of flour and water with the mother starter, which is the starter that you are working with that has already fermented and ripened. The point of doing this is to build up the concentration of yeast in the culture. (Sourdough "starter" should really be called sourdough "culture," because it is the yeast culture that starts your sourdough loaf.)

The most important factor in the success of ripening a starter from scratch or maintaining a starter, besides feeding it every day, is temperature. The ideal water and air temperature for ripening starter is about 75°F. If the water or air is too cold, the yeast won't thrive, and you won't notice much activity. Likewise, if you forget to feed your starter, it will start to look gray and liquidy and sad.

A healthy, ripened sourdough starter that is ready to use to make bread will have grown in volume, and there will be bubbles, lots of bubbles. If you use a clear container you will be able to see the bubbles on the sides and you will also notice bubbles on the top of the starter when you remove the lid from the container.

Sourdough starter is constantly growing and changing. The yeast will start feeding on the starches and sugars immediately. When you first feed it, the starter will look like a thick paste with no bubbles. As the yeast grows and the starter ripens, bubbles form and become more voluminous, and the gluten proteins break down, taking the starter from a stiff paste to a light, airy, bubbly slurry.

Sourdough starter is ripe and ready to use in a bread recipe when the concentration of yeast is high enough and you see bubbles on the surface of the starter. How long the starter takes to get to this point depends on how much ripened starter is used to make the sourdough culture. If you use a lot of ripened starter, your sourdough starter could be ready in as little as 2 hours. This is because the ratio of ripened starter to flour is very high. If you use very little ripened starter, your starter could be ready in 12 hours because the ratio of ripened starter to flour is much lower, meaning it will take longer to build up the concentration of yeast. I use a float test (see Float Test, page xxxi) to determine when the yeast concentration is high enough. I take a piece of the ripened starter and check that it floats in a bowl of water. Floating means enough carbon dioxide has been produced, which is directly related to the amount of yeast. If you make sourdough starter regularly, you will find that there is a large window of 4 to 6 hours when the starter will float. Hopefully this gives you some reassurance that there is some flexibility with the timing of making your sourdough loaves. There is no need to rush around right when your starter has reached the 12-hour mark of growing and ripening. What I have found is that when you use your starter when it is "young," meaning it passes the float test at the earliest point of ripening, it creates a bread with explosive activity in the oven. There is a lot of bread spring, and the bread has beautiful large irregular holes. When you use your starter when it is "older," it still functions in fermenting and proofing your loaf, but the loaf will not have as much oven spring, and it will have fewer large, irregular holes. I like to use a younger starter for all of my sourdough loaves. For other breads, like bagels, rolls, or brioche, I find that an older starter works better, primarily because these breads use a combination of starter and instant yeast.

I can't tell you how many people tell me, "I killed my starter!" But in fact, once you've got it going, a starter is nearly impossible to kill. To revive a seemingly dead starter, first, drain any liquid that has formed on top. Then feed the starter according to Maintaining a Mother Starter (page xxxi). If the starter is not active, wait a full day before feeding it again. At this point, you may want to double or triple the amount of ripened starter (the mother) you add to the feed. Wait another full day before feeding it again, and within a day or two, you will start to see some activity. Once you can see that the starter is beginning to bubble and grow, resume feeding it twice a day.

You can make sourdough starter in a glass or plastic container; the important thing is that it have a tight-fitting lid and that it hold at least 1½ quarts. (If you use a one-quart container, when the starter expands, the pressure of it will cause it to explode out of the container.) It's ideal to have two such containers, as when you feed the starter, you move it from one container to the other.

Making a Sourdough Starter from Scratch

The following formula is for what is known as a "liquid starter," as opposed to a biga, or "stiff starter."

Day One: Morning

Organic rye grains have natural yeast on them, so starting with stone-ground flour from this grain is key to developing yeast in the starter. The honey acts as a vitamin booster for the yeast. You will give the starter a full day to begin to ferment before feeding it again. Still, this is the beginning stage and there won't be a high enough concentration of yeast in the mixture for you to notice a visible difference after the first day.

For the starter		
Water (70°– 75°F)	1½ cups	352 grams
Organic stone-ground rye flour	1½ cups	300 grams
Mild-flavored honey, such as wildflower or clover	1 teaspoon	7 grams

Put the water in a 1½-quart or larger container with a tight-fitting lid. Add the flour and honey and stir with a spoon to combine. Cover the container and set it in a warm place (about 75°F), such as near or on your stove, for 24 hours.

Day Two: Morning Feed

Your starter will still look like flour mixed with water. To continue to encourage the yeasts to grow, take a portion of the yeast culture—this is called "ripened starter" or "mother"—and mix it with flour and water. This is called "feeding" your starter.

When feeding your starter, you start with a small amount (about 1 tablespoon) of the mother starter. Although it might feel wasteful to discard the remainder, it does not have enough concentration of yeast to bake with yet. If you were to feed the entire starter instead of just this small amount, the amount of flour you would add would not be enough food for the yeast and the yeast would eventually starve; your bread volume would shrink, and your starter would stop rising as a result. Starting with a small amount of ripened starter helps the yeast to grow at a good rate without starving it.

For the morning feed		
Water (70°–75°F)	1 cup	235 grams
Mother (the mixture from Day One)	1 cup	200 grams
Organic stone-ground rye flour	1 cup	110 grams
Bread flour or all-purpose flour	¾ cup	90 grams

Put the water in a 1½-quart (or larger) container with a tight-fitting lid. Scoop out 200 grams (1 cup) of the original starter and add it to the container; discard the remaining starter. Add the rye flour and bread flour and stir with a metal spoon to combine. Cover the container and set the starter in a warm place (about 75°F) for about 12 hours.

Day Two: Evening Feed

Depending on how warm it is in your home and other factors, such as humidity, by this time, your starter may already be very active. If it is active, you will see bubbles on the top of the starter (and from the side if you are using a glass container); yeast produces carbon dioxide and alcohol, and those bubbles indicate that there is yeast activity. The starter may also be rising considerably in the container: That is the carbon dioxide at work. Some gluten has formed in the starter, and the carbon dioxide is getting trapped inside the gluten network. (Be warned: When I recently made starter in a too-small vessel, I came home on the evening of Day Two to find my starter exploding out of the container.)

Water (70°–75°F)	½ cup	118 grams
Ripened starter	½ cup	113 grams
Organic rye flour	½ cup	55 grams
Bread flour or all-purpose flour	½ cup	60 grams

Put the water in a 1½-quart (or larger) container with a tight-fitting lid. Scoop out 100 grams (½ cup) of the ripened starter and add it to the container; discard the remaining ripened starter. Add the rye flour and bread flour and stir with a metal spoon to combine. Cover the container and set the starter in a warm place (about 75°F) for about 12 hours.

Days Three, Four, and Five

At this point, you switch from rye flour to whole wheat flour because the yeast from the rye flour has already begun growing. I use a combination of whole wheat flour instead of all bread flour because the whole wheat flour contains natural yeast. So as the days go on and the yeast in my starter becomes more concentrated, I am gradually moving from yeast-containing grains to more refined bread flour, which does not contain the natural yeast.

For the morning feed

Water (70°–75°F)	½ cup	118 grams
Ripened starter	⅔ cup	113 grams
Organic whole wheat flour	½ cup	60 grams
Bread flour or all-purpose flour	½ cup	60 grams

Put the water in a 1½-quart (or larger) container with a tight-fitting lid. Measure out 100 grams (½ cup) of the ripened starter and add it to the container; discard the remaining ripened starter. Add the whole wheat flour and bread flour and stir with a metal spoon to combine. Cover the container and set the starter in a warm place (about 75°F) for about 12 hours.

For the evening feed

Water (70°–75°F)	½ cup	118 grams
Ripened starter	⅔ cup	113 grams
Organic whole wheat flour	½ cup	60 grams
Bread flour or all-purpose flour	½ cup	60 grams

Put the water in a 1½-quart (or larger) container with a tight-fitting lid. Measure out 113 grams (⅔ cup) of the ripened starter and add it to the container; discard the remaining ripened starter. Add the whole wheat flour and bread flour and stir with a metal spoon to combine. Cover the container and set the starter aside at room temperature (70°F) for about 12 hours.

Day Six

Your starter is now ready to use. From here out, refer to the feed schedule in Maintaining a Mother Starter (page xxxi).

Float Test

To test whether your starter is ready to use, fill a small bowl with water. Wet the fingers of one hand and use them to carefully pinch off a piece of the starter, taking care not to deflate the starter in the process. Place the starter in the water. If it floats, the starter is good to use. The reason it is floating is that the yeast has produced a sufficient amount of carbon dioxide. If the concentration of yeast has produced enough carbon dioxide to cause the starter to float, it is also high enough to leaven dough. If the starter sinks, feed it for a few more days, testing it every day, until it floats. This is called the float test. I ask the bakers who work with me to make sure the starter passes the float test each time before adding it to dough.

Maintaining a Mother Starter

Now that you have built a starter, you have to maintain it, which means feeding it on a regular basis. If you are maintaining your starter just to have on hand to use someday, it is enough to feed it once a day. If you are actively baking with it or are getting ready to bake with it in the very near future, feed it twice a day. This ensures less bacteria and more active yeast in the starter, which results in a higher rise in your baked goods.

For the morning maintenance feed

Water (70°–75°F)	⅔ cup	157 grams
Ripened starter	1 tablespoon	25 grams
Bread flour or all-purpose flour	1⅓ cups	160 grams

Put the water in a 1½-quart (or larger) container with a tight-fitting lid. Measure out 25 grams (1 tablespoon) of the ripened starter and add it to the container; discard the remaining ripened starter. Add the flour and stir with a metal spoon to combine. Cover the container and set the starter aside in a warm place (about 75°F) for about 12 hours.

For the evening maintenance feed

Water (70°–75°F)	⅔ cup	157 grams
Ripened starter	1 tablespoon	25 grams
Bread flour or all-purpose flour	1⅓ cups	160 grams

Put the water in a 1½-quart (or larger) container with a tight-fitting lid. Measure out 25 grams (1 tablespoon) of the ripened starter and add it to the container. Discard the remaining ripened starter. Add the flour and stir with a metal spoon to combine. Cover the container and set the starter in a warm place (about 75°F) for about 12 hours.

Saving Your Starter

If you are unable to feed your starter because you are leaving town, put the ripened starter in the refrigerator until you return. Do not put just-fed starter in the refrigerator. Starter that was just fed has a low (or no) concentration of yeast; the yeast hasn't had time to feed and grow. If you do this, when you remove the starter from the refrigerator, it may not come back to life. To prevent this from happening, put your starter in the refrigerator at its ripest point, when it is very active and bubbly.

When you are ready to resume a maintenance feeding schedule, remove the starter from the refrigerator and drain off any liquid that has formed on top. Resume feeding the starter twice a day using the feed routine for Maintaining a Mother Starter (page xxxi) until the yeast has concentrated enough that the starter passes the Float Test (page xxxi).

**Using Sourdough Starter in the Recipes in the Book,
i.e., Very Important Information**

Throughout the book, you'll refer back to this starter recipe. Once you
have grown your starter and have it on regular maintenance feedings (see
Maintaining a Mother Starter, page xxxi), you will continue to maintain it
separately from the bread recipes. Each recipe that uses sourdough starter
calls for you to take some of the ripened mother starter and feed it separately
from your regularly maintained starter. This separate feeding makes just the
right amount of sourdough starter for each recipe.

Very Good Bread

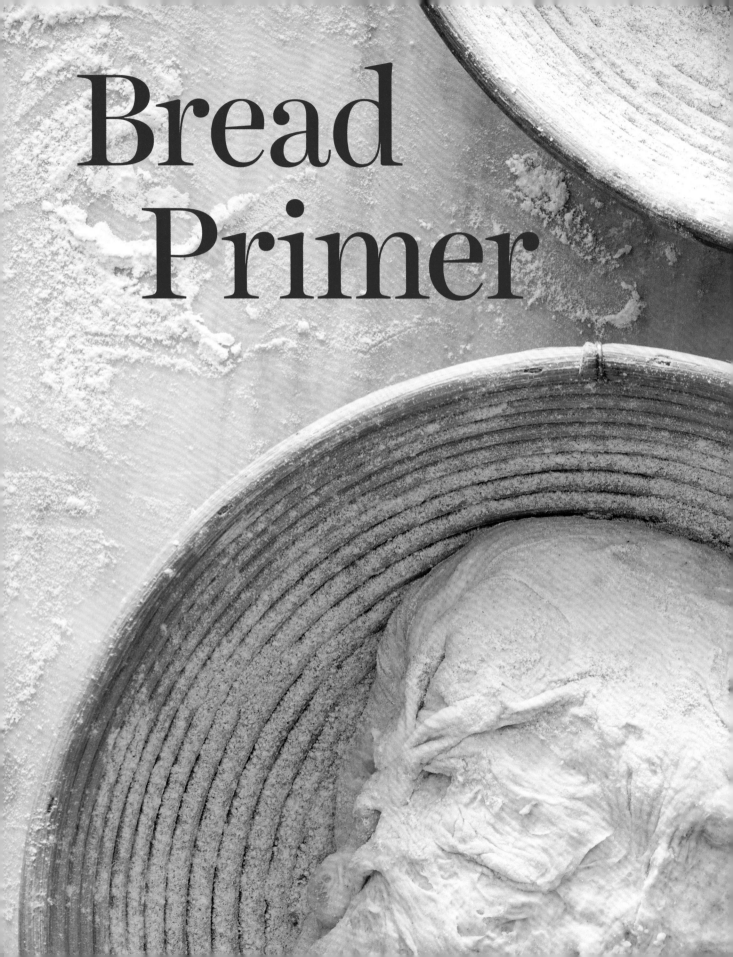

Bread
Primer

The first loaf of bread I made at home, some twenty-five years ago now, came from a recipe in a book called *Crust & Crumb,* by Peter Reinhart. It was a simple loaf of bread, and the recipe was not a complicated one. I followed the instructions diligently, shaping the dough into a round and placing it in the refrigerator overnight. The next day it slightly collapsed in the oven, but the color of the crust was a beautiful deep amber brown, and the flavor was unbelievably good. I was immediately hooked on breadmaking, determined to make an even better loaf the next time.

What helped me understand the basics of breadmaking was a simple recipe—just flour, water, salt, and yeast. There was no preferment like sourdough starter or poolish, and the steps were straightforward. Breadmaking can feel overwhelming when you first get started, especially when working with sourdough starter or with a special shape like a baguette. Having a couple of building block recipes gives you the basic knowledge and practice from which to make more challenging loaves of bread.

The two recipes in this chapter focus on the fundamentals of breadmaking to give you the skill set to tackle more complex loaves.

Master Class
The Twelve Steps of Breadmaking

There are twelve steps to follow to make bread successfully. They are:

Mise en place

This is a French culinary term for "everything in place," and it refers to having all your ingredients in front of you and prepared. Get out all your ingredients, as well as the equipment and tools you are going to need for a recipe. Prep and measure your ingredients, and once you are done with them, put away the containers that those ingredients came in. Mise en place also means getting prepared, and with breadmaking that means making yourself a schedule of what happens when. Throughout this book you will find sample schedules to follow.

Mixing

Mixing begins as soon as the ingredients are combined. Mixing appears simple. You are simply combining ingredients to form a uniform mass of dough. But it is actually more complex. Mixing sets the stage for proper fermentation. Your dough needs to be a specific temperature for proper fermentation to occur. Achieving a specific dough temperature once mixing is complete means adjusting your water temperature while taking into account the temperatures of the flour and other major components like sourdough starter. Not only does your dough need to be a certain temperature once mixing is completed, it also needs to be developed to a certain point. Dough development is based on how much the gluten is formed during mixing. Some doughs, like bagel dough, are nearly fully developed during the mixing stage. If dough is refrigerated overnight, like bagels, gluten will continue to form, but most of the gluten is formed right away. Sourdough loaves are mixed by hand, and there is very little dough development at the mixing stage. Gluten will continue to form during the fermentation stage, and folding the dough will help to develop the dough.

An autolyse may also happen during mixing. **Autolyse** is a technique that was developed in France by a baker named Raymond Calvel, who discovered that—because both salt and yeast inhibit gluten formation—if you mix flour and water together and then let them rest before adding the salt and yeast, the gluten forms better. Better gluten formation produces bread with more volume and a better crumb structure. I use autolyse in doughs where crumb structure and stretch of gluten are important. In this book, I use it with the sourdough loaves, baguettes, ciabatta, and pizza. Most professional bakers autolyse their dough for about 30 minutes primarily due to time constraints. Some bakers, though, will autolyse doughs for 12 and up to 24 hours. I call for a two- to three-hour autolyse in most recipes because a longer autolyse benefits the dough. Realistically speaking, the recipes will turn out just fine with a shorter autolyse should you be pressed for time.

Fermenting

Professional bakers refer to the first rise as the "fermentation," and that is how I refer to it in this book. The first rise, or fermentation period, comes at the point in the process when you have just finished mixing the dough and the yeast has begun to feed on it. Your dough will be what we call "in bulk," which means it will be in a container, covered, and in a warm place, which allows the yeast to grow. Fermentation can also take place in the refrigerator, where, because of the colder temperature, the yeast growth slows down; this slow growth contributes a lot of flavor. Oftentimes, I like to start my fermentation in a warm room and then move the dough to the refrigerator to give it a long and slow rise; extending the time improves its flavor.

Folding

The dough is stretched and folded during the fermentation process. This is a more orderly method of what is also called "punching down" the dough. This movement helps to redistribute the yeast and develop, or strengthen, the dough. The dough at this point will be in a container, covered. To turn the dough (which I generally do every hour, meaning in the middle of a two-hour fermentation, or at the end of a 1-hour fermentation), first, uncover the bowl. Wet your hands, which prevents the dough from sticking to them, and pick up one edge of the dough and bring it toward the center. Do the same with the opposite edge of the dough, then with the top and bottom edges. Different doughs call for different numbers of stretches and folds. The wetter or more loose the dough is after mixing, the more stretches and folds there are. If the dough is very developed after the mixing is finished, it will not need any folding. Dough that uses only sourdough benefits from folding over a longer period of time because the fermentation happens more slowly.

Dividing

At the end of fermentation, the dough is divided into pieces using a scale and a bench knife. This is also called scaling. Each piece should weigh the same within a small range. If the dough is being scaled at 50 grams, the pieces should weigh between 47 and 53 grams.

Preshaping

After the dough is divided, the pieces are given a first shape, called a preshape. The preshape helps the final shape to be as even and uniform as possible. Preshapes are usually rounds, cylinders, or football shapes. A baguette preshape is cylindrical, and a large round loaf will have a round preshape. Not all bread will be preshaped. Bagels are a great example. Their low hydration and high gluten makes them easier to form into their final shape. Baguette dough, on the other hand, is wetter, and the dough must be formed into a long even length, and so the preshape helps the final shape be more even.

Resting   Preshaping the dough works the gluten, so the preshapes must rest to let the gluten relax before the final shaping. A beginning baker may not get as much tension in the preshape as a more experienced baker. Without a lot of tension in the preshape, the dough does not need to rest much at all before shaping.

Shaping   Shaping transforms the dough into its final shape. Getting the right amount of tension in the final shape helps it to hold its form while the bread proofs and bakes, and achieving an even form is the hardest part of breadmaking to teach. If there is too much flour on the work surface, the dough will slide around and you won't be able to create the right amount of tension for the dough to holds its shape. Not enough flour, and the dough sticks to the work surface and your hands.

Proofing   This refers to the second rise of dough. Once dough is shaped, it goes through a second fermentation and rises. Bakers use aids like banneton forms, linen fabric, or bread pans to help the dough expand in a particular shape during proofing. One question I am frequently asked is how much dough goes into a specific banneton. I like to use 8- to 9-inch bannetons to proof round loaves that weigh between 800 and 1,200 grams and that's what I call for in these recipes. Time and the size of a product help the baker to judge when something is proofed properly, but this can be tricky to judge for the novice baker. When you are starting out, the best way to tell if something is proofed is by poking it with your fingertip. Bread proofs from the outside toward the center, so you want to poke the dough in two places: the tip or end of the loaf or piece, and also in the center. When it's done proofing, the tip should really hold the indentation, while the center should hold the indentation but spring back a little.

The same dough, shaped into a small roll, will take less time to proof than that dough shaped into a large loaf. The longer you proof an enriched dough (any dough that has fat like oil or butter or eggs in it), the lighter and fluffier and bigger it will be. At a certain point in proofing any dough, you will reach the point of no return, where the dough will proof no more and will start to collapse either before it goes into the oven or during the bake.

Scoring   Just before baking, the loaf is cut or slashed to control where the bread will expand in the oven. As a loaf bakes, an outside crust begins to form. The interior of the loaf will continue to expand. Without scoring the bread in particular spots, the interior will continue to expand and pop out of the crust in an unorganized way, creating deformed shapes. Not all bread needs to be scored. Breads baked in pans or ciabatta are not typically scored.

Baking   Baking is the most important part of breadmaking. It transforms dough into bread. During the first part of the bake, bread expands. This expansion is called oven spring. When the bread is loaded into the oven, the increased temperature initially causes more activity from the yeast, which produces more carbon dioxide. The carbon dioxide, produced during proofing and during the last bit of yeast activity, expands from the heat in the oven. Water becomes steam, which also expands. These gases are trapped within a gluten network. So as the gases expand, the gluten is stretched and the bread volume increases. Professional bakers use bread ovens with hearth stones and steam to bake bread. Without steam, a crust would form prematurely, limiting the volume that the loaf could achieve. To mimic the steam in a professional bread oven, I call for either a Dutch oven for large loaves or a roaster lid and spritz water bottle for baguettes. The lids trap the steam and help the bread expand. I also use a rectangular baking stone, which I set on a rack in my oven. I can achieve almost identical results baking at home with these adjustments as I can in a professional bakery. About halfway through the bake, the lids are removed so the crust can form.

Cooling   Even though it is tempting to break into a warm loaf of bread before it has completely cooled, please wait. Cooling is an important step in the breadmaking process. As the bread cools, steam continues to be released, and the starch continues to set up. The sourdough loaves in this book have high hydrations. If they are not cooled properly and are sliced too soon, they will seem gummy because the steam has not finished evaporating. Allowing bread to cool also enhances its flavor profile. We perceive more flavor from bread as it changes from hot to room temperature. (Of course, if the bread gets too cold, there is also a loss of flavor perception!)

Pain Ordinaire

Makes 2 round loaves

This is a variation of the first loaf of bread I made at home, long before I attended culinary school or worked in bakeries. I think it is perfect for a beginner because it covers all of the basics of making bread in one simple recipe. There are only four ingredients—flour, water, salt, and instant yeast. The mixing is done entirely by hand—you don't need a mixer. And there is no kneading. Kneading, which develops the gluten, is replaced by folding the dough throughout the fermentation.

This recipe does not use sourdough starter to leaven the bread. As much as I love sourdough, I love this recipe for its simplicity and the lovely, fresh, wheat-y loaves it produces.

One aspect that makes these "ordinary loaves" special is that they are placed in the refrigerator overnight before being baked the next day. This is called retarding, and the first time I tried it at home was a revelation. Retarding slows down the proofing of the loaves, and as a result, the bread is more flavorful and has a deeper caramel crust. When you slow down the proofing, you are really slowing down the yeast activity. The yeast growth is impeded, but the enzymes that are present in the dough continue to break down the starches into simple sugars. Those simple sugars contribute to the flavor of the bread dough and also cause it to brown more in the oven.

If this is the first bread recipe you are making, please read the Twelve Steps of Breadmaking (page 5) to set yourself up for success.

Equipment Two 8- to 9-inch linen-lined bannetons or two 3-quart bowls lined with lightweight kitchen towels and a 5-quart Dutch oven with a lid.

For the dough			Baker's %
Water (75°–80°F)	3 cups	705 grams	78
Instant yeast	1½ teaspoons	5 grams	0.6
Fine sea salt	3¾ teaspoons	22.5 grams	2.5
Bread flour	6½ cups + more for dusting	780 grams	87
Whole wheat flour	1 cup + more for dusting	120 grams	13

Mix the dough

• Put the water in a deep bowl. Sprinkle the yeast on top and let rest for 5 minutes to help dissolve the yeast. Then whisk the yeast into the water. Whisk in the salt and then add the bread and whole wheat flours on top. Use a wooden spoon to mix the dough until it becomes a shaggy mass and too stiff to stir. Remove the spoon, scrape it clean with your fingers, and set it aside. Finish mixing the dough by hand, scooping and squeezing the dough between your hands until there are no dry patches, and the dough forms a rough, homogeneous blob.

Ferment the dough

- Measure the temperature of the dough. It should be between 75° and 80°F. Cover the bowl tightly with plastic wrap. Put the bowl aside (somewhere cool if the dough is too warm and somewhere warm if the dough is too cold) for 30 minutes.

Make 2 stretch and folds

- Remove the plastic wrap and set aside. With wet hands, scoop underneath the top edge of the dough and fold it two-thirds of the way toward the bottom edge. Fold the bottom edge to meet the top edge, as if you were folding a letter, pressing on the dough just enough to get it to stay in place, but not patting it. Do the same with the two sides, folding the right edge two-thirds of the way toward the left edge, and folding the left edge to meet the right edge. Then flip the dough upside down. Re-cover the bowl and set the dough aside for 30 minutes.
- Repeat stretching and folding the dough a second time for a second fold. Re-cover the bowl with plastic and set the dough aside for 1 hour.

Controlling the temperature is an important part of making this bread. Insulating the dough by mixing and fermenting it in a deep container helps it to stay at a good fermentation temperature (ideally between 75° and 80°F).

Divide and shape the loaves

- Line two 3-quart bowls each with a large, clean, lightweight kitchen towel and dust the towels heavily with whole wheat flour.
- Dust a large work surface heavily with bread flour. Use a plastic dough scraper or rubber spatula to scoop the dough onto the floured surface. With a bench knife, divide the dough in half.

It's important when working with bread dough that is not kneaded that you handle it gently. Although we usually develop the gluten by kneading, or mixing, this dough relies solely on the gluten that is formed during fermentation and stretch and folds. We don't want to deflate that by overhandling the dough.

- Working with one piece of dough at a time, fold the left and right sides into the center to create tautness. To do this, gently coax the dough into a rough, squarish shape. Begin at the top right corner and fold the corner two-thirds of the way across the top. Fold the top left corner to meet the right edge. Repeat the folding from right to left and then from left to right working your way down the loaf until you reach the bottom closest to you. This should be accomplished in three to four complete folds. Then fold the loaf like a letter, folding the top edge of the loaf two-thirds of the way down and folding the bottom edge up to meet it, pressing on the dough just enough to get it to stay in place. Pick the loaf up and place it with the seam facing up into one of the prepared bowls. Repeat the shaping for the second loaf.

Proof the loaves
- Cover the loaves with the overhanging towel and then wrap the bowls in plastic so that they do not dry out. Place them in the refrigerator to proof overnight, or for at least 8 hours, until the dough does not bounce back when you indent it with your finger.

Bake the bread
- About 30 minutes before you plan to bake, arrange an oven rack in the center position with no racks above it. Place the Dutch oven in the oven and preheat to 500°F.
- Take one of the bowls of dough out from the refrigerator and remove the plastic. Open the towel and dust the top of the loaf with bread flour. Open the oven and carefully slide the rack out partway. Remove the Dutch oven lid. Use the towel to flip the ball of dough into the palm of your free hand. Place the dough bottom-side up into the Dutch oven. Score the bread decoratively with a lame or a small sharp serrated knife. Replace the lid and slide the oven rack back into the oven.
- Bake the bread for 25 minutes.
- Reduce the oven temperature to 450°F. Carefully remove the lid and bake the bread for 20 to 25 minutes, until it has a deeply burnished crust. Remove the Dutch oven from the oven. Slide a large metal spatula under the bread and, holding the bread with your other hand, protected by a clean kitchen towel, remove it from the Dutch oven. Place the bread on a cooling rack to cool completely. Return the Dutch oven to the oven and reheat the oven to 500°F. Repeat the process for the second loaf of bread.

Shaping a round loaf

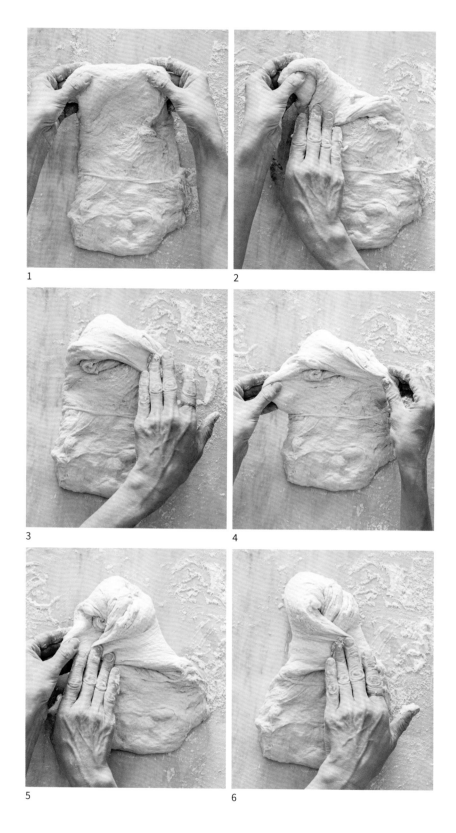

1

2

3

4

5

6

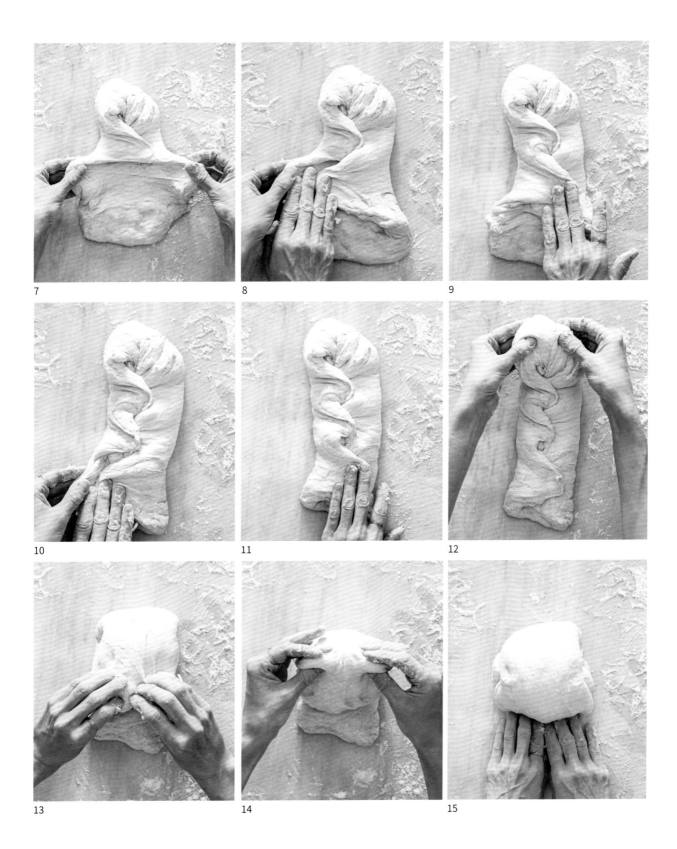

7

8

9

10

11

12

13

14

15

Honey Whole Wheat Loaf

Makes one 9 × 4-inch rounded top loaf

I like to bake this bread to use in sandwiches for my son's lunch. It is a straightforward and easy recipe to use, and that is why I have included it in the first chapter. Where the Pain Ordinaire (page 11) is shaped into a round loaf and placed in the refrigerator overnight, this dough goes into a pan and is mixed and baked the same day. You can bake any dough in a pan, from straightforward doughs like this recipe to more complicated sourdoughs. This recipe calls for a Pullman loaf pan, which has straight sides and often comes with a lid to make square tops. You can always substitute a regular loaf pan for the Pullman pan as long as it has similar dimensions.

Equipment One 9 × 4-inch Pullman loaf pan, 9 × 5-inch regular loaf pan, or 8 × 4-inch regular loaf pan

For the dough			Baker's %
Water (85°–90°F)	1 cup	235 grams	53
Instant yeast	¾ teaspoon	4.5 grams	1.0
Buttermilk, cold	⅔ cup	167 grams	38
Honey	2 tablespoons	40 grams	9.0
Fine sea salt	2 teaspoons	12 grams	2.7
Whole wheat bread flour	2⅔ cups	320 grams	73
Bread flour	1 cup + more for dusting	120 grams	27
For baking the loaf			
Egg, large	1	50 grams	
Fine sea salt	big pinch		

Mix the dough

· Put the water in a deep bowl. Sprinkle the yeast on top and let rest for 5 minutes to help dissolve the yeast. Then whisk the yeast into the water. Whisk in the buttermilk, honey, and salt, and then add the whole wheat and bread flours. Use a wooden spoon to mix the dough until it becomes a shaggy mass and too stiff to stir. Remove the spoon, scrape it clean with your fingers, and set it aside. Finish mixing the dough by hand, scooping and squeezing it between your hands until there are no dry patches and the dough forms a rough, homogeneous blob.

Ferment the dough

· Measure the temperature of the dough. It should be between 75° and 80°F. Cover the bowl with plastic wrap or a linen kitchen towel. Put the bowl aside—somewhere cool if the dough is too warm (above 82°F) and somewhere warm if the dough is too cold (below 75°F) or at room temperature if it's within its desired temperature range—for 1 hour.

Stretch and fold	· Uncover the dough. With wet hands, scoop underneath the top edge of the dough and fold it two-thirds of the way toward the bottom edge. Fold the bottom edge to meet the top edge, as if you were folding a letter, pressing on the dough just enough to get it to stay in place, but not patting it. Then fold the right edge of the dough two-thirds of the way toward the left edge, and fold the left edge to meet the right. Flip the dough upside down. Re-cover the bowl and set the dough aside for 1 hour.
Shape the loaf	· Lightly spray the insides of a 9 × 4-inch Pullman loaf pan (or regular loaf pan) with nonstick cooking spray. · Lightly dust a large flat work surface with flour. Use a plastic bowl scraper to scoop the dough out onto the floured work surface. Gently pat the dough into a rectangle about the length of the pan you will be baking it in, with a long side facing to you. Use your hands to get underneath the top edge of the dough and fold it down about two-thirds of the way from the top. Scoop your hands under the bottom edge of the dough (the edge closest to you) and fold it up over so the bottom edge is even with the top edge. Lift the dough and flip it over into the pan so the seam is on the bottom. Use your hands to pat the dough into the corners of the pan and even out the surface.
Proof the loaf	· Cover the dough with a damp lightweight kitchen towel and set aside at room temperature for about 2 hours, until the dough has risen and is about ¼ inch from the top rim of the pan.
Bake the bread	· Arrange an oven rack in the center position and preheat the oven to 400°F. · Whisk the egg with a pinch of salt to make an egg wash. Brush the top of the loaf with the egg wash. · Put the loaf on the center rack and bake for about 45 minutes, or until the top is a beautiful mahogany brown, rotating the pan from front to back halfway through. · Remove the loaf from the oven. Invert the loaf so it falls onto a cooling rack. Turn the loaf right-side up and let it cool completely. Slice as desired.

Bagels and Bialys

I first made bagels at home before I became a professional baker. They were fun to make and looked so professional. After I had struggled with shaping baguettes and proofing sourdough loaves just the right amount, the bagels seemed easy and looked stunning on my first try! I was convinced that part of the secret was the sourdough starter and the overnight retardation.

When the time came in my professional career to make bagels, I was working at Per Se. I went back to the recipe I had first made at home and began to make bagels for staff meal. I was responsible for making staff meal on Fridays, which I called Deli Day, since it comprised making a fun bread, slicing meats and cheeses to make sandwiches, and then making a pasta salad with bits and pieces of leftover vegetable trim. The number of staff "eating in" for Deli Day quadrupled, particularly when bagels were made. It was fun, and that is how I feel bagels should be to make—FUN.

The first bagels I made and sold over ten years ago looked like bagels a breadmaker might create. They were uniformly even, with perfect center holes, and they had beautiful amber crusts. My delivery driver pointed out that they had too much crust. In his opinion, bagels were soft and squishy with a much paler outside than mine were, and he was correct. Bagels need to be soft and squishy, which means they should be properly proofed. They may float in the water while you boil them, but if they are not proofed enough, they will still be too dense once they are baked. A good bagel balances soft and squishy with chewiness. The chewiness comes from the high-protein flour and low hydration of the dough.

In a traditional bagel bakery, the baker uses a revolving tray oven. This oven is made up of 4 to 6 stone hearths that rotate around like a Ferris wheel. This movement provides convective heat, which is what gives the bagels their shine. The type of airflow in a revolving tray oven inhibits caramelization of the crust, which results in bagels that are shiny but blond once baked. Bagel bakeries get around this lack of browning by adding some type of sugar to their kettle water. Some bakeries add dark brown sugar, others add barley malt syrup, and they all seem to have a secret formula on what and how much sugar they add to the water. At home, there is no need to add anything to the water. If the bagels are properly fermented, they will brown beautifully in the oven. (The same holds true for a standard professional convection oven. This type of airflow results in beautiful amber-brown bagel crusts.)

When the bagels come out of the kettle in a bagel bakery, they are unloaded onto a trough in front of the bagel oven. The baker will hose down the bagels with cold water to stop them from overproofing, and then they will load the bagels onto burlap-lined bagel boards. Time is money, and the more bagels per bagel board, the more efficient the bake. Squishing the bagels onto the boards to fit more bagels into the oven results in squished bagel holes and "kissing" bagels (when the sides of the bagels touch and bake together). The squished, kissing bagels are perfection to me. It means efficiency of the craft.

Bagels are loaded on the burlap-lined boards upside down so that their bottoms dry out. Otherwise, the wet bagels will glue themselves onto the oven hearth. After a minute or two the baker flips the boards, the bagels land right-side up on the hearth, and the boards are pulled out of the oven (and hosed down). I often look at the side profile of those bagels—the curvature of the bottom and top is equal because the bottom rises and bakes before the bagel is flipped over. There is no shame in baking bagels on a baking sheet, especially if you don't have bagel boards, but the bottoms will be flat with little curvature. A perfect bagel in my world has a uniform curvature between the top and bottom.

Perfection aside, the most important part of bagel making is to have fun, and I hope this chapter of recipes provides you with the information you need to make great-tasting bagels and have fun while doing it!

Master Class
A Guide to Successful Bagel Making

Mixing and kneading

Bagels use high-gluten bread flour and have low hydration. In my sourdough bagel recipe, the ratio of water to flour is 45%, not counting the water and flour from the sourdough starter, whereas baguettes and sourdough loaves are traditionally 70% hydration and higher. Bagels are meant to be boiled before baking, and this low hydration helps ensure they do not fall apart while they are boiling.

High-gluten bread flour gives bagels their chewy texture. I use bread flours with a protein content from 12.7% up to 14.2% for my bagels. Because bagel dough does not use a lot of water and uses high-protein bread flour, the dough is exceptionally thick and tough. In a professional bakery, we use a spiral mixer to knead the dough properly, which essentially just means developing all the potential gluten strands.

At home I believe the best way to develop the gluten is to use a food processor. I prefer to combine the ingredients in a stand mixer, although this could be done by hand, and then to divide the dough into portions and process them in a food processor. The trick is to not overheat the dough in the food processor. I like to use 30-second increments with rests in between.

To mix bagel dough at home, start by whisking all of the dissolvable ingredients into the water before you add the flour so that everything is nice and homogeneous. Once the flour is added, the dough becomes stiff. At this point dump the dough onto a work surface and begin the kneading.

Additional flour for dusting

Bagel dough is not a wet dough, and when you divide and shape the bagels, you should not add any additional dusting flour. Once the gluten has formed any initial stickiness will go away.

Water for boiling

When I boil bagels, I do not add anything to my water—no sugar or malt syrup or baking soda. Perhaps you think that, since I am making my bagels at home in Brooklyn, I have access to tap water that is especially good for bagel making? Rest assured, I have also used tap water in Rhode Island, California, and Sweden to make my bagels and have not found that it particularly affects the quality of either the dough or in the boiling. In my opinion, the most important factor affecting the bagels is the fermentation and proofing.

"Float Test" and proofing

Bagels are ready to be boiled and baked when they float in water (remember, carbon dioxide is produced from the yeast feeding on the sugars and starches in the dough, and it becomes trapped in the gluten structure of the bagels, causing the bagels to float). How they float helps me determine when to boil them. First, I fill a small bowl with water. I pick up one of the proofed bagels and drop it in the bowl. If it sinks, it has not proofed enough, and if boiled and baked, it will be too dense. If the bagel starts to sink and then gradually rises within a few seconds, it is ready, but slightly underproofed. Or if the bagel immediately floats, it is proofed and ready.

Boiling

When I drop the bagels into the boiling water, I aim to drop them so they float right-side down. I let them boil for 1 minute and then use tongs or a spider to flip them right-side up and boil for another 30 seconds to 1 minute. I boil the bagels based on how much they have proofed. If they are slightly underproofed, that is they sink a little and then float, I boil them for 2 minutes total, about 1 minute per side. If the bagels have overproofed and are puffy and "super floaters," I cut the boiling time down to 30 seconds per side (1 minute total), because the heat from the water will continue to proof the bagels.

Baking bagels on a baking stone

This is the fun part. The recipes are written so that you bake the bagels on baking sheets, and this works perfectly well. But for truly authentic bagels, you can construct your own bagel flipping boards. Traditionally bagels are baked on a hearth. You can't place the boiled bagels immediately onto the hearth because they are wet and will stick to the hearth, so bagels are first placed, upside down, on burlap-covered boards and then placed into the oven. Their bottoms dry out and begin to rise while in the oven. As soon as the bottoms are dry enough, about 2 minutes at home, they are flipped using the board right-side up and finish baking on the hearth. Baking them this way means that they have a uniform curvature and are not flat-bottomed.

To bake the bagels in this way, you will need a baking stone about 20 × 13 inches. And you will need to make three flipping boards from 1 × 4 lumber. The dimensions of each board should be 13 inches long by 3½ inches wide by ¾ inch thick. You will also need a burlap roll specifically for bagel boards. These rolls of burlap are 3½ inches wide. Cut the burlap into three 14½-inch lengths. Staple or hammer the ends of the burlap into the ¾-inch sides of the boards so that the length of each board is completely covered with the burlap.

Arrange the racks in the oven so that one rack is in the bottom third and no racks are above it. Place the baking stone on the rack and preheat the oven to 450°F. Note that this is a higher temperature than with the baking sheets because the baking sheets transfer heat to the bagels faster than the stone.

Before using the flipping boards, soak them in a container of water for 30 minutes. Pull them from the water and set them close to where the bagels will be boiled. Boil the bagels according to the recipe, and with a slotted spoon or spider, transfer the bagels to a baking sheet. Seed the bagels if desired. Place three bagels upside down on one flipping board, and place the board immediately into the oven on the hearth stone. Set a timer for two minutes. While the bottoms are drying, continue to boil more bagels.

After 2 minutes, flip the bagels right-side up onto the baking stone by holding on to the flipping board with a clean kitchen towel and turning the bagels right-side up in a quick motion. The bagels are done when their tops are golden brown and they sound hollow when tapped. Use a bread peel or large spatula to remove the bagels from the oven and onto a cooling rack.

Bagel Size

Bagels have increased in size over time. At the beginning of the twentieth century they were about 3 ounces (85 grams), and their size was controlled by Bagel Bakers Local 338, a trade union in New York City. The union also mandated that the bagels be shaped by hand. As bagels grew in popularity, so did the bakery technology to mass-produce them. Once the union workers were replaced by machines, bagels grew in size. Bagels today are closer to 4.5 to 6 ounces (130 to 170 grams).

When I first began to make bagels at the Smorgasburg, I made them close to the bagel union 3-ounce size. Each piece of dough weighed 110 grams, which was between 3.5 and 4 ounces. I kept my bagels at that weight for a long time. They weighed 110 grams when I opened Sadelle's and taught many bagel classes, and the recipe I handed out would make a baker's dozen!

During the pandemic, I worked with the restaurant Gertie, in Brooklyn. Nate, the owner, grew up on the Upper West Side eating bagels from Absolute Bagels. Those were the quintessential bagel for him, and they weighed about 4.5 ounces. We both came to agree that 4.5 ounces was reminiscent of a more recent New York bagel—not too large, not too small.

Each of the bagel recipes in this chapter makes 11 bagels, each weighing 130 grams (4.5 ounces). It might seem odd that the recipes do not make a dozen bagels. But hopefully you'll forgive me by understanding this bit of background in my recipe development.

Sourdough Bagels

Makes 11 bagels

I have been tinkering with recipes for bagels both at home and professionally for a long time and the result of all the tinkering is this recipe, which produces professional-looking and -tasting bagels at home. Please read through A Guide to Successful Bagel Making (page 23) before beginning this recipe.

Plan ahead Mix your starter 12 hours before you plan to make the dough. I suggest you mix the starter in the evening, and then mix the bagels the next morning.

Note You may end up with a small amount of dough left over; make a mini bagel, perfect for snacking.

			Baker's %
Sourdough Starter			
Water (70°–75°F)	½ cup	118 grams	98
Mother sourdough starter	1 tablespoon	25 grams	21
Bread flour	1 cup	120 grams	100
For the dough			
Water (65°–70°F)	1½ cups	355 grams	46
Instant yeast	2½ teaspoons	7.5 grams	1.0
Sourdough Starter (above)	1½ cups	263 grams	34
Barley malt syrup	1 tablespoon	21 grams	2.7
Fine sea salt	4 teaspoons	24 grams	3.0
Granulated sugar	3 tablespoons	39 grams	5.0
High-gluten bread flour	5¾ cups	776 grams	100
Nonstick cooking spray			

Mix the starter

• Mix the sourdough starter the evening (or at least 12 hours) before you plan to make the bagel dough. Put the water in a 1-quart container with a lid and add 25 grams (1 tablespoon) of the mother sourdough starter. Add the flour and stir with a metal spoon to combine. Cover the container and set aside in a warm place (about 75°F).

Mix the dough

• Put the water in the bowl of a stand mixer. Sprinkle the yeast on the top and let rest for 5 minutes to help dissolve the yeast. Then whisk the yeast into the water. Add the sourdough starter, barley malt syrup, salt, and sugar and whisk everything together until the liquid is homogeneous. Add the bread flour, fit the mixer with the dough hook, and mix on low for 2 minutes.

Knead the dough

• Dump the dough out onto a work surface and divide it into 4 pieces with a bench knife. Working with one piece of dough at a time, process in a food processor fitted with the metal blade for about 30 seconds, returning the dough to the work surface before processing the next piece. Once you have processed all the pieces of dough once, repeat until each piece has gone through the food processor three or four times. Recombine the pieces on the work surface once they have all been processed. Cover the dough with plastic wrap and let it rest for 10 minutes.

Divide and shape the bagels

· Spray the bottoms of two baking sheets with nonstick cooking spray. Line with parchment paper and spray the parchment with nonstick cooking spray.

· Use a bench knife to divide the dough into 11 (130-gram) pieces (see Note on previous page). Put a piece of dough on the work surface in front of you. Use both hands to shape the dough into a log. To do this, pick up the top edge and fold it down toward the middle, pinching the edge into the middle with the tips of your fingers. Repeat two or three more times, picking up the top edge and pinching it into the middle until you reach the bottom of the log.

· Roll the log back and forth with the palms of your hands to lengthen it until it is 10 inches long. Then wrap the log around the palm of your hand, overlapping the ends by about 2 inches. Use your palm to roll the overlapped ends back and forth on your work surface to seal them together. Place the shaped bagel on a prepared baking sheet. Continue shaping the remaining pieces of dough in the same way. Put 6 bagels on one sheet and 5 on the other, spacing them evenly apart and leaving at least 2 inches between them.

Proof the bagels

· Wrap both baking sheets with plastic wrap, spraying the plastic wrap with nonstick cooking spray to prevent the bagels from sticking to it. Let the bagels proof at room temperature for 30 minutes, and then place them in the refrigerator to proof overnight, or a minimum of 8 hours.

To store the baking sheets of bagels more efficiently in your refrigerator, put another baking sheet, upside down, on top of them to create enclosed proofing boxes. Carefully stack these boxes on top of each other in the refrigerator.

Boil and bake the bagels

· Arrange oven racks in the top third and bottom third of the oven and preheat the oven to 400°F.

· Fill a 5-quart pot with water and bring to a boil over high heat. While the water is coming up to a boil, remove the baking sheets from the refrigerator and unwrap them. Gently place one bagel in a small bowl of water. If it floats to the top, the bagels are proofed enough to boil and bake. If the bagel sinks, set a timer for 20 minutes and check again. Do not boil the bagels until they pass this float test.

· Gently pick up and drop 2 or 3 bagels into the boiling water. Boil for 1 minute and then turn them over using tongs and boil for another 30 to 60 seconds. Use a spider or slotted spoon to remove the bagels, one at a time, from the boiling water and place them back on the baking sheet. Continue until all the bagels have been boiled.

- When all of the bagels are boiled, place a baking sheet on each oven rack and bake for 28 to 33 minutes, until they are lightly browned and emit a hollow sound when you tap on the bottom of one with your finger, switching racks and rotating the baking sheets front to back halfway through the baking time. (Watch out to make sure that the bottoms do not brown too quickly. If they are getting too brown before they are done, slip a second baking sheet directly under each baking sheet to create a doubled baking sheet, shielding the dough from the direct heat.)

Cool the bagels
- Remove the bagels from the oven and let them cool on their baking sheets. To store the bagels, place in zippered plastic bags in the freezer for up to 3 weeks. Thaw the bagels (I use my microwave for about 20 seconds), slice, and toast.

Mixing and shaping bagels

1

2

3

4

5

6

Boiling and preparing to bake bagels

7

8

9

10

Everything Bagels

Makes 11 bagels

When I first began selling my bagels at the Williamsburg Smorgasburg, I had no idea what flavor would be the most popular, so I made an equal number of plain, sesame, and everything bagels. Very quickly it became obvious that the everything ones were the favorite, followed closely by plain and then much more distantly by sesame. Since I am a sesame seed lover, I was a bit disappointed, but quickly changed my bagel seeding so that there would be more everything bagels and fewer sesame seed ones.

At first, I didn't even know what was in an everything bagel topping. I remember having a conversation with Max Sussman, then the chef de cuisine at Roberta's. Together we guessed that it included sesame, poppy, caraway, fennel, onion, and pretzel salt. We were almost right. It turns out, the topping is even simpler: sesame, poppy, garlic, onion, and pretzel salt.

When I opened Sadelle's I kept my original everything topping with caraway and fennel and named the bagel, Everything 2.0. We also made a traditional everything, Everything 1.0.

Instead of using traditional pretzel salt in the topping mix, I like to use a nicer, flaky sea salt, like Maldon. You can tinker with the everything mix to your liking.

A note on the dehydrated onion and garlic: When buying dehydrated onion pieces, seek out minced onion. The pieces are small but are not pulverized. The same goes for garlic. Look for minced garlic. Sometimes it is called granulated garlic, so be careful. Oftentimes granulated garlic is closer to garlic powder and the pieces are too small to use as a bagel topping. My preferred source for all the bagel toppings is nuts.com.

Plan ahead Mix your starter 12 hours before you plan to make the dough. I suggest you mix the starter in the evening, and then mix the bagels the next morning.

Note You may end up with a small amount of dough left over; make a mini bagel, perfect for snacking.

Sourdough Starter			Baker's %
Water (70°–75°F)	½ cup	118 grams	98
Mother sourdough starter	1 tablespoon	25 grams	21
Bread flour	1 cup	120 grams	100
For the dough			
Water (65°–70°F)	1½ cups	355 grams	46
Instant yeast	2½ teaspoons	7.5 grams	1.0
Sourdough Starter (above)	1½ cups	263 grams	34
Barley malt syrup	1 tablespoon	21 grams	2.7
Fine sea salt	4 teaspoons	24 grams	3.0
Granulated sugar	3 tablespoons	39 grams	5.0
High-gluten bread flour	5¾ cups	776 grams	100
Nonstick cooking spray			
For the seed topping			
Sesame seeds	2 ounces	56 grams	
Poppy seeds	2 ounces	56 grams	
Dehydrated minced onion	2 ounces	56 grams	
Dehydrated minced garlic	2 ounces	56 grams	
Flaky salt	1 ounce	28 grams	

Mix the starter

· Mix the sourdough starter the evening (or at least 12 hours) before you plan to make the bagel dough. Put the water in a 1-quart container with a lid and add 25 grams (1 tablespoon) of the mother sourdough starter. Add the flour and stir with a metal spoon to combine. Cover the container and set aside in a warm place (about 75°F).

Mix the dough

· Put the water in the bowl of a stand mixer. Sprinkle the yeast on top and let rest for 5 minutes to help dissolve the yeast. Then whisk the yeast into the water. Add the sourdough starter, barley malt syrup, salt, and sugar and whisk everything together until the liquid is homogeneous. Add the bread flour, fit the mixer with the dough hook, and mix on low for 2 minutes.

Knead the dough

· Dump the dough out onto a work surface and divide it into 4 pieces with a bench knife. Working with one piece of dough at a time, process in a food processor fitted with the metal blade for about 30 seconds, returning the dough to the work surface before processing the next piece. Once you have processed all the pieces of dough once, repeat until each piece has gone through the food processor three or four times. Recombine the pieces on the work surface once they have all been processed. Cover the dough with plastic wrap and let it rest for 10 minutes.

Divide and shape the bagels

· Spray the bottoms of two baking sheets with nonstick cooking spray. Line with parchment paper and spray the parchment with nonstick cooking spray.
· Use a bench knife to divide the dough into 11 (130-gram) pieces (see Note on page 32). Put a piece of dough on the work surface in front of you. Use both hands to shape the dough into a log. To do this, pick up the top edge and fold it down toward the middle, pinching the edge into the middle with the tips of your fingers. Repeat two or three more times, picking up the top edge and pinching it into the middle until you reach the bottom of the log.
· Roll the log back and forth with the palms of your hands to lengthen it until it is 10 inches long. Then wrap the log around the palm of your hand, overlapping the ends by about 2 inches. Use your palm to roll the overlapped ends back and forth on your work surface to seal them together. Place the shaped bagel on a prepared baking sheet. Continue shaping the remaining pieces of dough in the same way. Put 6 bagels on one sheet and 5 on the other, spacing them evenly apart and leaving at least 2 inches between them.

Proof the bagels

· Wrap both baking sheets with plastic wrap, spraying the plastic wrap with nonstick cooking spray to prevent the bagels from sticking to it. Let the sheets of bagels proof at room temperature for 30 minutes, and then place them in the refrigerator to proof overnight, or a minimum of 8 hours.

To store the baking sheets of bagels more efficiently in your refrigerator, put another baking sheet, upside down, on top of them to create enclosed proofing boxes. Carefully stack these boxes on top of each other in the refrigerator.

Make the seed topping

· In a small bowl, mix together the sesame seeds, poppy seeds, onion, garlic, and salt with a metal spoon. Sprinkle ⅔ cup (85 grams) of the topping in an even layer on a large plate. Place the remaining topping in a small bowl and set aside.

Boil, coat, and bake the bagels

· Arrange oven racks in the top third and bottom third of the oven and preheat the oven to 400°F.
· Fill a 5-quart pot with water and bring to a boil over high heat. While the water is coming up to a boil, remove the baking sheets of bagels from the refrigerator and unwrap them. Gently place one bagel in a small bowl of water. If it floats to the top, the bagels are proofed enough to boil and bake. If the bagel sinks, set a timer for 20 minutes and check again. Do not boil the bagels until they pass this float test.
· Gently drop 2 or 3 bagels into the boiling water. Boil for 1 minute and then turn them over using tongs and boil for another 30 to 60 seconds. Use a spider or slotted spoon to remove the bagels, one at a time, from the boiling water

and place them right-side up on the large plate with the seed topping. Take the small bowl of topping and use your fingers to generously sprinkle the tops of the bagels with the mix. With both hands, pick up one bagel at a time and transfer it back to the baking sheet. Continue until all the bagels have been boiled and coated.

Baking bagels coated in seeds often takes several minutes longer than uncoated bagels because the heat transfer from the oven to the bagel must pass through the seeds first.

- Place a baking sheet on each oven rack and bake the bagels for 28 to 33 minutes, until they are lightly browned and emit a hollow sound when you tap on the bottom with your finger, switching racks and rotating the baking sheets from front to back halfway through the baking time. (Watch out that the bottoms do not brown too quickly. If they are getting too brown before they are done, slip a second baking sheet directly under each baking sheet to create a doubled baking sheet, shielding the dough from the direct heat.)

Cool the bagels
- Remove the bagels from the oven and let them cool on their baking sheets. To store the bagels, place in zippered plastic bags in the freezer for up to 3 weeks. Thaw the bagels (I use my microwave for about 20 seconds), slice, and toast.

Sesame Bagels

Makes 11 bagels

Sesame bagels are my favorite type of bagel. I love the nuttiness and texture the seeds add. When buying sesame seeds, I prefer those that haven't been hulled because they have more flavor and more texture. You can find the unhulled seeds online and at many large supermarkets; however, failing that, just use hulled. You will need 6 ounces of sesame seeds to coat the bagels in this recipe.

Plan ahead Mix your starter 12 hours before you plan to make the dough. I suggest you mix the starter in the evening, and then mix the bagels the next morning.

Note You may end up with a small amount of dough left over; make a mini bagel, perfect for snacking.

			Baker's %
Sourdough Starter			
Water (70°–75°F)	½ cup	118 grams	98
Mother sourdough starter	1 tablespoon	25 grams	21
Bread flour	1 cup	120 grams	100
For the dough			
Water (65°–70°F)	1½ cups	355 grams	46
Instant yeast	2½ teaspoons	7.5 grams	1.0
Sourdough Starter (above)	1½ cups	263 grams	34
Barley malt syrup	1 tablespoon	21 grams	2.7
Fine sea salt	4 teaspoons	24 grams	3.0
Granulated sugar	3 tablespoons	39 grams	5.0
High-gluten bread flour	5¾ cups	776 grams	100
Nonstick cooking spray			
For the seed topping			
Sesame seeds	6 ounces	168 grams	

Mix the starter

• Mix the sourdough starter the evening (or at least 12 hours) before you plan to make the bagel dough. Put the water in a 1-quart container with a lid and add 25 grams (1 tablespoon) of the mother sourdough starter. Add the flour and stir with a metal spoon to combine. Cover the container and set aside in a warm place (about 75°F).

Mix the dough

• Put the water in the bowl of a stand mixer. Sprinkle the yeast on top and let it rest for 5 minutes to help the yeast to dissolve. Then whisk the yeast into the water. Add the sourdough starter, barley malt syrup, salt, and sugar and whisk everything together until the liquid is homogeneous. Add the bread flour, fit the mixer with the dough hook, and mix on low for 2 minutes.

Knead the dough
· Dump the dough out onto a work surface and divide it into 4 pieces with a bench knife. Working with one piece of dough at a time, process in a food processor fitted with the metal blade for about 30 seconds, returning the dough to the work surface before processing the next piece. Once you have processed all the pieces of dough once, repeat until each piece has gone through the food processor three or four times. Recombine the pieces on the work surface once they have all been processed. Cover the dough with plastic wrap and let it rest for 10 minutes.

Divide and shape the bagels
· Spray the bottoms of two baking sheets with nonstick cooking spray. Line with parchment paper and spray the parchment with nonstick cooking spray.
· Use a bench knife to divide the dough into 11 (130-gram) pieces (see Note on previous page). Put a piece of dough on the work surface in front of you. Use both hands to shape the dough into a log. To do this, pick up the top edge and fold it down toward the middle, pinching the edge into the middle with the tips of your fingers. Repeat two or three more times, picking up the top edge and pinching it into the middle until you reach the bottom of the log.
· Roll the log back and forth with the palms of your hands to lengthen it until it is 10 inches long. Then wrap the log around the palm of your hand, overlapping the ends by about 2 inches. Use your palm to roll the overlapped ends back and forth on your work surface to seal them together. Place the shaped bagel on a prepared baking sheet. Continue shaping the remaining pieces of dough in the same way. Put 6 bagels on one sheet and 5 on the other, spacing them evenly apart and leaving at least 2 inches between them.

Proof the bagels
· Wrap both baking sheets with plastic wrap, spraying the plastic wrap with nonstick cooking spray to prevent the bagels from sticking to it. Let the sheets of bagels proof at room temperature for 30 minutes, and then place them in the refrigerator to proof overnight, or a minimum of 8 hours.

To store the baking sheets of bagels more efficiently in your refrigerator, put another baking sheet, upside down, on top of them to create enclosed proofing boxes. Carefully stack these boxes on top of each other in the refrigerator.

Boil, coat, and bake the bagels
· Arrange oven racks in the top third and bottom third of the oven and preheat the oven to 400°F.
· Sprinkle one-third of the sesame seeds in an even layer on a large plate. Place the remaining sesame seeds in a small bowl and set aside.
· Fill a 5-quart pot with water and bring to a boil over high heat. While the water is coming up to a boil, remove the baking sheets of bagels from the refrigerator and unwrap them. Gently place one bagel in a small bowl of water.

If it floats to the top, the bagels are proofed enough to boil and bake. If the bagel sinks, set a timer for 20 minutes and check again. Do not boil the bagels until they pass this float test.

- Gently drop 2 or 3 bagels into the boiling water. Boil for 1 minute and then turn them over using tongs and boil for another 30 to 60 seconds. Use a spider or slotted spoon to remove the bagels, one at a time, from the boiling water and place them right-side up on the large plate with sesame seeds. Take the small bowl of sesame seeds and use your fingers to generously sprinkle the tops of the bagels with the seeds. With both hands, pick up one bagel at a time and transfer it back to the baking sheet. Continue until all the bagels have been boiled and coated.

Baking bagels coated in seeds often takes several minutes longer than uncoated bagels because the heat transfer from the oven to the bagel must pass through the seeds first.

- Place a baking sheet on each oven rack and bake the bagels for 28 to 33 minutes, until they are lightly browned and emit a hollow sound when you tap on the bottom of a bagel with your finger, switching racks and rotating the baking sheets from front to back halfway through the baking time. (Watch out that the bottoms do not brown too quickly. If they are getting too brown before they are done, slip a second baking sheet directly under each baking sheet to create a doubled baking sheet, shielding the dough from the direct heat.)

Cool the bagels   - Remove the bagels from the oven and let them cool on their baking sheets. To store the bagels, place in zippered plastic bags in the freezer for up to 3 weeks. Thaw the bagels (I use my microwave for about 20 seconds), slice, and toast.

Onion Bagels

Makes 11 bagels

Onion bagels are traditionally made from plain bagels coated with dehydrated minced onion. When I first made these, I thought it would be clever to put the onion into the dough instead of on top of it for more flavor. I rehydrated the minced onion and added it to the dough. (Any time you add a dried or dehydrated item to a dough, it should be rehydrated so that it does not pull moisture away from the dough. You want the dough hydration to remain the same with any additions.) Then I decided to add fresh onion for more flavor, so I sweated some onion and added that to the dough . . . but it broke down into a pureed mess in the mixer. So next, I dehydrated the onion to toughen its cell walls to prevent it from breaking down during mixing. I soaked it in a little water before adding it to the dough so as not to affect the dough hydration. The result is a sweet and savory delicious onion bagel!

Plan ahead Mix your starter 12 hours before you plan to make the dough. I suggest you mix the starter in the evening, and then mix the bagels the next morning.

Note You may end up with a small amount of dough left over; make a mini bagel, perfect for snacking.

			Baker's %
For the dehydrated onions			
Yellow onions	3 large (about 2½ pounds)	1.14 kilograms	
Sourdough Starter			
Water (70°–75°F)	½ cup	118 grams	98
Mother sourdough starter	1 tablespoon	25 grams	21
Bread flour	1 cup	120 grams	100
For the dough			
Dehydrated onions (above)	1½ cups	135 grams	20
Water (65°–70°F)	1 cup + 1 tablespoon	251 grams	37
Instant yeast	2½ teaspoons	7.5 grams	1.1
Sourdough Starter (above)	1½ cups	263 grams	39
Barley malt syrup	1 tablespoon + 1 teaspoon	28 grams	4.0
Fine sea salt	1 tablespoon + 1 teaspoon	24 grams	3.5
High-gluten bread flour	5⅔ cups	680 grams	100
Fresh chives, finely chopped	½ ounce	14 grams	2
Nonstick cooking spray			

Dehydrate the onions

- Arrange oven racks in the top third and bottom third of the oven and preheat the oven to 200°F. Line two baking sheets with parchment paper.
- Trim and halve the onions from root to tip. Cut the onions into ½-inch cubes and spread them out over the surface of the two prepared baking sheets.
- Place a baking sheet on each oven rack and cook the onions for about 4 hours, until they have shriveled and are almost completely dried out, stirring them every hour so the onions around the edges of the baking sheet don't

burn. Remove the onions from the oven and set them aside to cool to room temperature. If you are making the onions in advance of making the dough, consolidate them on one baking sheet and set them aside, for as long as several hours, until you're ready to use them. Or transfer them to a zippered plastic bag and refrigerate for up to 2 days.

Mix the starter

• Mix the sourdough starter the evening (or at least 12 hours) before you plan to make the bagel dough. Put the water in a 1-quart container with a lid and add 25 grams (1 tablespoon) of the mother sourdough starter. Add the flour and stir with a metal spoon to combine. Cover the container and set aside in a warm place (about 75°F).

Mix the dough

• Put the dehydrated onion in a small bowl and cover it with warm water. Let the onion soak for 5 minutes. Drain the onion in a sieve.
• Put the water in the bowl of a stand mixer. Sprinkle the yeast on top and let rest for 5 minutes to help dissolve the yeast. Then whisk the yeast into the water. Add the sourdough starter, barley malt syrup, and salt and whisk everything together until the liquid is homogeneous. Add the bread flour, chopped chives, and drained rehydrated onion. Fit the mixer with the dough hook and mix on low for 2 minutes. Increase the speed to medium and mix for 5 minutes. Turn off the mixer and remove the bowl from the stand. Dump the dough onto a work surface.

The onion and chives are added to the dough at the beginning of the mixing process because of their small size. This dough is not processed in the food processor so that the small pieces are not pulverized.

Divide and shape the bagels

• Spray the bottoms of two baking sheets with nonstick cooking spray. Line with parchment paper and spray the parchment with nonstick cooking spray.
• Use a bench knife to divide the dough into 11 (130-gram) pieces (see Note on previous page). Put a piece of dough on the work surface in front of you. Use both hands to shape the dough into a log. To do this, pick up the top edge and fold it down toward the middle, pinching the edge into the middle with the tips of your fingers. Repeat two or three more times, picking up the top edge and pinching it into the middle until you reach the bottom of the log.
• Roll the log back and forth with the palms of your hands to lengthen it until it is 10 inches long. Then wrap the log around the palm of your hand, overlapping the ends by about 2 inches. Use your palm to roll the overlapped ends back and forth on your work surface to seal them together. Place the shaped bagel on a prepared baking sheet. Continue shaping the remaining pieces of dough in the same way. Put 6 bagels on one sheet and 5 on the other, spacing them evenly apart and leaving at least 2 inches between them.

Proof the bagels

· Wrap both baking sheets with plastic wrap, spraying the plastic wrap with nonstick cooking spray to prevent the bagels from sticking to it. Let the sheets of bagels proof at room temperature for 30 minutes, and then place them in the refrigerator to proof overnight, or a minimum of 8 hours.

To store the baking sheets of bagels more efficiently in your refrigerator, put another baking sheet, upside down, on top of them to create enclosed proofing boxes. Carefully stack these boxes on top of each other in the refrigerator.

Boil and bake the bagels

· Arrange oven racks in the top third and bottom third of the oven and preheat the oven to 400°F.

· Fill a 5-quart pot with water and bring to a boil over high heat. While the water is coming up to a boil, remove the baking sheets of bagels from the refrigerator and unwrap them. Gently place one bagel in a small bowl of water. If the bagel floats to the top, the bagels are proofed enough to boil and bake. If the bagel sinks, set a timer for 20 minutes and check again. Do not boil the bagels until they pass this float test.

· Gently pick up and drop 2 or 3 bagels into the boiling water. Boil for 1 minute and then turn them over, using tongs, and boil for another 30 to 60 seconds. Use a spider or slotted spoon to remove the bagels, one at a time, from the boiling water and place them back on the baking sheet. Continue until all the bagels have been boiled.

· Place a baking sheet on each oven rack and bake the bagels for 28 to 33 minutes, until they are lightly browned and emit a hollow sound when you tap on the bottom of a bagel with your finger, switching racks and rotating the baking sheets from front to back halfway through the baking time. (Watch out that the bottoms do not brown too quickly. If they are getting too brown before they are done, slip a second baking sheet directly under each baking sheet to create a doubled baking sheet, shielding the dough from the direct heat.)

Cool the bagels

· Remove the bagels from the oven and let them cool on their baking sheets. To store the bagels, place in zippered plastic bags in the freezer for up to 3 weeks. Thaw the bagels (I use my microwave for about 20 seconds), slice, and toast.

Salt and Pepper Bagels

Makes 11 bagels

These are my riff on the traditional salt bagel. I add cracked butcher's pepper to the dough and sprinkle flaky sea salt on top. Butcher's pepper, which is a larger grind, is sold in specialty food stores and butcher shops. You can make your own by coarsely grinding peppercorns in a spice grinder. Pass the mixture through a fine-mesh sieve and use the coarse pieces.

Plan ahead Mix your starter 12 hours before you plan to make the dough. I suggest you mix the starter in the evening, and then mix the bagels the next morning.

Note You may end up with a small amount of dough left over; make a mini bagel, perfect for snacking.

			Baker's %
Sourdough Starter			
Water (70°–75°F)	½ cup	118 grams	98
Mother sourdough starter	1 tablespoon	25 grams	21
Bread flour	1 cup	120 grams	100
For the dough			
Water (65°–70°F)	1½ cups	355 grams	46
Instant yeast	2½ teaspoons	7.5 grams	1.0
Sourdough Starter (above)	1½ cups	263 grams	34
Barley malt syrup	1 tablespoon	21 grams	3.0
Granulated sugar	3 tablespoons	39 grams	5.0
Fine sea salt	4 teaspoons	24 grams	3.1
High-gluten bread flour	5¾ cups	776 grams	100
Cracked butcher's pepper	1 tablespoon + 1 teaspoon	12 grams	1.5
Nonstick cooking spray			
For the salt topping			
Flaky salt	1 tablespoon + 1 teaspoon	13 grams	

Mix the starter

· Mix the sourdough starter the evening (or at least 12 hours) before you plan to make the bagel dough. Put the water in a 1-quart container with a lid and add 25 grams (1 tablespoon) of the mother sourdough starter. Add the flour and stir with a metal spoon to combine. Cover the container and set aside in a warm place (about 75°F).

Mix the dough

· Put the water in the bowl of a stand mixer. Sprinkle the yeast on top and let rest for 5 minutes to help dissolve the yeast. Then whisk the yeast into the water. Add the sourdough starter, barley malt syrup, sugar, and sea salt and whisk everything together until the liquid is homogeneous. Add the bread flour and cracked butcher's pepper, fit the mixer with the dough hook, and mix on low for 2 minutes.

Knead the dough

· Dump the dough out onto a work surface and divide it into 4 pieces with a bench knife. Working with one piece of dough at a time, process in a food processor fitted with the metal blade for about 30 seconds, returning the dough to the work surface before processing the next piece. Once you have processed all the pieces of dough once, repeat until each piece has gone through the food processor three or four times. Recombine the pieces on the work surface once they have all been processed. Cover the dough with plastic wrap and let it rest for 10 minutes.

Divide and shape the bagels

· Spray the bottoms of two baking sheets with nonstick cooking spray. Line with parchment paper and spray the parchment with nonstick cooking spray.
· Use a bench knife to divide the dough into 11 (130-gram) pieces (see Note on page 43). Put a piece of dough on the work surface in front of you. Use both hands to shape the dough into a log. To do this, pick up the top edge and fold it down toward the middle, pinching the edge into the middle with the tips of your fingers. Repeat two or three more times, picking up the top edge and pinching it into the middle until you reach the bottom of the log.
· Roll the log back and forth with the palms of your hands to lengthen it until it is 10 inches long. Then wrap the log around the palm of your hand, overlapping the ends by about 2 inches. Use your palm to roll the overlapped ends back and forth on your work surface to seal them together. Place the shaped bagel on a prepared baking sheet. Continue shaping the remaining pieces of dough in the same way. Put 6 bagels on one sheet and 5 on the other, spacing them evenly apart and leaving at least 2 inches between them.

Proof the bagels

· Wrap both baking sheets with plastic wrap, spraying the plastic wrap with nonstick cooking spray to prevent the bagels from sticking to it. Let the sheets of bagels proof at room temperature for 30 minutes, and then place them in the refrigerator to proof overnight, or a minimum of 8 hours.

To store the baking sheets of bagels more efficiently in your refrigerator, put another baking sheet, upside down, on top of them to create enclosed proofing boxes. Carefully stack these boxes on top of each other in the refrigerator.

Boil and bake the bagels

· Arrange oven racks in the top third and bottom third of the oven and preheat the oven to 400°F.
· Fill a 5-quart pot with water and bring to a boil over high heat. While the water is coming up to a boil, remove the baking sheets of bagels from the refrigerator and unwrap them. Gently place one bagel in a small bowl of water. If the bagel floats to the top, the bagels are proofed enough to boil and bake. If the bagel sinks, set a timer for 20 minutes and check again. Do not boil the bagels until they pass this float test.

• Gently pick up and drop 2 or 3 bagels into the boiling water. Boil for 1 minute and then turn them over using tongs and boil for another 30 to 60 seconds. Use a spider or slotted spoon to remove the bagels, one at a time, from the boiling water and place them back on the baking sheet. Continue until all the bagels have been boiled.

• Generously sprinkle the tops of the bagels with flaky salt. Place a baking sheet on each oven rack and bake the bagels for 28 to 33 minutes, until they are lightly browned and emit a hollow sound when you tap on the bottom of a bagel with your finger, switching racks and rotating the baking sheets from front to back halfway through the baking time. (Watch out that the bottoms do not brown too quickly. If they are getting too brown before they are done, slip a second baking sheet directly under each baking sheet to create a doubled baking sheet, shielding the dough from the direct heat.)

Cool the bagels

• Remove the bagels from the oven and let them cool on their baking sheets. To store the bagels, place in zippered plastic bags in the freezer for up to 3 weeks. Thaw the bagels (I use my microwave for about 20 seconds), slice, and toast.

Pumpernickel Raisin Bagels

Makes 11 bagels

There are three things that define pumpernickel bagels: They are squishy, darkly colored, and taste of caraway. Squishiness is a characteristic of gluten, and since rye and pumpernickel flours contain very little gluten, it stands to reason that pumpernickel bagels are not actually made with much, if any, of those flours. When we think of the flavor "pumpernickel," we are mostly thinking of the flavor from caraway seeds. Pumpernickel is both the name of a sourdough loaf of bread made with roughly ground rye flour, as well as being the name for the roughly ground rye flour. Most commercially made pumpernickel bagels use caramel coloring to achieve their dark color. In Europe, dark-roasted malted barley flour is a common ingredient in pumpernickel loaves. The dark-roasted malted barley flour adds a rich, earthy cocoa and coffee flavor without overpowering.

To pull all these things together, I use a small percentage, just 4% baker's percentage, of rye flour in the bagel dough. I also toast caraway seeds, grinding half into a powder to give these bagels their flavor. And I add dark-roasted malted barley flour to the dough for flavor and coloring. This, while readily available in Europe, is more difficult to locate in the United States. I have purchased mine at beer brewing supply shops or online. I buy it as a whole grain and then grind it at home with a flour mill. It also can be processed in a coffee or spice grinder, though in that case, it needs to be sifted to remove the coarse pieces until you are left with a fine powder. If this is too much work, cocoa powder can also be substituted, although the bagels may have more of a chocolaty taste to them. If you choose to use cocoa powder in place of the malted barley flour, reduce the amount from ½ cup (60 grams) to ¼ cup (30 grams) and increase the rye flour to ½ cup (60 grams).

Plan ahead Mix your starter 12 hours before you plan to make the dough. I suggest you mix the starter in the evening, and then mix the bagels the next morning.

Note You may end up with a small amount of dough left over; make a mini bagel, perfect for snacking.

			Baker's %
Sourdough Starter			
Water (70°–75°F)	½ cup	118 grams	98
Mother sourdough starter	1 tablespoon	25 grams	21
Bread flour	1 cup	120 grams	100
For the dough			
Caraway seeds	5 tablespoons	40 grams	5.0
Raisins	1⅓ cups	200 grams	26
Water (65°–70°F)	1½ cups	355 grams	46
Instant yeast	2½ teaspoons	7.5 grams	1.0
Sourdough Starter (above)	1½ cups	225 grams	29
Barley malt syrup	1½ tablespoons	32 grams	4.0
Fine sea salt	4 teaspoons	24 grams	3.1
High-protein bread flour	5⅔ cups	679 grams	88
Rye flour	¼ cup	30 grams	4.0
Dark-roasted malted barley flour	½ cup	60 grams	8.0

Mix the starter	• Mix the sourdough starter the evening (or at least 12 hours) before you plan to make the bagel dough. Put the water in a 1-quart container with a lid and add 25 grams (1 tablespoon) of the mother sourdough starter. Add the flour and stir with a metal spoon to combine. Cover the container and set aside in a warm place (about 75°F).
Prepare the caraway seeds	• In a medium skillet, toast the caraway seeds over medium-high heat for 2 to 3 minutes, shaking the pan frequently so they toast evenly and don't burn, until they are fragrant and begin popping. Pour the seeds out of the skillet into a medium bowl to cool to room temperature.
	• Once cool, put 2½ tablespoons (20 grams) of the seeds in a spice grinder and pulse to pulverize. Put the ground caraway back in the bowl with the caraway seeds.
Mix the dough	• Place the raisins in a small bowl and cover with warm water. Set aside to soak for 5 minutes. Drain the raisins in a sieve and let them sit in the sieve to continue to drain while you mix the dough.
	• Put the water in the bowl of a stand mixer. Sprinkle the yeast on top and let rest for 5 minutes to help dissolve the yeast. Then whisk the yeast into the water. Add the sourdough starter, barley malt syrup, and salt and whisk everything together until the liquid is homogeneous. Add the bread flour, rye flour, roasted barley flour, and the caraway mixture, fit the mixer with the dough hook, and mix on low for 2 minutes.
Knead the dough	• Dump the dough out onto a work surface and divide it into 4 pieces with a bench knife. Working with one piece of dough at a time, process in a food processor fitted with the metal blade for about 30 seconds, returning the dough to the work surface before processing the next piece. Once you have processed all the pieces of dough once, repeat until each piece has gone through the food processor three or four times. Recombine the pieces on the work surface once they have all been processed. Cover the dough with plastic wrap and let it rest for 10 minutes.
Fold in the raisins	• Remove the plastic from the dough and stretch the dough out onto the work surface to make it into a squarish shape as flat and wide as possible. Sprinkle the raisins on top. To encase the raisins, fold the top third of the dough down halfway and fold the bottom third of the dough up to meet the top in the middle, like folding a letter. Press the dough down and flip it over. Take the right half of the dough and fold it in to the center. Take the left half and fold it in to the center to meet the right half. Press the dough down firmly to spread out the raisins. Continue to fold and press several more times until the raisins are mixed in. If the dough resists folding, re-cover it with plastic and let it rest

10 minutes. Once the folding is finished, cover the dough with plastic and let it rest on the work surface for 15 minutes to relax the gluten before proceeding.

Divide and shape the bagels

• Spray the bottoms of two baking sheets with nonstick cooking spray. Line with parchment paper and spray the parchment with nonstick cooking spray.
• Use a bench knife to divide the dough into 11 (130-gram) pieces (see Note on page 47). Put a piece of dough on the work surface in front of you. Use both hands to shape the dough into a log. To do this, pick up the top edge and fold it down toward the middle, pinching the edge into the middle with the tips of your fingers. Repeat two or three more times, picking up the top edge and pinching it into the middle until you reach the bottom of the log.
• Roll the log back and forth with the palms of your hands to lengthen it until it is 10 inches long. Then wrap the log around the palm of your hand, overlapping the ends by about 2 inches. Use your palm to roll the overlapped ends back and forth on your work surface to seal them together. Place the shaped bagel on a prepared baking sheet. Continue shaping the remaining pieces of dough in the same way. Put 6 bagels on one sheet and 5 on the other, spacing them evenly apart and leaving at least 2 inches between them.

Proof the bagels

• Wrap both baking sheets with plastic wrap, spraying the plastic wrap with nonstick cooking spray to prevent the bagels from sticking to it. Let the sheets of bagels proof at room temperature for 30 minutes, and then place them in the refrigerator to proof overnight, or a minimum of 8 hours.

To store the baking sheets of bagels more efficiently in your refrigerator, put another baking sheet, upside down, on top of them to create enclosed proofing boxes. Carefully stack these boxes on top of each other in the refrigerator.

Boil and bake the bagels

• Arrange oven racks in the top third and bottom third of the oven and preheat the oven to 400°F.
• Fill a 5-quart pot with water and bring to a boil over high heat. While the water is coming up to a boil, remove the baking sheets of bagels from the refrigerator and unwrap them. Gently place one bagel in a small bowl of water. If the bagel floats to the top, the bagels are proofed enough to boil and bake. If the bagel sinks, set a timer for 20 minutes and check again. Do not boil the bagels until they pass this float test.
• Gently pick up and drop 2 or 3 bagels into the boiling water. Boil for 1 minute and then turn them over using tongs and boil for another 30 to 60 seconds. Use a spider or slotted spoon to remove the bagels, one at a time, from the boiling water and place them back on the baking sheet. Continue until all the bagels have been boiled.

- Place a baking sheet on each oven rack and bake the bagels for 28 to 33 minutes, until they are lightly browned and emit a hollow sound when you tap on the bottom of a bagel with your finger, switching racks and rotating the baking sheets from front to back halfway through the baking time. (Watch out that the bottoms do not brown too quickly. If they are getting too brown before they are done, slip a second baking sheet directly under each baking sheet to create a doubled baking sheet, shielding the dough from the direct heat.)

Cool the bagels

- Remove the bagels from the oven and let them cool on their baking sheets. To store the bagels, place in zippered plastic bags in the freezer for up to 3 weeks. Thaw the bagels (I use my microwave for about 20 seconds), slice, and toast.

Pumpernickel Everything Bagels

Makes 11 bagels

When I made bagels for the Smorgasburg outdoor market, I included these pumpernickel everything bagels in the lineup. These were the least popular but had the most devoted following. Like the pumpernickel raisin bagels, these get their flavor from toasted caraway, dark-roasted malted barley flour, and rye flour, but instead of the sweetness from raisins, these are savory with the garlicky everything topping. If you choose to use cocoa powder in place of the malted barley flour, reduce the amount from ½ cup (60 grams) to ¼ cup (30 grams) and increase the rye flour to ½ cup (60 grams).

Plan ahead Mix your starter 12 hours before you plan to make the dough. I suggest you mix the starter in the evening, and then mix the bagels the next morning.

Note You may end up with a small amount of dough left over; make a mini bagel, perfect for snacking.

Sourdough Starter			Baker's %
Water (70°–75°F)	½ cup	118 grams	98
Mother sourdough starter	1 tablespoon	25 grams	21
Bread flour	1 cup	120 grams	100
For the dough			
Caraway seeds	5 tablespoons	40 grams	5.0
Water (65°–70°F)	1½ cups	355 grams	46
Instant yeast	2½ teaspoons	7.5 grams	1.0
Sourdough Starter (above)	1½ cups	225 grams	29
Barley malt syrup	1½ tablespoons	32 grams	4.0
Fine sea salt	4 teaspoons	24 grams	3.1
High-protein bread flour	5⅔ cups	679 grams	88
Rye flour	¼ cup	30 grams	4.0
Dark-roasted malted barley flour	½ cup	60 grams	8.0
For the seed topping			
Sesame seeds	2 ounces	56 grams	
Poppy seeds	2 ounces	56 grams	
Dehydrated minced onion	2 ounces	56 grams	
Dehydrated minced garlic	2 ounces	56 grams	
Flaky salt	1 ounce	28 grams	

Mix the starter

· Mix the sourdough starter the evening (or at least 12 hours) before you plan to make the bagel dough. Put the water in a 1-quart container with a lid and add 25 grams (1 tablespoon) of the mother sourdough starter. Add the flour and stir with a metal spoon to combine. Cover the container and set aside in a warm place (about 75°F).

Prepare the caraway seeds

· In a medium skillet, toast the caraway seeds over medium-high heat for 2 to 3 minutes, shaking the pan frequently so they toast evenly and don't burn, until they are fragrant and begin popping. Pour the seeds out of the skillet into a medium bowl to cool to room temperature.

▪ Once cool, put 2½ tablespoons (20 grams) of the seeds in a spice grinder and pulse to pulverize. Put the ground caraway back in the bowl with the unground caraway seeds.

Mix the dough
▪ Put the water in the bowl of a stand mixer. Sprinkle the yeast on top and let rest for 5 minutes to help dissolve the yeast. Then whisk the yeast into the water. Add the sourdough starter, barley malt syrup, and salt and whisk everything together until the liquid is homogeneous. Add the bread flour, rye flour, roasted barley flour, and the caraway mixture. Fit the mixer with the dough hook and mix on low for 2 minutes.

Knead the dough
▪ Dump the dough out onto a work surface and divide it into 4 pieces with a bench knife. Working with one piece of dough at a time, process in a food processor fitted with the metal blade for about 30 seconds, returning the dough to the work surface before processing the next piece. Once you have processed each piece of dough once, repeat until each piece has gone through the food processor three or four times. Recombine the pieces on the work surface once they have all been processed. Cover the dough with plastic wrap and let it rest for 10 minutes.

Divide and shape the bagels
▪ Spray the bottoms of two baking sheets with nonstick cooking spray. Line with parchment paper and spray the parchment.

▪ Use a bench knife to divide the dough into 11 (130-gram) pieces (see Note on previous page). Put a piece of dough on the work surface in front of you. Use both hands to shape the dough into a log. To do this, pick up the top edge and fold it down toward the middle, pinching the edge into the middle with the tips of your fingers. Repeat two or three more times, picking up the top edge and pinching it into the middle until you reach the bottom of the log.

▪ Roll the log back and forth with the palms of your hands to lengthen it until it is 10 inches long. Then wrap the log around the palm of your hand, overlapping the ends by about 2 inches. Use your palm to roll the overlapped ends back and forth on your work surface to seal them together. Place the shaped bagel on a prepared baking sheet. Continue shaping the remaining pieces of dough in the same way. Put 6 bagels on one sheet and 5 on the other, spacing them evenly apart and leaving at least 2 inches between them.

Proof the bagels
▪ Wrap both baking sheets with plastic wrap, spraying the plastic wrap with nonstick cooking spray to prevent the bagels from sticking to it. Let the sheets of bagels proof at room temperature for 30 minutes, and then place them in the refrigerator to proof overnight, or a minimum of 8 hours.

To store the baking sheets of bagels more efficiently in your refrigerator, put another baking sheet, upside down, on top of them to create enclosed proofing boxes. Carefully stack these boxes on top of each other in the refrigerator.

Make the seed topping
- In a small bowl, mix together the sesame seeds, poppy seeds, onion, garlic, and salt with a metal spoon. Sprinkle ⅔ cup (85 grams) of the topping in an even layer onto a large plate. Place the remaining topping in a small bowl and set aside.

Boil and bake the bagels
- Arrange oven racks in the top third and bottom third of the oven and preheat the oven to 400°F.
- Fill a 5-quart pot with water and bring to a boil over high heat. While the water is coming up to a boil, remove the baking sheets of bagels from the refrigerator and unwrap them. Gently place one bagel in a small bowl of water. If it floats to the top, the bagels are proofed enough to boil and bake. If the bagel sinks, set a timer for 20 minutes and check again. Do not boil the bagels until they pass this float test.
- Gently drop 2 or 3 bagels into the boiling water. Boil for 1 minute and then turn them over using tongs and continue to boil for another 30 to 60 seconds. Use a spider or slotted spoon to remove the bagels, one at a time, from the boiling water and place them right-side up on the plate with the seed topping. Take the small bowl of reserved topping and use your fingers to generously sprinkle it over the tops of the bagels. With both hands, pick up one bagel at a time and transfer it back to the baking sheet. Continue until all the bagels have been boiled and coated.

Baking bagels coated in seeds often takes several minutes longer than baking uncoated bagels because the heat from the oven to the bagel must pass through the seeds first.

- Place a baking sheet on each oven rack and bake the bagels for 28 to 33 minutes, until they emit a hollow sound when you tap on the bottom with a finger, switching racks and rotating the baking sheets from front to back halfway through the baking time.

Cool the bagels
- Remove the bagels from the oven and let them cool on their baking sheets. To store the bagels, place in zippered plastic bags in the freezer for up to 3 weeks. Thaw the bagels (I use my microwave for about 20 seconds), slice, and toast.

Marbled Rye Bagels

Makes 12 bagels

I started making marbled rye bagels as a nod to classic marbled rye bread. First, I mix doughs for both plain and pumpernickel bagels. The fun begins when you combine the pieces and get creative, swirling and twisting to your heart's content.

Plan ahead Mix your starter 12 hours before you plan to make the dough. I suggest you mix the starter in the evening, and then mix the bagels the next morning.

Note You may end up with a small amount of dough left over; make a mini bagel, perfect for snacking.

			Baker's %
Sourdough Starter			
Water (70°–75°F)	⅓ cup	78 grams	100
Mother sourdough starter	2 tablespoons	50 grams	62.5
Bread flour	⅔ cup	80 grams	100
For the plain dough			
Water (68°–78°F)	¾ cup	173 grams	44
Instant yeast	1½ teaspoons	4.5 grams	1.2
Sourdough Starter (above)	Scant ½ cup	104 grams	27
Barley malt syrup	2 teaspoons	14 grams	3.6
Fine sea salt	2 teaspoons	12 grams	3.1
Granulated sugar	2 tablespoons	25 grams	6.0
High-protein bread flour	3¼ cups	390 grams	100
For the pumpernickel dough			
Caraway seeds	2 tablespoons + 1½ teaspoons	20 grams	6.0
Water (68°–78°F)	¾ cup	173 grams	45
Instant yeast	1½ teaspoons	4.5 grams	1.2
Sourdough Starter (above)	Scant ½ cup	104 grams	27
Barley malt syrup	2 teaspoons	14 grams	3.6
Fine sea salt	2 teaspoons	12 grams	3.1
High-protein bread flour	2½ cups + ⅓ cup	340 grams	88
Rye flour	2 tablespoons	16 grams	4.0
Dark-roasted malted barley flour	¼ cup	31 grams	8.0

Mix the starter

· Mix the sourdough starter the evening (or at least 12 hours) before you plan to make the bagel dough. Put the water in a 1-quart container with a lid and add 50 grams (2 tablespoons) of the mother sourdough starter. Add the flour and stir with a metal spoon to combine. Cover the container and set aside in a warm place (about 75°F).

Mix the plain dough

· Put the water in the bowl of a stand mixer. Sprinkle the yeast on top and let rest for 5 minutes to help dissolve the yeast. Then whisk the yeast into the water. Add the sourdough starter, barley malt syrup, and salt and whisk everything together until the liquid is homogeneous. Add the sugar and bread flour, fit the mixer with the dough hook, and mix on low for 2 minutes. Dump the dough out onto a work surface and cover it with a sheet of plastic wrap while you make the pumpernickel dough. Save the stand mixer bowl for the pumpernickel dough; no need to clean it.

Mix the pumpernickel dough
- In a medium skillet, toast the caraway seeds over medium-high heat for 2 to 3 minutes, shaking the pan frequently so they toast evenly and don't burn, until they are fragrant and begin popping. Pour the seeds out of the skillet into a medium bowl to cool to room temperature.
- Once cool, put 1 heaping tablespoon (10 grams) of the seeds in a spice grinder and pulse to pulverize. Put the ground caraway back in the bowl with the unground caraway seeds and set aside.
- Put the water in the stand mixer bowl, sprinkle the yeast on top, and let it rest for 5 minutes to help the yeast to dissolve. Whisk the yeast into the water. Add the sourdough starter, barley malt syrup, and salt and whisk everything together until the liquid is homogeneous. Add the bread flour, rye flour, roasted barley flour, and the caraway mixture. Fit the mixer with the dough hook and mix on low for 2 minutes. Dump the dough out onto a work surface and cover it with a sheet of plastic wrap.

Knead the doughs
- Remove the plastic wrap from the plain dough and divide it into 4 pieces with a bench knife. Working with one piece of dough at a time, process in a food processor fitted with the metal blade for about 30 seconds, returning the dough to the work surface before processing the next piece. Once you have processed all the pieces of dough once, repeat until each piece has gone through the food processor three or four times. Recombine the pieces on the work surface once they have all been processed. Cover the dough with plastic wrap. Repeat the process with the pumpernickel dough.

Divide and shape the bagels
- Spray the bottoms of two baking sheets with nonstick cooking spray. Line with parchment paper and spray the parchment with nonstick cooking spray.
- Remove the plastic wrap from the plain bagel dough and use a bench knife to divide the dough into 12 (55-gram) pieces (see Note on previous page). Do the same for the pumpernickel dough, cutting it into 12 (55-gram) pieces.
- Pick up one piece of the pumpernickel dough and put it down on the work surface in front of you. Flatten it with the palm of your hand. Take a piece of plain dough and put it on top of the flattened pumpernickel dough. With your palm, press down on both pieces so that they stick to each other.
- Use both hands to shape the dough into a log. To do this, pick up the top edge and fold it down toward the middle, pinching the edge into the middle

with the tips of your fingers. Repeat two or three more times, picking up the top edge and pinching it into the middle until you reach the bottom of the log.
· Roll the log back and forth with the palms of your hands to lengthen it until it is 10 inches long. Then wrap the log around the palm of your hand, overlapping the ends by about 2 inches. Use your palm to roll the overlapped ends back and forth on your work surface to seal them together. Place the shaped bagel on a prepared baking sheet and continue shaping the remaining pieces of dough in the same way. Put 6 bagels on one sheet and 6 on the other, spacing them evenly apart and leaving at least 2 inches between them.

Proof the bagels

· Wrap both baking sheets with plastic wrap, spraying the plastic wrap with nonstick cooking spray to prevent the bagels from sticking to it. Let the sheets of bagels proof at room temperature for 30 minutes, and then place them in the refrigerator to proof overnight, or a minimum of 8 hours.

To store the baking sheets of bagels more efficiently in your refrigerator, put another baking sheet, upside down, on top of them to create enclosed proofing boxes. Carefully stack these boxes on top of each other in the refrigerator.

Boil and bake the bagels

· Arrange oven racks in the top third and bottom third of the oven and preheat the oven to 400°F.
· Fill a 5-quart pot with water and bring to a boil over high heat. While the water is coming up to a boil, remove the baking sheets of bagels from the refrigerator and unwrap them. Gently place one bagel in a small bowl of water. If it floats to the top, the bagels are proofed enough to boil and bake. If the bagel sinks, set a timer for 20 minutes and check again. Do not boil the bagels until they pass this float test.
· Gently drop 2 or 3 bagels into the boiling water. Boil for 1 minute and then turn them over using tongs and boil for another 30 to 60 seconds. Use a spider or slotted spoon to remove the bagels, one at a time, from the boiling water and place them right-side up back on the baking sheet. Continue until all the bagels have been boiled.
· Place a baking sheet on each oven rack and bake the bagels for 28 to 33 minutes, until they emit a hollow sound when you tap on the bottom with your finger, switching racks and rotating the baking sheets from front to back halfway through the baking time.

Cool the bagels

· Remove the bagels from the oven and let them cool on their baking sheets. To store the bagels, place in zippered plastic bags in the freezer for up to 3 weeks. Thaw the bagels (I use my microwave for about 20 seconds), slice, and toast.

Whole Wheat Bagels

Makes 11 bagels

There is always someone who would like a whole wheat or whole-grain bagel. When I worked at Per Se, I learned a lot about service and the art of providing your guests with a positive experience. Here is the recipe I created for all those who requested whole wheat bagels. Using whole wheat and whole grains changes the texture of the bagel. Here the whole wheat is one-third of the flour, which gives the bagels plenty of whole grain without changing their texture from soft and squishy to heavy and cardboard-like.

Plan ahead Mix your starter 12 hours before you plan to make the dough. I suggest you mix the starter in the evening, and then mix the bagels the next morning.

Note You may end up with a small amount of dough left over; make a mini bagel, perfect for snacking.

			Baker's %
Sourdough Starter			
Water (70°–75°F)	½ cup	118 grams	98
Mother sourdough starter	1 tablespoon	25 grams	21
Bread flour	1 cup	120 grams	100
For the dough			
Water (65°–75°F)	1½ cups	355 grams	46
Instant yeast	2½ teaspoons	7.5 grams	1.0
Sourdough Starter (above)	1½ cups	263 grams	34
Barley malt syrup	1 tablespoon	21 grams	2.7
Granulated sugar	3 tablespoons	39 grams	5.0
Fine sea salt	4 teaspoons	24 grams	3.1
High-gluten bread flour	4¼ cups	510 grams	65
Whole wheat bread flour	2¼ cups	270 grams	35
Nonstick cooking spray			
For the topping			
Old-fashioned rolled oats	¼ cup	23 grams	

Mix the starter · Mix the sourdough starter the evening (or at least 12 hours) before you plan to make the bagel dough. Put the water in a 1-quart container with a lid and add 25 grams (1 tablespoon) of the mother sourdough starter. Add the flour and stir with a metal spoon to combine. Cover the container and set aside in a warm place (about 75°F).

Mix the dough · Put the water in the bowl of a stand mixer. Sprinkle the yeast on top and let rest for 5 minutes to help dissolve the yeast. Then whisk the yeast into the water. Add the sourdough starter, barley malt syrup, sugar, and salt and whisk everything together until the liquid is homogeneous. Add the bread flour and whole wheat flour, fit the mixer with the dough hook, and mix on low for 2 minutes.

Knead the dough
· Dump the dough out onto a work surface and divide it into 4 pieces with a bench knife. Working with one piece of dough at a time, process in a food processor fitted with the metal blade for about 30 seconds, returning the dough to the work surface before processing the next piece. Once you have processed all the pieces of dough once, repeat until each piece has gone through the food processor three or four times. Recombine the pieces on the work surface once they have all been processed. Cover the dough with plastic wrap and let it rest for 10 minutes.

Divide and shape the bagels
· Spray the bottoms of two baking sheets with nonstick cooking spray. Line with parchment paper and spray the parchment with nonstick cooking spray.
· Use a bench knife to cut the dough into 11 (130-gram) pieces (see Note on previous page). Put a piece of dough on the work surface in front of you. Use both hands to shape the dough into a log. To do this, pick up the top edge and fold it down toward the middle, pinching the edge into the middle with the tips of your fingers. Repeat two or three more times, picking up the top edge and pinching it into the middle until you reach the bottom of the log.
· Roll the log back and forth with the palms of your hands to lengthen it until it is 10 inches long. Then wrap the log around the palm of your hand, overlapping the ends by about 2 inches. Use your palm to roll the overlapped ends back and forth on your work surface to seal them together. Place the shaped bagel on a prepared baking sheet and continue shaping the remaining pieces of dough in the same way. Put 6 bagels on one sheet and 5 on the other, spacing them evenly apart and leaving at least two inches between them.

Proof the bagels
· Wrap both baking sheets with plastic wrap, spraying the plastic wrap with nonstick cooking spray to prevent the bagels from sticking to it. Let the sheets of bagels proof at room temperature for 30 minutes, and then place them in the refrigerator to proof overnight, or a minimum of 8 hours.

To store the baking sheets of bagels more efficiently in your refrigerator, put another baking sheet, upside down, on top of them to create enclosed proofing boxes. Carefully stack these boxes on top of each other in the refrigerator.

Get the topping ready
· Sprinkle ⅔ cup (85 grams) of the oats in an even layer on a large plate. Place the remaining oats in a small bowl and set aside.

Boil and bake the bagels
· Arrange oven racks in the top third and bottom third of the oven and preheat the oven to 400°F.
· Fill a 3-quart pot with water and bring to a boil over high heat. While the water is coming up to a boil, remove the baking sheets of bagels from the

refrigerator and unwrap them. Gently place one bagel in a small bowl of water. If the bagel floats to the top, the bagels are proofed enough to boil and bake. If the bagel sinks, set a timer for 20 minutes and check again. Do not boil the bagels until they pass this float test.

• Gently pick up and drop 2 or 3 bagels into the boiling water. Boil for 1 minute and then turn them over using tongs and boil for another 30 to 60 seconds. Use a spider or slotted spoon to remove the bagels, one at a time, from the boiling water and place them right-side up on the large plate with the oat topping. Take the small bowl of oats and use your fingers to generously sprinkle the tops of the bagels with the oats. With both hands, pick up one bagel at a time and transfer it back to the baking sheet. Continue until all the bagels have been boiled and topped.

• Place a baking sheet on each oven rack and bake the bagels for 28 to 33 minutes, until they are lightly browned and emit a hollow sound when you tap on the bottom of a bagel with your finger, switching racks and rotating the baking sheets from front to back halfway through the baking time. (Watch out that the bottoms do not brown too quickly. If they are getting too brown before they are done, slip a second baking sheet directly under each baking sheet to create a doubled baking sheet, shielding the dough from the direct heat.)

Cool the bagels

• Remove the bagels from the oven and let them cool on their baking sheets. To store the bagels, place in zippered plastic bags in the freezer for up to 3 weeks. Thaw the bagels (I use my microwave for about 20 seconds), slice, and toast.

Cinnamon Raisin Bagels

Makes 11 bagels

Cinnamon swirl is the mark of a professionally baked cinnamon raisin bagel. That is done with a spiral mixer. At home this requires a different technique to accomplish. These cinnamon raisin bagels have cinnamon in the dough, plus a cinnamon swirl and loads of raisins. The cinnamon swirl is created by hydrating cinnamon to create a cinnamon paste and then swirling it into the dough. All cinnamon is ground differently, so please pay attention to how the paste feels. It should feel spongy and not dry and crumbly. If it is dry, add a little more water. Once you've baked them, I love spreading a tangy cream cheese on top to balance the sweetness from the raisins.

Plan ahead Mix your starter 12 hours before you plan to make the dough. I suggest you mix the starter in the evening, and then mix the bagels the next morning.

Note You may end up with a small amount of dough left over; make a mini bagel, perfect for snacking.

			Baker's %
Sourdough Starter			
Water (70°–75°F)	½ cup	118 grams	98
Mother sourdough starter	1 tablespoon	25 grams	21
Bread flour	1 cup	120 grams	100
For the cinnamon paste			
Ground cinnamon	3 tablespoons	18 grams	
Water (70°F)	2 tablespoons	30 grams	
For the dough			
Raisins	1 cup	150 grams	23
Water (70°–75°F)	1¼ cups	293 grams	44
Instant yeast	1 tablespoon	9 grams	1.4
Sourdough Starter (above)	1½ cups	220 grams	33
Barley malt syrup	3 tablespoons	63 grams	10
Fine sea salt	4 teaspoons	24 grams	3.6
High-gluten bread flour	5½ cups	660 grams	100
Ground cinnamon	4 teaspoons	8 grams	1.2

Mix the starter
- Mix the sourdough starter the evening (or at least 12 hours) before you plan to make the bagel dough. Put the water in a 1-quart container with a lid and add 25 grams (1 tablespoon) of the mother sourdough starter. Add the flour and stir with a metal spoon to combine. Cover the container and set aside in a warm place (about 75°F).

Make the cinnamon paste
- Put the ground cinnamon in a small bowl and cover with the water. Stir the mixture with a small metal spoon and let rest for 1 hour uncovered.

Mix the dough

- Place the raisins in a small bowl and cover with hot tap water and set aside to soak for about 5 minutes. Drain the raisins in a fine-mesh sieve and let them sit in the sieve to drain any remaining water while you make the dough.
- Put the water in the bowl of a stand mixer. Sprinkle the yeast on top and let rest for 5 minutes to help dissolve the yeast. Then whisk the yeast into the water. Add the sourdough starter, barley malt syrup, and salt and whisk everything together until the liquid is homogeneous. Add the bread flour and ground cinnamon, fit the mixer with the dough hook, and mix on low for 2 minutes.

Knead the dough

- Dump the dough out onto a work surface and divide it into 4 pieces with a bench knife. Working with one piece of dough at a time, process in a food processor fitted with the metal blade for about 30 seconds, returning the dough to the work surface before processing the next piece. Once you have processed all the pieces of dough once, repeat until each piece has gone through the food processor three or four times. Recombine the pieces on the work surface once they have all been processed. Cover the dough with plastic wrap and let it rest for 10 minutes.

Fold in the raisins

- Remove the plastic from the dough and stretch the dough out onto the work surface to make it into a squarish shape as flat and wide as possible. Sprinkle the raisins on top. Encase the raisins in the dough by folding the top third of the dough down halfway and fold the bottom third of the dough up to meet the top in the middle, like folding a letter. Press the dough down and flip it over. Take the right half of the dough and fold it in to the center. Take the left half and fold it in to the center to meet the right half, pressing the dough down firmly to spread out the raisins. Continue to fold and press several more times until the raisins are mixed in. If the dough resists folding, re-cover it with plastic and let it rest 10 minutes. Once the folding is finished, cover the dough with plastic and let it rest on the work surface for 15 minutes to relax the gluten before proceeding.

Swirl the cinnamon paste

- Remove the plastic wrap and pat the dough into a 12 × 5-inch rectangular slab with a long side facing you. Spread the cinnamon paste evenly over the top with your fingers. Roll the dough away from you to form a log as you would for cinnamon rolls.

Divide and shape the bagels

- Spray the bottoms of two baking sheets with nonstick cooking spray. Line with parchment paper and spray the parchment with nonstick cooking spray.
- With the seam of the log face down on the countertop, divide the dough with a bench knife into 11 (130-gram) pieces (see Note on previous page). Put a piece of dough on the work surface in front of you. Use both hands to shape the dough into a log. To do this, pick up the top edge and fold it down toward the middle, pinching the edge into the middle with the tips of your fingers. Repeat two or three more times, picking up the top edge and pinching it into the middle until you reach the bottom of the log.

- Roll the log back and forth with the palms of your hands to lengthen it until it is 10 inches long. Then wrap the log around the palm of your hand, overlapping the ends by about 2 inches. Use your palm to roll the overlapped ends back and forth on your work surface to seal them together. Place the shaped bagel on a prepared baking sheet and continue shaping the remaining pieces of dough in the same way. Put 6 bagels on one sheet and 5 on the other, spacing them evenly apart and leaving at least 2 inches between them.

Proof the bagels

- Wrap both baking sheets with plastic wrap, spraying the plastic wrap with nonstick cooking spray to prevent the bagels from sticking to it. Let the sheets of bagels proof at room temperature for 30 minutes, and then place them in the refrigerator to proof overnight, or a minimum of 8 hours.

To store the baking sheets of bagels more efficiently in your refrigerator, put another baking sheet, upside down, on top of them to create enclosed proofing boxes. Carefully stack these boxes on top of each other in the refrigerator.

Boil and bake the bagels

- Arrange oven racks in the top third and bottom third of the oven and preheat the oven to 400°F.
- Fill a 5-quart pot with water and bring to a boil over high heat. While the water is coming up to a boil, remove the baking sheets of bagels from the refrigerator and unwrap them. Gently place one bagel in a small bowl of water. If the bagel floats to the top, the bagels are proofed enough to boil and bake. If the bagel sinks, set a timer for 20 minutes and check again. Do not boil the bagels until they pass this float test.
- Gently pick up and drop 2 or 3 bagels into the boiling water. Boil for 1 minute and then turn them over using tongs and boil for another 30 to 60 seconds. Use a spider or slotted spoon to remove the bagels, one at a time, from the boiling water and place them back on the baking sheet. Continue until all the bagels have been boiled.
- Place a baking sheet on each oven rack and bake the bagels for 28 to 33 minutes, until they are lightly browned and emit a hollow sound when you tap on the bottom of a bagel with your finger, switching racks and rotating the baking sheets from front to back halfway through the baking time. (Watch out that the bottoms do not brown too quickly. If they are getting too brown before they are done, slip a second baking sheet directly under each baking sheet to create a doubled baking sheet, shielding the dough from the direct heat.)

Cool the bagels

- Remove the bagels from the oven and let them cool on their baking sheets. To store the bagels, place in zippered plastic bags in the freezer for up to 3 weeks. Thaw the bagels (I use my microwave for about 20 seconds), slice, and toast.

Onion Bialys

Makes 11 bialys

Bialys are chewy, crusty rolls with toasted onion and poppy seeds in the center. Their name is short for Bialystoker kuchen, because they came originally from Bialystok in northeastern Poland. They contain no sugar or barley malt syrup, and they are not boiled like bagels. They are shaped and then go directly into the oven to bake. While they are warm, spread their tops with either cream cheese or butter to enjoy.

Plan ahead Mix your starter 12 hours before you plan to make the dough. I suggest you mix the starter in the evening, and then mix the bialys the next morning. The onions can be made and kept refrigerated for up to 3 days before you use them.

			Baker's %
For the onions			
Yellow onions	2 pounds (2 to 3 large)	908 grams	
Unsalted butter	2 tablespoons	28 grams	
Fine sea salt	1¼ teaspoons	8 grams	
Sourdough Starter			
Water (70°–75°F)	¼ cup	59 grams	98
Mother sourdough starter	1 tablespoon	25 grams	21
Bread flour	½ cup	60 grams	100
For the dough			
Water (70°–75°F)	1½ cups + 1 tablespoon	368 grams	61
Instant yeast	½ teaspoon	1.5 grams	0.25
Sourdough Starter (above)	½ cup	110 grams	18
Fine sea salt	2½ teaspoons	15 grams	2.5
High-protein bread flour	4½ cups	540 grams	90
Whole wheat bread flour	½ cup	60 grams	10
For the topping			
Poppy seeds	½ teaspoon	1.5 grams	
Flaky sea salt	½ teaspoon	3 grams	
Bread crumbs	1 tablespoon	10 grams	

Cook the onions

· Arrange an oven rack in the lowest position and preheat the oven to 300°F.

· Trim and halve the onions from root to tip, then slice the onion into half-moons ⅛ inch thick.

· In a large Dutch oven or other ovenproof pot with a lid, melt the butter over medium heat. Add the onions and salt and cook, stirring frequently, without browning the onions for 10 minutes. (If the onions begin to brown, reduce the heat slightly.) Cover the pot, transfer to the oven, and bake the onions for 30 minutes.

· Remove from the oven and let rest, covered, for another 30 minutes. Remove the lid from the pot and put the onions in a large fine-mesh sieve to drain off the liquid. The onions can be prepared up to 3 days in advance. Refrigerate in an airtight container until you're ready to use them.

Mix the starter	• Mix the sourdough starter the evening (or at least 12 hours) before you plan to make the bialy dough. Put the water in a 1-quart container with a lid and add 25 grams (1 tablespoon) of the mother sourdough starter. Add the flour and stir with a metal spoon to combine. Cover the container and set aside in a warm place (about 75°F).
Mix the dough	• Put the water in the bowl of a stand mixer. Sprinkle the yeast on top and let rest for 5 minutes to help dissolve the yeast. Then whisk the yeast into the water. Add the sourdough starter, salt, bread flour, and whole wheat flour. Fit the mixer with the dough hook and mix on low speed for 2 minutes. Increase the speed to medium and mix for 5 minutes.
Ferment the dough	• Remove the dough hook and use a wet hand to clean off the dough. Cover the bowl with plastic wrap and set the bowl in a warm place (about 75°F) in your kitchen and let it ferment for 1 hour.
Divide and shape the bialys	• Line a baking sheet with parchment paper and spray the paper with nonstick cooking spray.

Under "Divide and shape the bialys":

• Line a baking sheet with parchment paper and spray the paper with nonstick cooking spray.

• Lightly dust your work surface with flour. Uncover the bowl and use a plastic bowl scraper to scoop the dough onto the floured surface. Dust the top of the dough with flour and use a bench knife to divide it into 11 (100-gram) pieces. Put one piece of dough on the work surface in front of you. Dust your hands lightly with flour. Gently rest your palm on the dough and roll it into a tight round ball. Put the ball on the prepared baking sheet and repeat with the remaining dough, leaving about 2 inches between the rounds.

• Spray a sheet of plastic wrap with nonstick cooking spray and place it, sprayed-side down, over the baking sheet. Place the baking sheet in the refrigerator to retard the bialys overnight, or for a minimum of 8 hours.

• The next day, flip two baking sheets upside down and place a piece of parchment paper on top of each. Lightly dust the paper with flour.

• Remove the baking sheet with the balls of dough from the refrigerator. Lightly dust your work surface with flour. Take one ball and put it on the work surface. Dust its top with flour. Make an indentation. Press down in the center of the ball using your index and middle fingers. Continue to press down and stretch the indentation, spreading the bialy out so that it is 4½ inches across and has an outer lip that is about ¾ to 1 inch wide. It will seem like you are shaping a mini pizza. While shaping, occasionally dust underneath the bialys with flour so that they do not stick to the work surface. Set the shaped bialy on the prepared parchment. Repeat, shaping the remaining balls of dough in the same way, placing 5 to 6 shaped bialys on each prepared baking sheet, and leaving about 2 inches between them.

- Put 1 heaping tablespoon (about 25 grams) of onions in the center of each bialy. Use your fingers to smoosh the onions down into the dough. Sprinkle the poppy seeds, flaky salt, and bread crumbs over the onions.

Proof and bake the bialys

- Put the two sheets of bialys in a warm place (about 75°F) to proof for 45 minutes to 1 hour.
- Arrange an oven rack in the center position. Place a baking stone on the rack and preheat the oven to 500°F.
- Working with one sheet of bialys at a time, place the baking sheet next to the baking stone and carefully shimmy the parchment paper and bialys directly onto the stone. Close the oven and set the baking sheet aside. Bake for 12 to 15 minutes, until the bialys are a light amber brown. Remove the bialys and paper from the oven with an oven peel or use the back side of the baking sheet and carefully pull the paper and bialys back onto it. Set the bialys onto a cooling rack.
- Bake the remaining bialys in the same way. Serve warm or at room temperature.

Bagel Platters
and Sandwiches

When I started selling bagels and cream cheese at the Smorgasburg outdoor food market in Brooklyn in early 2013, I would mix and shape bagels and make cream cheese the day before the market. The morning of the market I would arrive at the bakery by 3 a.m. to boil the bagels and then transport everything to the market to be ready by 9 a.m. It was quickly apparent that by selling bagels with a schmear for $3 each I was not making enough to break even, and so I began curing my own gravlax and assembling what I call "The Works," a bagel sandwich with chive cream cheese, gravlax, tomato, red onion, and capers.

By the fall of 2013, I had partnered with the Major Food Group to open a bagel and appetizing restaurant. Appetizing shops in New York City sell all types of smoked and cured fish, cream cheeses, and all other types of food served with bagels. (By kosher law, cheese and meat cannot be eaten together, whereas cheese and fish can.) This opened the door to creatively develop a menu of all types of cured fish and spreads that could be served with the bagels I had been making and perfecting.

Curing fish at home is gratifying and relatively simple. It does require some planning because you cure the fish over a couple of days. In this chapter you will find all the information you need to succeed in curing fish and making salads and cream cheeses to go with your delicious bagels. I am proud to share what I have learned over the years of appetizing making.

Master Class
Curating the Perfect Bagel Platter

The key to a creating the best smorgasbord of bagels, fish, and cream cheese is the variety you offer and the quantity of each thing. Here's what to consider as you plan it out:

The bagels Offer a variety of bagels and plan for 1 bagel per person. To do this for 4 to 6 people, make the dough for the Sourdough Bagels (page 27). Keep several bagels plain, and then coat several bagels with sesame seeds, several with everything seed mix, and a couple with a sprinkling of flaky salt. Once the bagels are made, slice them in half with a bread knife so that they can be mixed and matched. Store leftover bagels in a zippered plastic bag in the freezer. Have a toaster and a pair of toaster tongs handy for those who like a toasted bagel.

Fish Offer one cured fish and a salad, like whitefish salad. Slice enough of the cured fish to set out 2 to 3 ounces (56 to 85 grams) per person.

Egg Offering some egg notches the platter up. Prepare some sliced hard-boiled eggs with slightly jammy centers. And go even bigger by adding salmon roe or caviar to your offerings.

Cream cheese (and butter) Offer two types—plain and a flavored cream cheese. Also, soften some salted butter to have as an option.

Vegetables Offer tomatoes. Choose large, beautiful, ripe tomatoes, like big heirlooms, so that they cover the entire bagel half. Also offer thinly sliced cucumbers and red onion. Use a sharp knife or mandoline to get paper-thin slices. Soak the slices of red onion in cold water for a couple of minutes to remove their aggressiveness. Have a variety of complementary vegetables to add color, contrast, and texture. They can include capers, dill fronds, chives, grated radish, and microgreens. Have fun!

Slicing Fish
Like a Pro

If you've ever watched a professional slice cured fish, it seems like an art form. A super-thin slicing knife is used to slice long, paper-thin slices of fish. It can seem intimidating, but don't let that deter you. It's very approachable.

1. Use a long, sharp knife, ideally a fish fillet knife or salmon slicer. If you haven't sharpened your knife in a while, now is a good time. A sharper knife will let you slice thinner slices. Professionals use salmon slicing knives, which have long, flexible blades with beveled edges. The bevels prevent the fish from sticking to the knife as you slice, and the flexibility helps to keep the slices thin. A regular chef's knife is a perfectly acceptable substitute.

2. Work at an angle. Holding the knife at a 45-degree angle to the cutting board, use a back-and-forth sawing motion to cut a slice, beginning at the thickest part of the fish and ending at the thinnest part. If head and tail are attached, you would begin toward the head and move toward the tail.

3. Continue to slice following the angle you created with the first slice, keeping the slices as thin as possible.

Dill and Black Pepper Gravlax

Serves 8

Lox is salmon that has been cured in salt. (Contrary to what many believe, it is not smoked salmon.) Gravlax is a type of lox usually flavored with dill.

Curing salmon is a straightforward process, but there are a few rules to follow to set yourself up for success. Choose the freshest fish you can find. Use farmed salmon because it has more fat than wild-caught. The fat aids the salt in penetrating the flesh; less fatty fish tend to dry out on their surface and become leathery. When possible, choose sushi-grade fish for your cure, and preferably use Diamond Crystal kosher salt. Diamond Crystal contains no additives or anticaking agents, which means it is less dense, dissolves more easily—and is just salt.

Black peppercorns	3 tablespoons	27 grams
Granulated sugar	¼ cup	50 grams
Kosher salt	⅓ cup	46 grams
Fresh salmon, center-cut, skin-on, 1½ inches thick	1½ to 2 pounds	908 grams
Dill	1 large bunch, stems removed	

• Place the black peppercorns in a spice grinder and pulse about 10 times to coarsely grind. Put the peppercorns in a small bowl, add the sugar and salt, and stir to combine.

• Lay a long sheet of plastic wrap across your work surface. Spread one-third of the salt mixture evenly along the center of the plastic wrap. Place the salmon skin-side down on top of the salt mixture. Lay the dill on top of the salmon and pack the remaining salt mixture on top.

• Wrap the plastic wrap tightly around the fish. Wrap the fish in two more layers of plastic wrap. Place the salmon package on a baking sheet and place a heavy plate on top of the fish. Put the salmon in the refrigerator and refrigerate for 24 hours.

• After 24 hours, remove the plate and carefully flip the salmon skin-side up. Place the plate on top of the fish. Refrigerate for 24 more hours.

• Remove the salmon from the refrigerator and unwrap. Remove the dill and rinse the salmon under cold water and pat it dry with paper towels.

• Tightly wrap the gravlax in plastic wrap and refrigerate until ready to use, ideally within 3 to 4 days.

• To slice the salmon, unwrap it and place it on a cutting board. Using a long, sharp knife, slice thin pieces at a 45-degree angle, beginning at the thickest part of the fish and moving the knife in a back-and-forth sawing motion toward the thinnest part. (For more detail, see Slicing Fish Like a Pro, page 72.)

Togarashi-Cured Sable

Serves 8

Sablefish, also known as black cod, is a must when preparing a bagel platter. It was once called "poor man's sturgeon" because it was plentiful and cheap. Sable has a high fat content (rich in omega-3's!), which means it cures beautifully. Togarashi is a Japanese spice blend that includes ground chiles, sesame seeds, black pepper, and nori, and I think it works beautifully with cured sable. I get my togarashi from the spice shop SOS Chefs in New York City or at my local Japanese market. These days Amazon also carries togarashi in a dizzying number of choices.

Granulated sugar	½ cup	100 grams
Kosher salt	⅓ cup	46 grams
Togarashi	1 tablespoon	10 grams
Sable fillet, center-cut, skin-on	1½ pounds	908 grams

· In a small bowl, whisk together the sugar, salt, and togarashi. Lay a long sheet of plastic wrap down across your work surface. Spread one-quarter of the togarashi mixture evenly along the center of the plastic wrap. Place the sable skin-side down on top of the spice mixture. Spread the rest of the mixture on the top and sides of the sable.

· Wrap the plastic wrap tightly around the fish. Wrap the package in two more layers of plastic wrap. Place the sable package on a baking sheet and place a heavy plate on top of the fish. Place the sable in the refrigerator and refrigerate for 24 hours.

· After 24 hours, remove the plate and carefully flip the sable skin-side up. Place the plate on top of the fish and refrigerate for 24 more hours.

· To slice the sable, unwrap it and place it on a cutting board. Using a long, sharp knife, slice thin pieces at a 45-degree angle, beginning at the thickest part of the fish and moving the knife in a back-and-forth sawing motion toward the thinnest part. (For more detail, see Slicing Fish Like a Pro, page 72.)

· Use the sable immediately or keep it wrapped and refrigerated for up to 3 days.

Beet-Cured Salmon

Beet-cured salmon has an earthier, slightly sweeter taste than the Dill and Black Pepper Gravlax (page 75). The color the salmon takes from the beets also makes for a beautiful display.

Serves 8

Beet	1 medium (about 8 ounces)	230 grams
Granulated sugar	½ cup	100 grams
Kosher salt	1 cup	137 grams
Juniper berries	1 tablespoon	7 grams
White peppercorns	1 tablespoon	13 grams
Lemon	1	
Fresh salmon, center-cut, skin-on, 1½ inches thick	1½ to 2 pounds	908 grams

- Grate the beet into the food processor using the largest holes on a box grater and add the sugar and salt.
- In a medium skillet, toast the juniper and white peppercorns over medium-high heat for 2 to 3 minutes, shaking the pan frequently so they toast evenly and don't burn, until they are fragrant. Pour the spices out of the skillet into the food processor.
- Zest the lemon into the processor and then pulse the processor until the mixture resembles thick oatmeal—a few ticks away from being completely pureed.
- Lay a long sheet of plastic wrap down across your work surface. Spread one-quarter of the beet mixture evenly along the center of the plastic wrap. Place the salmon skin-side down on top of the beet mixture. Spoon the rest of the mixture on the top and sides of the salmon.
- Wrap the plastic wrap tightly around the fish. Wrap the package in two more layers of plastic wrap. Place the salmon package on a baking sheet and place a heavy plate on top of the fish. Place the salmon in the refrigerator and refrigerate for 24 hours.
- After 24 hours, remove the plate and carefully flip the salmon skin-side up. Place the plate on top of the fish and refrigerate for 24 more hours.
- Remove the salmon from the refrigerator and unwrap. Brush off the beet mixture and rinse the salmon under cold water. Pat the salmon dry with paper towels.
- Tightly wrap the salmon in plastic and refrigerate until ready to use, ideally within 3 to 4 days.
- To slice the salmon, unwrap it and place it on a cutting board. Using a long, sharp knife, slice thin pieces at a 45-degree angle, beginning at the thickest part of the fish and moving the knife in a back-and-forth sawing motion toward the thinnest part. (For more detail, see Slicing Fish Like a Pro, page 72.)

Chive and Scallion Cream Cheese

Makes 8 ounces (enough for 4 bagels)

If you have one flavored cream cheese recipe in your repertoire, it should be this classic. Philadelphia cream cheese is the brand I normally use to make it. I purchase the cream cheese block and whip it with the add-ins using the paddle attachment on my stand mixer.

Philadelphia cream cheese actually originated in New York state and got its name because of the high-quality dairy coming from Philadelphia at the time.

Cream cheese	8 ounces	226 grams
Scallions, thinly sliced	1 ounce	28 grams
Chives, finely chopped	1 ounce	28 grams

· Cube the cream cheese and place it in the bowl of a stand mixer fitted with the paddle attachment. Add the scallions and chives and beat the cream cheese on medium-high for several minutes until it is lightened and fluffy, scraping down the bowl with a rubber spatula once or twice to incorporate the scallions and chives. Scrape the cream cheese into a deli container, cover, and refrigerate until ready to use. The cream cheese will keep refrigerated for 3 to 4 days.

Veggie Cream Cheese

Makes 8 ounces (enough for 4 bagels)

Here is another delicious savory cream cheese recipe that you should include with any bagel platter spread. It is best used within 24 to 48 hours of making it, as the carrots and radish will weep some water into the cream cheese. If this happens, give the cream cheese a few solid stirs to recombine.

Cream cheese	8 ounces	226 grams
Carrot, peeled	1 medium	45 grams
Red radishes, tops trimmed	3 to 4 small	45 grams
Scallions, thinly sliced	1½ ounces	42 grams

· Cube the cream cheese and place it in the bowl of a stand mixer fitted with the paddle attachment.
· Shred the carrot and radishes on the medium holes of a box grater.
· Add the shredded vegetables to the cream cheese along with the sliced scallions. Beat the cream cheese on medium-high speed for several minutes until it is lightened and fluffy, scraping down the bowl with a rubber spatula once or twice to incorporate the veggies. Scrape the cream cheese into a deli container, cover, and refrigerate until ready to use. The cream cheese will keep for 1 to 2 days refrigerated.

Smoked Whitefish Salad

Makes 2 cups

Smoked whitefish salad is a staple of Jewish appetizing. You can get it at any appetizing store and also at many grocery stores. The benefit of making your own whitefish salad is that you can control the size of the chunks of fish, which I prefer on the larger, not mashed-up-to-bits, side. Appetizing stores also sell whole smoked whitefish. Whitefish is a deep freshwater fish known as lake whitefish, and it is primarily found in the Great Lakes; a large one weighs between 2 and 3 pounds. The whitefish has small bones, so take care to remove all of them. And don't add any salt to the salad. The fish will already be salty from the preserving process. I call for fresh lemon juice in the recipe to balance the saltiness.

Whole smoked whitefish	1 large (1 pound 14 ounces)	850 grams
Mayonnaise	3 tablespoons	45 grams
Sour cream	3 tablespoons	45 grams
Chives, finely chopped	2 tablespoons	6 grams
Lemon, juiced	1 tablespoon	15 grams

· Place the fish on a large cutting board. Pierce the skin on the top side with a small serrated knife. Peel off and discard the skin. Use a fork to lift the flaked fish gently off the tiny bones. Place the flaked fish into a medium bowl.

· Repeat on the other side, flipping the fish over and removing the skin and then using the fork to lift the flesh off the bones and into the bowl. Discard the fish carcass or reserve to make fish broth.

· Add the mayonnaise, sour cream, chives, and lemon juice to the bowl with the fish. Use the fork to mash the ingredients together a bit. Store in a covered container in the refrigerator for up to 1 week.

Baked Salmon Salad

Kippered salmon is baked, hot smoked salmon. And while this version is not smoked, it beats canned salmon any day.

Makes 2 to 3 cups

Fresh salmon, center-cut, skin-on, 1½ inches thick	1 pound	454 grams
Extra-virgin olive oil	1 tablespoon	13 grams
Fine sea salt	to taste	
Mayonnaise	½ cup	110 grams
Dill, chopped	3 tablespoons	18 grams
Freshly ground black pepper	to taste	
Lemon juice	to taste	

- Arrange an oven rack in the center position and preheat the oven to 400°F. Line a baking sheet with parchment paper.
- Brush the salmon fillets with the olive oil and sprinkle with salt. Place the baking sheet in the oven and bake the salmon for 15 minutes, or until it flakes easily when pressed with a fork. Remove from the oven and let cool.
- Use a fork to flake the salmon into a bowl, discarding the skin. Add the mayonnaise and dill and season with pepper and lemon juice to taste, gently mashing the salad with the fork to combine the ingredients. Refrigerate until ready to serve. Keeps refrigerated for 2 to 3 days.

My Favorite Egg Salad

Makes 1 quart

I have a few rules for egg salad:

1. Do not overcook the eggs. They need to be just slightly shy of fully hard-cooked.

2. Finely dice the eggs for the best texture—the egg salad will be more cohesive without big chunks of hard-cooked egg.

3. Don't go too heavy on the mayonnaise—a little goes a long way.

4. Add some acid for balance—I prefer apple cider vinegar. Dijon mustard is another good acid to use.

5. Always include freshly ground black pepper.

Eggs, large	12	
Mayonnaise	½ cup	115 grams
Fine sea salt	¼ teaspoon	2 grams
Apple cider vinegar	1 tablespoon	15 grams
Freshly ground black pepper	⅛ teaspoon	1 gram

- In a 6-quart pot wide enough to hold the eggs in a single layer, arrange the eggs and add cold water to cover by 1 inch. Bring the water to a full boil and then turn off the heat. Let the eggs cook in the hot water for 8 minutes.
- While the eggs are in the hot water, fill a bowl with ice and water to make an ice bath. Use a spider strainer or slotted spoon and transfer the eggs to the ice bath. Let the eggs rest in the ice bath for about 10 minutes, until they are cool.
- Peel the eggs, rinsing them in the ice bath to remove any bits of shell. Dry the eggs with a kitchen towel.
- Dice the eggs into ¼-inch pieces and place in a medium bowl. Add the mayonnaise, salt, vinegar, and pepper and stir together with a rubber spatula.
- If not using the egg salad right away, cover and refrigerate for up to 3 days.

Chopped Chicken Liver

Serves 6 to 8

Chopped chicken liver is a Jewish delicatessen classic. Schmaltz is rendered chicken fat, and it can be purchased from a butcher, or you can make it yourself by pulling off the skin and fat from a package of chicken thighs. Put the skin and fat in a saucepan with about 1 tablespoon water and cook slowly over very low heat to render the fat. You can also use the fat left over from a roast chicken.

Schmaltz	3 tablespoons	38 grams
Chicken livers, trimmed and separated into lobes	½ pound	226 grams
Shallot, finely minced	1 large	
Garlic, finely minced	1 clove	
Fine sea salt	1 teaspoon	6 grams
Freshly ground black pepper	¼ teaspoon	2 grams
White wine	2 tablespoons	30 grams
Ruby port	2 tablespoons	30 grams

• In a large skillet, heat the schmaltz over medium-high heat. When it is hot, add the chicken livers, followed by the shallot, garlic, salt, and pepper. Sear the livers on one side for about 2 minutes. Turn the livers over with tongs and cook for 30 more seconds. Add the wine and the port and cook for about 30 more seconds.

• Remove from the heat and transfer the mixture to a food processor. Pulse several times until the mixture is partly creamy with some remaining chunks.

• Transfer the mixture to an airtight container and refrigerate for up to 3 days.

The Works

Makes 2 bagel sandwiches

The works means an everything bagel filled with the classic combination of chive cream cheese, lox, tomato, red onion, and capers. It is *the* quintessential bagel sandwich. In New York, it is common to order "The Works, hold the onion," or "The Works, just a few capers, not too many," or "The Works, sub plain cream cheese for the chive." You get the idea.

Everything Bagels (page 32)	2	
Chive and Scallion Cream Cheese (page 80)	3 ounces	85 grams
Dill and Black Pepper Gravlax (page 75), sliced	6 ounces	170 grams
Tomato, thinly sliced	1 large	
Red onion, thinly sliced	1 medium	
Capers, roughly chopped	2 teaspoons	

- Slice the bagels in half horizontally with a serrated bread knife. Dividing evenly, spread the bottom half of each with the chive cream cheese and then layer each bagel with sliced gravlax, draping it over the cream cheese. Place slices of tomato and red onion on top of the gravlax, followed by the capers.
- Place the top bagel halves on top.

Everything Bagel Tuna Crunch Sandwiches

Makes 2 sandwiches

In my mind, nothing makes a tuna salad sandwich better than adding a layer of kettle potato chips to bring some salty, fatty crunch. A tablespoon or two of sweet pickle relish in the tuna salad adds a sweet and sour note and, to take things to the next level, I encourage you to toast the bagel.

Ingredient	Amount	Weight
Tuna, good-quality, extra-virgin olive oil–packed	1 (5-ounce) can	
Red onion, finely minced	1 tablespoon	10 grams
Parsley, finely chopped	1 tablespoon	5 grams
Mayonnaise	¼ cup	50 grams
Sweet pickle relish	1½ tablespoons	23 grams
Fine sea salt	¼ teaspoon	2 grams
Lemon juice, fresh	1 teaspoon	5 grams
Freshly ground black pepper	Several grinds	
Everything Bagels (page 32)	2	
Kettle potato chips	1 ounce	28 grams

- Place the tuna in a bowl and add the red onion, parsley, mayonnaise, pickle relish, salt, lemon juice, and black pepper. Use a fork to mash everything together.
- Slice the bagels in half horizontally and toast as desired.
- Scoop half of the tuna salad onto each bottom bagel half and top with a handful of potato chips. Place the top bagel halves on top.

Lox, Eggs, and Onion

Makes 2 sandwiches

L.E.O.—lox, scrambled eggs, and sautéed onions—is a classic Jewish breakfast staple. I head to Barney Greengrass, the iconic Jewish deli on the Upper West Side, when I crave one—lox scrambled with the eggs and onion and served with a bagel and cream cheese on the side. When I worked at the restaurant High Street on Hudson in New York, I created this playful version: an onion bialy sandwich filled with a 2-egg omelet, slices of gravlax, and a schmear of scallion and chive cream cheese.

Onion Bialys (page 65)	2	
Chive and Scallion Cream Cheese (page 80)	1 ounce	28 grams
Dill and Black Pepper Gravlax (page 75), sliced	4 ounces	113 grams
Eggs, large	4	200 grams
Fine sea salt	to taste	
Freshly ground black pepper	to taste	
Unsalted butter	1 tablespoon	14 grams

- Slice each bialy in half horizontally. Set the top halves aside, using an offset spatula, if needed, to keep the onion intact.
- Spread the bottom half of each bialy with 1 tablespoon cream cheese. Divide the gravlax between the bialy halves.
- In a medium bowl, whisk the eggs together with a couple of pinches of salt and a couple of grinds of black pepper.
- In an 8-inch nonstick skillet, melt the butter over medium heat. Add the eggs and shake the pan vigorously while using the tines of a fork to break up the curds. Continue cooking for 1 to 2 minutes, until the eggs appear soft-scrambled. Spread out the eggs with the fork and let them continue to cook for a few more seconds to set the bottom.
- Remove the skillet from the heat and tilt it at an angle over a plate. Use the fork to gently roll the omelet down over itself and onto the plate. Divide the omelet in half and, using a spatula, place each omelet half onto a bialy sandwich.
- Place the bialy tops onto each sandwich using an offset spatula to keep the onions in place.

Flatbreads

Making flatbreads is one of my favorite

things to do. I started making flour tortillas at home when my son was very young. Because I was used to buying tortillas at the grocery store, I was dumbfounded at how good the homemade ones were, and I became hooked. I began making them regularly because they turned out to be both easy and really enjoyable to make.

Flatbreads can be leavened or unleavened, and they can be cooked any number of ways: in the oven, in a skillet, or deep-fried. One of the most forgiving elements of flatbreads is their greater crust-to-crumb ratio. Because they are spread or rolled out, they are thinner, with less crumb inside and more outside "crust." So there does not need to be as much precision as with making baguettes or sourdough loaves of bread.

This chapter consists of recipes for four flatbreads plus accompanying savory dishes. The flatbreads are all intentionally cooked in a skillet so that the setup and cooking are kept simple. The savory recipes that accompany the flatbreads are some of my favorite things to make at home.

M'smen with Labneh and Dukkah

Makes 11 m'smen

M'smen is a laminated flatbread from Morocco. It is traditionally served with butter and honey or with fresh cheese; it is eaten at breakfast or at teatime. When I was working on my recipes to open Sadelle's, my friend Kaoutar Benabdelkader, who shared a kitchen space with me, was making these delicious flatbreads. I would watch how she made them, stretching the rounded balls into thin flat discs and then folding them up into a packet before they were stretched out again. I would exchange my pastries for her m'smen. Labneh and dukkah are not traditionally Moroccan, but they are some of my favorite accompaniments to have when I make these flatbreads.

Bread flour	4¼ cups + more for dusting	510 grams
Coarse semolina	1⅓ cups	193 grams
Granulated sugar	2 tablespoons + 2 teaspoons	35 grams
Fine sea salt	2½ teaspoons	15 grams
Water (75°–80°F)	1¾ cups	411 grams
Canola oil	9 tablespoons	117 grams
Unsalted butter, melted	6 tablespoons	84 grams
Flaky sea salt	for sprinkling	
Labneh (recipe follows)		
Extra-virgin olive oil	for drizzling	
Dukkah (recipe follows)		

Mix and round the dough

· In a large bowl, whisk together the flour, 1 cup (145 grams) of the semolina, the sugar, and salt.

· In a stand mixer fitted with the dough hook, combine the water and 1 tablespoon of the canola oil. Add the flour mixture and mix on low speed for 10 minutes. Remove the dough hook and wipe it clean with a wet hand.

· Pour 2 tablespoons of canola oil onto a baking sheet and spread it around with your fingers to completely coat the bottom and sides.

· Lightly flour a large work surface and use a plastic bowl scraper to scrape the dough onto the floured surface. Lightly dust the top of the dough with flour and use a bench knife to divide it into 11 (100-gram) pieces.

· Put one piece of dough in front of you. Dust your hands lightly with flour. Gently rest your palm on the dough and roll it into a tight round ball. Put the ball on the prepared baking sheet. Repeat the process with the remaining portions of dough.

· Spray a sheet of plastic wrap with nonstick cooking spray and place it, sprayed-side down, over the baking sheet. Let the balls rest for 30 minutes at room temperature.

Stretch and laminate the rounds

· In a small bowl, combine the remaining 6 tablespoons canola oil and melted butter. Drizzle 1 tablespoon of the butter-oil mixture onto a large work surface. Use your fingers to spread it evenly around. Remove the plastic wrap covering the balls of dough and set it aside for later. Pick up one of the balls of dough and place it onto the oiled surface. Use your fingers to stretch and spread the ball out to a flat round 10 inches in diameter. If the dough sticks to your fingers, coat your fingers with some of the oil on the work surface and continue stretching.

· Drizzle 1 tablespoon of the butter-oil mixture on top of the round and use your fingers to spread it evenly across it. Sprinkle 1 teaspoon of semolina over the round.

· Pick up the top edge of the round and fold it down two-thirds. Fold the bottom edge to meet the top edge, so the dough is folded into thirds, like a letter. Fold the sides inward—folding the right side two-thirds to the left, and the left side to meet the right—in the same way to form a sort of packet. Place the packet, seam-side down, back onto the oiled baking sheet. Repeat the process with the remaining balls.

Rest the dough

· Re-cover the baking sheet with the reserved plastic wrap. Let the packets rest for 30 minutes to allow the gluten to relax.

Shape and cook the m'smen

· Preheat a 12-inch skillet over medium-low heat. Flip a baking sheet upside down and drizzle a little of the remaining butter-oil mixture on its backside. Spread the oil around with your fingers. Remove the plastic from the dough packets. Pick up one packet and place it on the butter-oil mixture. Use your fingers to stretch and spread the packet out to a flat 8-inch square. If the dough sticks to your fingers, coat your fingers with some of the oil on the work surface and continue stretching.

· Bring the baking sheet with m'smen as close to the heated skillet as possible. Working quickly, lift up the top two corners of the m'smen and lay it down flat into the pan. Cook the m'smen for 2 minutes, or until the underside is golden brown. With a metal spatula, lift the m'smen up, flip it over, and cook on the second side for 2 to 3 minutes. Using the metal spatula, transfer the m'smen to a cooling rack. Repeat the process with the remaining m'smen.

Finish and serve

· Place the finished m'smen on a serving platter. Sprinkle generously with flaky salt. Scoop the labneh into a large serving bowl and create a well in the center. Drizzle extra-virgin olive oil into the well. Sprinkle generously with dukkah.

Labneh

Makes about 2½ cups

Labneh is a savory thickened Middle Eastern yogurt and an excellent dip. I begin with an already thick Greek yogurt, and then drain it further.

Whole-milk Greek yogurt	24 ounces	680 grams
Lemon, zested and juiced	1	
Fine sea salt	½ teaspoon	3 grams

- In a medium bowl, stir together the yogurt, lemon zest, and lemon juice.
- Set a fine-mesh sieve over a bowl and line the sieve with cheesecloth. Scoop the yogurt mixture into the lined sieve. Set the yogurt in the refrigerator to drain for 12 to 24 hours. (The longer is sits, the more liquid will drain off and the thicker the mixture will be.)
- Dump the drained yogurt into a medium bowl and stir in the salt with a rubber spatula. Serve immediately or store in a covered container in the refrigerator for up to 1 week.

Dukkah

Makes about 1 cup

Dukkah is a popular Egyptian nut and spice blend that is traditionally sprinkled on bread, but it can also be added to dips like labneh and sprinkled on vegetables.

Shelled pistachios	½ cup	70 grams
Cumin seeds	1 tablespoon	8 grams
Coriander seeds	1 tablespoon	5 grams
Caraway seeds	1 tablespoon	7 grams
Nigella seeds	1½ teaspoons	4 grams
Sesame seeds	1 tablespoon	8 grams
Dried mint	1 tablespoon	3 grams
Aleppo pepper	1 tablespoon	8 grams
Flaky sea salt	1 teaspoon	4 grams

▪ Arrange an oven rack in the center position and preheat the oven to 300°F.

▪ Spread the pistachios on a baking sheet and toast for 20 minutes, or until they are golden brown and fragrant, shaking the pan at least once. Set the pistachios aside to cool slightly, then coarsely chop them.

▪ In a medium skillet, toast the cumin, coriander, and caraway seeds over medium-high heat for 1 to 2 minutes, shaking the pan frequently so they toast evenly and don't burn, until they are fragrant and begin popping in the pan. Pour the seeds out of the skillet into a medium bowl to cool to room temperature.

▪ Scoop the cooled seeds into a spice grinder and pulse to break them up without pulverizing them (3 quick pulses). Put the ground seeds in a medium bowl and add the chopped pistachios, nigella seeds, sesame seeds, mint, Aleppo pepper, and salt. Stir them together with a metal spoon.

▪ Place the dukkah in an airtight container until ready to use. It will keep covered for 2 weeks before beginning to stale.

M'smen with Short Rib Confit

Makes 11 m'smen

When I told my friend Ben Chekroun that I was including a m'smen recipe in this book, he told me that his favorite way to eat them was slathered with a spicy Moroccan preserved meat called khliî. The meat is salted and dried and then cut up and cooked in fat with water until the water evaporates. The fat is then used to cover and preserve the meat, like duck confit. This is my quick recipe for khliî. It can be spread on top of the m'smen, but I have found it to be even more delicious when it is folded into the dough before, which is what I do here. The flavor from the meat and spices perfumes the m'smen, and it goes perfectly with a couple of fried eggs sprinkled with cumin and flaky salt.

For the khliî		
Coriander seeds	1 tablespoon	5 grams
Ground cumin	2 teaspoons	4 grams
Garlic, peeled but whole	4 cloves	
Salt	1½ teaspoons	12 grams
Lemon juice	1 tablespoon	15 grams
Extra-virgin olive oil	¼ cup	55 grams
Beef short ribs, bone-in	2½ pounds	1.13 kilograms
Beef tallow	1 cup	55 grams
Water	6 cups	1.4 kilograms
Ras el hanout	1 teaspoon	2 grams
For the m'smen		
Bread flour	4¼ cups + more for dusting	510 grams
Coarse semolina	1⅓ cups	193 grams
Sugar	2 tablespoons + 2 teaspoons	35 grams
Fine sea salt	2½ teaspoons	15 grams
Water (75°–80°F)	1¾ cups	411 grams
Canola oil	9 tablespoons	117 grams
Unsalted butter, melted	6 tablespoons	84 grams
Flaky sea salt	for sprinkling	

Make the khliî

- In a medium skillet, toast the coriander seeds over medium-high heat for 2 to 3 minutes, shaking the pan frequently so they toast evenly, don't burn, and are fragrant. Pour the seeds out of the skillet into a medium bowl to cool to room temperature.
- Put the toasted coriander seeds, 1 teaspoon of the cumin, the garlic cloves, and 1 teaspoon of the salt into a mortar and crush with the pestle to make a paste. Stir in the lemon juice and olive oil. Place the short ribs in a 5-quart Dutch oven and spoon the marinade over them. Let rest at room temperature for 2 hours.
- Place the Dutch oven over medium-high heat to begin browning the short ribs, turning them with kitchen tongs to brown all sides, about 5 minutes.

- In a small saucepan, combine the beef tallow and 2 cups (470 grams) of the water and heat over medium heat for just a few minutes to melt the tallow. Pour the fat mixture over the short ribs along with the remaining 4 cups (945 grams) water. Bring to a simmer, then reduce the heat to low and cook for 3 hours uncovered.
- Remove the short ribs from the Dutch oven and place them on a cutting board to cool. Once they are cool enough to handle, remove the bones and any gristle and chop the meat up into fine pieces. Place the chopped meat into a medium bowl and add the ras el hanout and the remaining 1 teaspoon cumin and ½ teaspoon salt.

Mix and round the m'smen dough

- In a large bowl, whisk together the flour, 1 cup (145 grams) of the semolina, the sugar, and salt.
- In a stand mixer fitted with the dough hook, combine the water and 1 tablespoon of the canola oil. Add the flour mixture and mix on low speed for 10 minutes. Remove the dough hook and wipe it clean with a wet hand.
- Pour 2 tablespoons of canola oil onto a baking sheet and spread it around with your fingers to completely coat the bottom and sides.
- Lightly flour a large work surface and use a plastic bowl scraper to scrape the dough onto the floured surface. Lightly dust the top of the dough with flour and use a bench knife to divide it into 11 portions of 100 grams each.
- Put one portion of dough in front of you. Dust your hands lightly with flour. Gently rest your palm on the dough and roll it into a tight round ball. Put the ball on the prepared baking sheet. Repeat the process with the remaining portions of dough.
- Spray a sheet of plastic wrap with nonstick cooking spray and place the plastic wrap, sprayed-side down, over the baking sheet. Let the dough rest for 30 minutes at room temperature.

Stretch and laminate the rounds

- In a small bowl, combine the remaining 6 tablespoons canola oil and the melted butter. Drizzle 1 tablespoon of the butter-oil mixture onto a large work surface. Use your fingers to spread it evenly around. Remove the plastic wrap covering the balls of dough and set it aside for later. Pick up one of the balls of dough and place it onto the oiled surface. Use your fingers to stretch and spread the ball out to a flat round 10 inches in diameter. If the dough sticks to your fingers, coat your fingers with some of the oil on the work surface and continue stretching.
- Drizzle 1 tablespoon of the butter-oil mixture on top of the round and use your fingers to spread it evenly across it. Sprinkle 1 teaspoon of semolina over the round and dot 2 tablespoons of the short rib confit evenly over the surface of the round.

• Pick up the top edge of the round and fold it down two-thirds of the way from the top. Fold the bottom edge to meet the top edge, so the dough is folded into thirds, like a letter. Fold the sides of the dough inward—folding the right side two-thirds to the left, and the left side to meet it—to form a sort of packet. Place the packet, seam-side down, back onto the oiled baking sheet. Repeat the process with the remaining balls.

Rest the dough

• Re-cover the baking sheet with the reserved plastic wrap. Let the packets rest for 30 minutes to allow the gluten to relax.

Shape and cook the m'smen

• Preheat a 12-inch skillet over medium-low heat. Flip a baking sheet upside down and drizzle a little of the remaining butter-oil mixture on its backside. Spread the oil around with your fingers. Remove the plastic wrap from the dough packets. Pick up one packet and place it on the butter-oil mixture. Use your fingers to stretch and spread the packet out to a flat 9 × 7-inch rectangle. If the dough sticks to your fingers, coat them with some of the oil on the work surface and continue stretching.

• Bring the baking sheet with m'smen as close to the heated skillet as possible. Working quickly, lift up the top two corners of a m'smen and lay it down flat into the pan. Cook the m'smen for 2 minutes, or until the underside is golden brown. With a metal spatula, lift the m'smen up, flip it over, and cook on the second side for 2 to 3 minutes. Using the metal spatula, transfer the m'smen to a cooling rack. Repeat the process with the remaining m'smen.

Fresh Flour Tortillas

Makes 20 tortillas

Fresh flour tortillas are soft, easy to make, and versatile. They stand out when they are made with lard, which adds flavor and flakiness. Lard is pure fat, unlike butter, which contains a percentage of water, and a pure fat will make a flakier bread. Choose lard that is fresh, either rendered back lard or leaf lard.

For the dough			Baker's %
Bread flour	3¾ cups + more for dusting	450 grams	100
Fine sea salt	1 teaspoon	6 grams	1.3
Lard, cold	½ cup	113 grams	25
Water (70°–75°F)	1 cup	235 grams	52

Mix and round the dough

- In a stand mixer fitted with the paddle, combine the flour and salt and mix on low speed for about 30 seconds to combine the ingredients. Add the cold lard 1 tablespoon at a time and mix on low for 2 to 3 minutes to completely blend into the flour mixture.
- With the mixer running, slowly stream in the water and mix until the dough is homogeneous and there are no dry crumbs at the bottom of the bowl.
- Dust a large work surface with flour. Use a plastic bowl scraper to scoop the dough onto the floured surface. Gather the dough together with your hands and press it together form a single mass. Use a bench knife to divide the dough into 20 (40-gram) pieces.
- Working with one piece of dough at a time, gently rest your palm on the dough and roll it into a tight round ball. Place the ball on a lightly flour dusted corner of your work surface, away from where you are rolling, and continue rolling the remaining pieces in the same way. Cover the balls loosely with plastic wrap and let them rest for 30 to 60 minutes.

Fresh Flour Tortillas continues

Cook the tortillas
- Preheat a 12-inch skillet over medium-low heat.
- Dust a work surface with flour and place one of the balls of dough in front of you. Dust the top of the ball with more flour, and using a rolling pin, roll it out to 6 inches in diameter.
- Pick up the tortilla and place it into the preheated skillet. Cook for 1 to 2 minutes, until it has puffed up and is beginning to char on its bottom side. Using tongs, flip the tortilla over and cook for an additional 1 to 2 minutes. Remove the tortilla from the skillet to a cooling rack.
- Continue to roll out and cook the remaining tortillas in the same way. Serve warm or at room temperature.

Tacos with Pulled Pork and Salsa Ranchera

Serves 6 to 8

I keep a binder of recipes at home that I turn to over and over again. These are recipes for dishes that I cook for my son, like lasagne and shepherd's pie. My flour tortilla recipe (page 101) is in this binder, as is this pulled pork recipe and all its accompaniments. The salsa ranchera takes the tacos to a special place. The tomatoes are roasted and passed through a food mill, then cooked down with onion and serrano pepper into a most delicious sauce, which I also like to serve with eggs and warm tortillas in the morning. If you don't feel like making tortillas, the pulled pork is also good on potato rolls.

Pulled Pork (recipe follows)		
Salsa Ranchera (recipe follows)		
Fresh Flour Tortillas (page 101)	20	
Sour cream	1 cup	250 grams
Queso fresco, crumbled	4 ounces	113 grams
Cilantro, finely chopped	¼ cup	15 grams

• Prepare the pulled pork early in the day. Once the pork is out of the oven and resting, prepare the salsa ranchera. The flour tortillas can be prepared a day or two in advance, or made fresh while the pork is roasting.

• To assemble the tacos, spoon the shredded pork onto the tortillas. Serve with salsa ranchera, sour cream, queso fresco, and cilantro.

Pulled Pork

Makes 4 to 5 cups

Fine sea salt	1 tablespoon + 1 teaspoon	24 grams
Smoked paprika	1 tablespoon	8 grams
Cayenne pepper	1 teaspoon	2 grams
Freshly ground black pepper	1 teaspoon	2 grams
Ground cumin	1 teaspoon	2 grams
Boneless pork butt	4 pounds	1,816 grams
Vegetable oil	1 tablespoon	14 grams
Large yellow onion, finely diced	6 ounces	170 grams
Water	1 cup	235 grams
Apple cider vinegar	2 tablespoons	29 grams

• Arrange an oven rack in the lowest position with no racks above it and preheat the oven to 300°F.

• In a small bowl, combine 1 tablespoon of the salt, the smoked paprika, cayenne, pepper, and cumin and stir to blend the rub completely.

• Place the pork butt on a cutting board and sprinkle all over with the rub, massaging it into the meat.

• Heat a Dutch oven over medium-high heat. Add the oil and place the pork into the pot. Cook for about 5 minutes, turning the pork with tongs so that it browns on all sides. Add the diced onion and continue cooking for 1 to 2 minutes longer. Add the water, bring the water to a simmer, cover the Dutch oven, and transfer to the oven. Braise for 4 hours, or until the pork is tender and the internal temperature is at least 195°F. Remove the pork from the oven and let it rest in the liquid for 30 minutes.

• Use a fork to pull the meat apart, transferring the pieces to a large bowl.

• Adjust the seasoning by adding the apple cider vinegar, remaining 1 teaspoon salt, and 3 to 4 tablespoons of the seasoned cooking liquid.

Salsa Ranchera

Makes about 2 cups

Note For a less spicy salsa, cut the serrano in half and discard the membranes and seeds.

Medium red tomatoes	1 pound	454 grams
Serrano pepper, stemmed (see Note)	1	
Extra-virgin olive oil	3 tablespoons	43 grams
Yellow onion, finely diced	½ medium	
Garlic, finely diced	1 clove	
Fine sea salt	½ teaspoon	3 grams

- Arrange an oven rack in the top position and preheat the broiler.
- Toss the tomatoes and serrano with 1 tablespoon of the olive oil and place in a shallow broilerproof baking dish. Broil for 20 minutes, or until the tomatoes and chile are charred and just slightly soft when poked.
- Let the tomatoes cool for about 5 minutes, then pass the tomatoes and chile through a food mill into a bowl.
- In a saucepan, heat the remaining 2 tablespoons olive oil over medium heat. Add the onion and garlic and cook over medium heat, stirring often, for 5 minutes, or until the onion is translucent. Add the pureed tomato-chile mixture and simmer for 5 minutes. Season with the salt and transfer to a small bowl.

Whole Wheat Pitas

Makes 12 pitas

Pitas are relatively easy to make at home. The trick to perfect pitas is getting them to puff up. The pita dough needs to hit the heat hard so that the water in the dough quickly turns to steam to help push up a layer of the dough. I prefer using a 12-inch cast-iron skillet to make these because the cast iron retains heat so well.

			Baker's %
Water (70°–75°F)	1⅔ cups	392 grams	69
Instant yeast	2½ teaspoons	7.5 grams	1.3
Extra-virgin olive oil	2½ tablespoons	35 grams	6
Bread flour	3½ cups + more for dusting	420 grams	74
Whole wheat flour	1¼ cups	150 grams	26
Fine sea salt	2 teaspoons	12 grams	2.1

Make the dough

- Put the water in the bowl of a stand mixer. Sprinkle the yeast on top and let stand for 5 minutes to help dissolve the yeast. Then whisk the yeast into the water.
- Add the olive oil, followed by the bread flour, whole wheat flour, and salt. Fit the mixer with the dough hook and mix the ingredients on low speed for 3 minutes. Increase the speed to medium and mix for 5 minutes to develop the gluten. Remove the dough hook and wipe it clean with a wet hand.

Ferment and stretch and fold the dough

- Cover the bowl with a clean kitchen towel or plastic wrap and set aside in a warm place (about 75°F) to ferment the dough for 1 hour 30 minutes. At the 30-minute mark, uncover the bowl and use a wet hand to fold the top edge of the dough down two-thirds and the bottom edge up to meet it, so the dough is folded like a letter. Fold the sides inward in the same way to form a sort of ball, then re-cover the bowl. Then at the 60-minute mark, repeat the stretching and folding.

Divide and shape the pitas

- Line a baking sheet with parchment paper and spray the paper with nonstick cooking spray.
- Lightly dust a work surface with flour. Using a plastic bowl scraper, scoop the dough onto the floured surface. Dust the top of the dough with flour and use a bench knife to divide it into 10 (100-gram) pieces. Put one piece of dough in front of you. Dust your hands lightly with flour. Gently rest your palm on the dough and roll it into a tight round ball. Put the ball on the prepared baking sheet. Repeat the process with the remaining pieces, adding them to the baking sheet and leaving about 2 inches between the balls.
- Cover the baking sheet with a damp lightweight kitchen towel and set it aside in a warm place (75° to 80°F) for 20 to 30 minutes to relax the gluten.

Roll out and cook the pitas

- Preheat a 12-inch skillet (preferably cast-iron) over medium-high heat.
- Lightly flour a work surface, uncover the balls, and place one on the floured work surface. Dust the dough and the rolling pin with flour and roll the dough to a 6-inch round. Pick up the pita and place it in the skillet. Cook for about 2 minutes, or until it has puffed up. Using tongs, flip the pita over and cook for an additional 30 seconds. Remove the pita from the skillet with tongs to a cooling rack.
- Continue to roll out and cook the remaining pitas in the same way. Serve warm or at room temperature.

Lamb Meatballs with Yogurt and Pickled Onion

This is my favorite recipe to make when I crave something savory and comforting. The lamb meatballs are tender, flavorful, and moist, and they are also fairly quick to make. The yogurt sauce is quick to whip up, and the red onions are a quick pickle.

Makes 8 pita sandwiches

For the red onion pickles

Apple cider vinegar	½ cup	118 grams
Water, room temperature	1 cup	237 grams
Granulated sugar	1 tablespoon	13 grams
Fine sea salt	1½ teaspoons	9 grams
Red onion, halved and thinly sliced	1 medium	

For the yogurt sauce

Whole-milk Greek yogurt	2 cups	480 grams
Scallions, thinly sliced	½ cup	50 grams
Dill, chopped	¼ cup	15 grams
Fine sea salt	1½ teaspoons	9 grams
Extra-virgin olive oil	4 tablespoons	60 grams
Lemon, juiced	1	25 grams
Champagne vinegar	1 tablespoon	13 grams

For the lamb meatballs

Ground lamb	2 pounds	908 grams
Scallions, thinly sliced	1 cup	100 grams
Cilantro, chopped	½ cup	20 grams
Garlic, grated	3 cloves	
Fine sea salt	2 teaspoons	12 grams
Ground cumin	1 teaspoon	2 grams
Dried thyme	½ teaspoon	1 gram
Extra-virgin olive oil	2 tablespoons	26 grams

For assembling the sandwiches

Parsley	1 bunch
Mint	1 bunch
Dill	1 bunch
Cilantro	1 bunch
Scallions	1 bunch
Whole Wheat Pitas (page 108)	8

Make the red onion pickles
- In a medium bowl, whisk together the vinegar, water, sugar, and salt until dissolved. Add the red onion slices and let the onion mixture sit at room temperature for 1 hour. Refrigerate until needed.

Make the yogurt sauce
- In a medium bowl, whisk together the yogurt, scallions, dill, and salt. Drizzle in the olive oil, followed by the lemon juice and champagne vinegar. Scoop the sauce into a lidded container and refrigerate for 1 hour to let the flavors meld together before serving.

Make the meatballs
- In a large bowl, combine the lamb, scallions, cilantro, grated garlic, salt, cumin, and thyme. Use your hands to combine the ingredients well. Divide this mixture into 24 balls weighing 1½ ounces (44 grams) each.
- In a 12-inch skillet, heat 1 tablespoon of the olive oil over medium heat until it shimmers. Working in batches, add some of the meatballs to the pan and cook, turning regularly with a spatula, for about 10 minutes, or until the meatballs are evenly browned on all sides. Transfer the meatballs to a paper towel–lined plate. Wipe the burned bits from the pan, add the remaining 1 tablespoon olive oil, and cook the rest of the meatballs in the same way.

Assemble the sandwiches
- Chop the herbs and place in a large bowl.
- Thinly slice the scallions on a bias and add them to the bowl. Toss the herbs and scallions with your fingers.
- Slice the pita open on one side. Place 3 meatballs into the pocket. Spoon 2 to 3 generous tablespoons of yogurt sauce over the meatballs. Sprinkle with pickled red onion and herb mix. Repeat to make more sandwiches.

Sourdough Loaves

In 1996 I purchased *Nancy Silverton's Breads from the La Brea Bakery,* a book entirely devoted to making bread with sourdough starter. I was an enthusiastic novice home baker, and I followed the instructions for making your own starter using organic grapes submerged in a slurry of flour and water. I didn't make it past growing the sourdough starter, and I put the book away, pulling it out every so often for inspiration. By 2006 I was working at Babbo restaurant in New York City as a pastry assistant. I had more knowledge in bread, but still no experience with sourdough. I decided that I was going to make the starter and every recipe in the book and write a blog about it (blogs were a new thing at that time—remember *The Julie/Julia Project*?). I grew the starter at home using the organic grapes and made the first bread recipe in the book, Country White, and it was successful—it didn't collapse in the oven like I feared it would. Also, it was tasty! And so I kept going. I bought a dried starter online— the person who sold it to me claimed it was one hundred years old or something like that—and I fed this new/old starter, which was stronger and more robust than the one I cultivated from scratch. One by one I went through all the recipes in the book, making a bread schedule for myself so that I could stay on track. I learned more in those months of making bread at home than I could have imagined. Making sourdough bread regularly helped me get comfortable with the different stages a starter goes through, from the time you feed it to the time you add it to your dough, and even the moments when you feed it but don't have time to make a loaf of bread. Making sourdough bread is a cathartic experience when you do it regularly.

The sourdough recipes in this chapter are truly my favorite breads to make. I make them at home, over and over again. I often double the City Sourdough (page 118) to make two loaves, which I then slice and freeze, so that I have slices to pull out from the freezer for toast. The Toasted Sesame Durum Sourdough (page 141) is particularly delicious for grilled cheese or dipping into fondue. I am completely smitten with the Einkorn Pan Bread (page 147), especially when I focus on healthy eating. The breads in this chapter offer variety from more neutral sourdough loaves like the City Sourdough and the Whole Wheat Sourdough (page 122) to the fruit- and nut-studded Cherry Pecan Anadama (page 156) to the caraway-inflected Marbled Rye (page 129). I couldn't be happier to be able to share all of the recipes in this chapter.

Master Class
Sourdough Loaves
Keys to Success

There are several keys to success when making this and the other sourdough loaves in this chapter.

Making the starter
Each recipe begins by taking a small amount of your existing mother starter to make the starter needed for the bread. That starter should be made early in the day and used when it is young (see Sourdough Starter Tutorial, page xxvi). It should just pass the Float Test (see page xxxi). A younger starter is stronger and more active and will give the loaf better oven spring (See The Twelve Steps of Breadmaking, page 5) and a beautiful crumb.

Saving your mother starter
All of the starter you make for a recipe will be used in that recipe, but don't throw away the remainder of your mother starter. Keep that starter on its maintenance schedule (see Maintaining a Mother Starter, page xxxi).

Autolyse
Autolyse the flours and first water addition (see Double Hydration, below) for 2 to 3 hours before you add the ripened starter to the dough. More gluten forms with the longer autolyse. (If you are pinched for time, a 30-minute autolyse is okay.)

Double hydration
Some of the sourdough bread recipes use a double hydration, which is helpful when the dough has a lot of water in it. A double hydration means there are two water additions. The first water is added during the autolyse (see above). By holding back some of the water during the autolyse, usually around 7%, it is easier for the dough to form a strong gluten structure and it is easier to handle the dough. The second water is added after the autolyse and starter are added to the dough.

Adding salt
Add the salt after the autolyse. Salt interferes with gluten formation, so it is best to add it at the end of the mixing.

City Sourdough

Makes 1 loaf

This is the first loaf of bread I made in the wood-fired oven at Roberta's. It is a quintessential pain de campagne, a large round country-style (rustic) French loaf, made with a combination of bread and whole wheat flours, and leavened naturally with sourdough starter. Because I was making this in Brooklyn, I thought City Sourdough was a perfect name.

			Baker's %
Sourdough Starter			
Water (70°–75°F)	2 tablespoons + 2 teaspoons	40 grams	100
Mother sourdough starter	1 tablespoon	25 grams	62.5
Bread flour	⅓ cup	40 grams	100
For the dough			
First water (85°–95°F)	1⅔ cups	392 grams	73
Bread flour	4 cups + more for dusting	480 grams	89
Whole wheat bread flour	½ cup	60 grams	11
Sourdough Starter (above)	½ cup + 1 tablespoon	105 grams	19
Second water (85°–95°F)	2 tablespoons + 2 teaspoons	40 grams	7.0
Fine sea salt	2 teaspoons	12 grams	2.2
For dusting the towel-lined bowl			
Brown rice flour	4 tablespoons		

Mix the starter

· Mix the sourdough starter 4 to 5 hours before adding it to the dough. Put the water in a 1-quart container with a lid and add 25 grams (1 tablespoon) of ripened mother sourdough starter. Add the flour and stir with a metal spoon to combine. Cover the container and set the starter aside in a warm place (about 75°F) until it is ripe and passes the Float Test (page xxxi).

Autolyse the dough

· In a shallow 3- to 4-quart container, stir together the first water, bread flour, and whole wheat flour with a metal spoon to combine. Cover the container and set aside in a warm place (about 75°F) for 2 to 3 hours to autolyse.

For more information on why we are resting the dough before mixing the sourdough starter and salt into the dough, see Autolyse (page 5).

Add the starter to the dough

· As soon as the starter is ripe, uncover the dough and add the starter, mixing it by scooping your hand under the dough and folding the dough into the center until the starter is thoroughly mixed in. Measure the temperature of the dough. It should be between 78° and 82°F. Re-cover the container and let the dough rest for 30 minutes.

Add the second water and salt to the dough

· Uncover the dough. Add the second water and salt; scoop under the dough with a wet hand and fold the dough into the center until it is homogeneous. Re-cover the container and let the dough rest for 30 minutes.

Make 4 stretch and folds

• Uncover the dough. With wet hands, scoop underneath the top edge of the dough, stretch it out, and fold it down two-thirds of the way toward the bottom edge. Stretch out and fold the bottom edge up to meet the top edge, as if you were folding a letter, pressing on the dough just enough to get it to stay in place. Do the same with the two sides, stretching and folding the right edge two-thirds of the way toward the left edge, and stretching and folding the left edge to meet the right edge. Then flip the dough upside down. This is your first fold. Re-cover the container and set the dough aside for 30 minutes.

• Repeat stretching and folding the dough a second time for a second fold. Re-cover and set the dough aside for 30 minutes.

• Repeat stretching and folding the dough a third time for a third fold. Re-cover and set the dough aside for 30 minutes.

• Repeat stretching and folding one last time for a fourth fold. Re-cover and set the dough aside for 1 hour for a total fermentation time of 3½ hours.

Shape and retard the loaf

• Line a 3-quart bowl with a lightweight kitchen towel (or use a linen-lined banneton) and dust with brown rice flour. Set aside.

• Dust a large work surface with bread flour. Use a plastic dough scraper or rubber spatula to scoop the dough onto the floured surface. Gently coax the dough into a rough, squarish shape.

• First, to create tautness: Begin at the top right corner of the dough and fold the corner two-thirds of the way across the top. Fold the top left corner to meet the right edge. Repeat the folding from right to left and then from left to right, working your way down the loaf until you reach the bottom closest to you. This should be accomplished in three to four complete folds.

• Then fold the loaf like a letter, folding the top edge of the loaf two-thirds of the way down and folding the bottom edge up to meet it, pressing on the dough just enough to get it to stay in place. Pick the loaf up and place it into the lined bowl seam side up.

- Wrap the bowl in plastic wrap and place it in the refrigerator to proof overnight, or for at least 8 hours.

Score and bake the bread

- Thirty minutes before you plan to bake, arrange an oven rack in the center position with no racks above it. Place a 5-quart Dutch oven on the rack and preheat the oven to 500°F.
- Take the bowl of dough out of the refrigerator and remove the plastic. Dust the top of the loaf with brown rice flour. Open the oven and carefully slide the oven rack out partway. Remove the Dutch oven lid. Use the towel to gently flip the dough into the palm of your free hand. Place the dough seam-side down into the Dutch oven. Score the bread decoratively with a lame or a small, sharp serrated knife. Replace the lid and slide the oven rack back into the oven.
- Bake the bread for 25 minutes. Reduce the oven temperature to 450°F and carefully remove the lid. Bake the bread for 25 minutes longer, until it has a deeply burnished crust.

Cool the bread

- Remove the Dutch oven from the oven. Slide a large metal spatula under the bread and, holding the bread with your other hand (protected by a clean kitchen towel), remove it from the Dutch oven. Place the bread on a cooling rack to cool completely.

Whole Wheat Sourdough

Makes 1 loaf

This wonderfully delicious loaf of bread is composed of 70% whole wheat bread flour to 30% white bread flour. Because the whole wheat bread flour contains the bran and germ in addition to the endosperm, it absorbs more water. The hydration for this recipe is higher than it is for the City Sourdough, 84% baker's percentage compared to 80% baker's percentage, although the baked loaf will seem equally moist. Whole-grain flours ferment more quickly than white flours, so this loaf has a shorter fermentation time and a lower fermentation temperature in order that it not overproof.

Sourdough Starter			Baker's %
Water (70°–75°F)	2 tablespoons + 2 teaspoons	40 grams	100
Mother sourdough starter	1 tablespoon	25 grams	62.5
Bread flour	⅓ cup	40 grams	100
For the dough			
First water (70°–80°F)	1⅔ cups	392 grams	73
Sourdough Starter (above)	½ cup + 1 tablespoon	105 grams	20
Whole wheat bread flour	3 cups + 2 tablespoons	378 grams	70
Bread flour	1⅓ cups	160 grams	30
Second water (70°–80°F)	¼ cup	59 grams	11
Fine sea salt	2¼ teaspoons	14 grams	2.6
For dusting the towel-lined bowl			
Brown rice flour	4 tablespoons		

Mix the starter

• Mix the sourdough starter 4 to 5 hours before adding it to the dough. Put the water in a 1-quart container with a lid and add 25 grams (1 tablespoon) of ripened mother sourdough starter to the container. Add the flour and stir with a metal spoon to combine. Cover the container and set the starter aside in a warm place (about 75°F) until it is ripe and passes the Float Test (page xxxi).

Autolyse the dough

• In a shallow 3- to 4-quart container, stir together the first water, whole wheat bread flour, and bread flour with a metal spoon to combine. Cover the container and set aside in a warm place (about 75°F) for 2 to 3 hours to autolyse.

For more information on why we are resting the dough before mixing the sourdough starter and salt into the dough, see Autolyse (page 5).

Add the starter to the dough
- As soon as the starter is ripe, uncover the dough and add the starter, mixing it by scooping your hand under the dough and folding the dough into the center until the sourdough is thoroughly mixed in. Measure the temperature of the dough. It should be between 72° and 76°F. Re-cover the container and let the dough rest for 30 minutes.

Add the second water and salt to the dough
- Uncover the dough. Add the second water and salt and scoop under the dough with a wet hand and fold the dough into the center until it is homogeneous. Re-cover the container and set aside. Let the dough rest for 30 minutes.

Make 2 stretch and folds
- Uncover the dough. With wet hands, scoop underneath the top edge of the dough, stretch it out, and fold it down two-thirds of the way toward the bottom edge. Stretch out and fold the bottom edge up to meet the top edge, as if you were folding a letter, pressing on the dough just enough to get it to stay in place. Do the same with the two sides, stretching and folding the right edge two-thirds of the way toward the left edge, and stretching and folding the left edge to meet the right edge. Then flip the dough upside down. This is your first fold. Re-cover the container and set the dough aside for 30 minutes.
- Repeat stretching and folding the dough a second time for a second fold. Re-cover and set the dough aside for 90 minutes for a total fermentation time of 3 hours.

Shape and retard the loaf
- Line a 3-quart bowl with a lightweight kitchen towel (or use a linen-lined banneton) and dust with brown rice flour. Set aside.
- Dust a large work surface with bread flour. Use a plastic dough scraper or rubber spatula to scoop the dough onto the floured surface. Gently coax the dough into a rough squarish shape.
- First, to create tautness: Begin at the right top corner of the dough and fold the corner two-thirds of the way across the top. Fold the top left corner to meet the right edge. Repeat the folding from right to left and then from left to right, working your way down the loaf until you reach the bottom closest to you. This should be accomplished in three to four complete folds.
- Then fold the loaf like a letter, folding the top edge of the loaf two-thirds of the way down and folding the bottom edge to meet it, pressing on the dough just enough to get it to stay in place. Pick the loaf up and place it seam-side up into the lined bowl.
- Wrap the bowl in plastic wrap and place it in the refrigerator to proof overnight, or for at least 8 hours.

Score and bake the bread
- Thirty minutes before you plan to bake, arrange an oven rack in the center position with no racks above it. Place a 5-quart Dutch oven on the rack and preheat the oven to 500°F.

- Take the bowl of dough out of the refrigerator and remove the plastic. Dust the top of the loaf with brown rice flour. Open the oven and carefully slide the oven rack out partway. Remove the Dutch oven lid. Use the towel to flip the ball of dough into the palm of your free hand. Place the dough seam-side down into the Dutch oven. Score the bread decoratively with a lame or small, sharp serrated knife. Replace the lid and slide the oven rack back into the oven.
- Bake the bread for 25 minutes. Reduce the oven temperature to 450°F and carefully remove the lid. Bake the bread for 25 minutes longer, until it has a deeply burnished crust.

Cool the bread

- Remove the Dutch oven from the oven. Slide a large metal spatula under the bread and, holding the bread with your other hand (protected by a clean kitchen towel), remove it from the Dutch oven. Place the bread on a cooling rack to cool completely.

Sprouted Rye Miche

Makes 1 loaf

Miche is a French word for a very large round sourdough loaf of bread made with a combination of flours that usually includes white wheat, whole wheat, and rye. Miches vary in size, ranging from 1 pound to more than 6 pounds! A miche should be large enough to last throughout the week. Since a 6-pound loaf of bread is difficult to master at home, this recipe makes a 1.2-kilogram (2⅔-pound) miche. This miche recipe includes sprouted rye berries, which add texture and nutrition. Rye berries are sprouted by first soaking them and then keeping them in a warm and moist environment until they begin to sprout (usually about 3 days). In the process of germinating, the phytate in the berries is broken down. Phytate decreases the absorption of vitamins and minerals in the body, so when it breaks down, the vitamins and minerals become available for the body to absorb.

Plan ahead   It takes 3 days to sprout the rye, plus one day to mix the dough before retarding it overnight. If you want to have your loaf ready on Sunday, plan to begin sprouting the berries on Wednesday.

For the sprouted rye			Baker's %
Rye berries	½ cup	40 grams	
Water (70°–75°F)	2 cups	470 grams	
Sourdough Starter			
Water (70°–75°F)	2 tablespoons + 2 teaspoons	40 grams	100
Mother sourdough starter	1 tablespoon	25 grams	62.5
Bread flour	⅓ cup	40 grams	100
For the dough			
Water (70°–80°F)	2 cups	470 grams	86
Bread flour	2¼ cups + more for dusting	270 grams	49.5
Whole wheat bread flour	1 cup + 2 tablespoons	138 grams	25
Whole rye flour	1 cup + 2 tablespoons	138 grams	25
Sourdough Starter (above)	½ cup + 1 tablespoon	105 grams	19
Fine sea salt	2½ teaspoons	15 grams	2.7
Sprouted rye berries (above)	1 cup	137 grams	25
For dusting the towel-lined bowl			
Brown rice flour	4 tablespoons		

Sprout the rye berries

• Place the rye berries in a large bowl, cover them with the water, and soak for 8 hours. Drain in a mesh sieve and return to the bowl. Cover the bowl with plastic wrap and let the berries rest at room temperature overnight, or for at least 8 hours.

• The next morning, to keep the berries moist, uncover the bowl and cover the berries with room temperature water (70°–75°F). Immediately drain in a mesh sieve. Return all the berries to the bowl. Re-cover the bowl and let the berries rest at room temperature for 12 hours.

- Repeat this rinsing process in the evening, uncovering the bowl, covering the berries with water, draining the water immediately, and re-covering the bowl. Let the berries rest at room temperature overnight.
- The third day, repeat rinsing the berries in the morning and evening. You should begin to see sprouts growing. Once sprouts begin to grow, refrigerate the sprouted rye in a covered container. The sprouted grain can stay refrigerated for up to 1 week before using. (Alternatively, it can be frozen and then thawed overnight in the refrigerator before using.)

Mix the starter

- Mix the sourdough starter 4 to 5 hours before adding it to the dough. Put the water in a 1-quart container with a lid and add 25 grams (1 tablespoon) of the ripened sourdough starter to the container. Add the flour and stir with a metal spoon to combine. Cover the container and set the starter aside in a warm place (about 75°F) until it is ripe and passes the Float Test (page xxxi).

Autolyse the dough

- In a shallow 3- to 4-quart container, stir together the water, bread flour, whole wheat flour, and rye flour with a metal spoon to combine. Cover the container and set it aside in a warm place (about 75°F) for 2 to 3 hours to autolyse.

For more information on why we are resting the dough before mixing the sourdough starter, salt, and rye berries into the dough, see Autolyse (page 5).

Add the starter to the dough

- As soon as the starter is ripe, uncover the dough and add the starter, mixing it by scooping your hand under the dough and folding the dough into the center until the sourdough is thoroughly mixed in. Measure the temperature of the dough. It should be between 72° and 76°F. Re-cover the container and let the dough rest for 30 minutes.

Add the salt and sprouted rye to the dough

- Uncover the dough. Add the salt and sprouted rye, scoop under the dough with a wet hand, and fold the dough into the center until it is homogeneous. Re-cover the container and let the dough rest for 30 minutes.

Make 4 stretch and folds

- Uncover the dough. With wet hands, scoop underneath the top edge of the dough, stretch it out, and fold it down two-thirds of the way toward the bottom edge. Stretch out and fold the bottom edge up to meet the top edge, as if you were folding a letter, pressing on the dough just enough to get it to stay in place. Do the same with the two sides, stretching and folding the right edge two-thirds of the way toward the left edge, and stretching and folding the left edge to meet the right edge. Then flip the dough upside down. This is your first fold. Re-cover the container and set the dough aside for 30 minutes.
- Repeat stretching and folding the dough a second time for a second fold. Re-cover and set the dough aside for 30 minutes.

- Repeat stretching and folding the dough a third time for a third fold. Re-cover and set the dough aside for 30 minutes.
- Repeat stretching and folding one last time for a fourth fold. Re-cover and set the dough aside for 1 hour, for a total fermentation time of 3½ hours.

Shape and retard the loaf

- Line a 3-quart bowl with a lightweight kitchen towel (or use a linen-lined banneton) and dust with brown rice flour. Set aside.
- Dust a large work surface with bread flour. Use a plastic dough scraper or rubber spatula to scoop the dough onto the floured work surface. Gently coax the dough into a rough squarish shape.
- First, to create tautness: Begin at the top right corner of the dough and fold the corner two-thirds of the way across the top. Fold the top left corner to meet the right edge. Repeat the folding from right to left and then from left to right until you reach the bottom closest to you. This should be accomplished in three to four complete folds.
- Then fold the loaf like a letter, folding the top edge two-thirds of the way down and folding the bottom edge up to meet the top edge, pressing on the dough just enough to get it to stay in place. Pick the loaf up and place it seam-side up into the lined bowl.
- Wrap the bowl in plastic wrap and place it in the refrigerator to proof overnight, or for at least 8 hours.

Score and bake the bread

- Thirty minutes before you plan to bake, arrange an oven rack in the center position with no racks above it. Place a 5-quart Dutch oven on the rack and preheat the oven to 500°F.
- Take the bowl of dough out of the refrigerator and remove the plastic. Dust the top of the loaf with brown rice flour. Open the oven and carefully slide the oven rack out partway. Remove the Dutch oven lid. Use the towel to flip the ball of dough into the palm of your free hand. Place the dough seam-side down into the Dutch oven. Score the bread decoratively with a lame or small, sharp serrated knife. Replace the lid and slide the oven rack back into the oven.
- Bake the bread for 25 minutes. Reduce the oven temperature to 450°F and carefully remove the lid. Bake the bread for 20 to 25 minutes longer, until it has a deeply burnished crust.

Cool the bread

- Remove the Dutch oven from the oven. Slide a large metal spatula under the bread and, holding the bread with your other hand (protected by a clean kitchen towel), remove it from the Dutch oven. Place the bread on a cooling rack to cool completely.

Marbled Rye

Makes 1 loaf

This sourdough loaf is made by mixing and fermenting two different doughs and then combining them during the latter part of the fermentation. The first dough is a light caraway rye dough, made with toasted caraway and a percentage of rye flour. The second dough is pumpernickel. It is also made with toasted caraway and a percentage of rye flour, but it also has dark-roasted malted barley flour, like the Pumpernickel Raisin Bagels (page 47). Because dark-roasted malted barley flour can be difficult to source, I grind my own from whole grains that I purchase from beer brewing supply stores. Though I make mine in a flour mill, it also can be ground in a coffee/spice grinder—though that produces a coarser grind and you will need to sift out the coarse pieces until you are left with a fine powder. Cocoa powder can be substituted, adding a chocolaty taste to the loaf.

			Baker's %
Sourdough Starter			
Water (70°–75°F)	2 tablespoons + 2 teaspoons	40 grams	100
Mother sourdough starter	1 tablespoon	25 grams	62.5
Bread flour	⅓ cup	40 grams	100
For the caraway seeds			
Caraway seeds	2 tablespoons + 1½ teaspoons	20 grams	
For the light caraway rye dough			
Water (80°–90°F)	1 cup + 4 teaspoons	255 grams	85
Bread flour	2 cups + more for dusting	240 grams	80
Rye flour	½ cup	60 grams	20
Sourdough Starter (above)	¼ cup + 1 tablespoon	52 grams	18
Fine sea salt	1¼ teaspoons	7.5 grams	2.5
For the pumpernickel dough			
Water (80°–90°F)	1 cup + 3 tablespoons	280 grams	85
Bread flour	1½ cups	180 grams	55
Rye flour	¾ cup	90 grams	27
Dark-roasted malted barley flour	½ cup	60 grams	18
Sourdough Starter (above)	¼ cup + 1 tablespoon	52 grams	16
Fine sea salt	1¼ teaspoons	7.5 grams	2.3
For dusting the cloth-lined bowl			
Brown rice flour	3 tablespoons		

Mix the starter

· Mix the sourdough starter 4 to 5 hours before adding it to the dough. Put the water in a 1-quart container with a lid and add 25 grams (1 tablespoon) of the ripened mother sourdough starter. Add the flour and stir with a metal spoon to combine. Cover the container and set the starter aside in a warm place (about 75°F) until it is ripe and passes the Float Test (page xxxi).

Prepare the caraway seeds

· In a medium skillet, toast the caraway seeds over medium-high heat for 2 to 3 minutes, shaking the pan frequently so they toast evenly and don't burn, until they are fragrant and begin popping. Pour the seeds out of the skillet into a medium bowl to cool to room temperature.

• Put 1 tablespoon (8 grams) of the seeds in a spice grinder and pulse to pulverize. Put the ground caraway in a small bowl and set aside.

Autolyse (light caraway rye dough)

• In a shallow 3- to 4-quart lidded container, stir together the water, bread flour, and rye flour with a metal spoon to combine. Cover the container and set aside in a warm place (about 75°F) for 2 to 3 hours to autolyse.

Autolyse (pumpernickel dough)

• In a another shallow 3- to 4-quart lidded container, stir together the water, bread flour, rye flour, and dark-roasted malted barley flour with a metal spoon to combine. Cover the container and set aside in a warm place (about 75°F) for 2 to 3 hours to autolyse.

For more information on why we are resting the dough before mixing the sourdough starter, salt, and caraway into the dough, see Autolyse (page 5).

Add the sourdough starter (both doughs)

• As soon as the starter is ripe, uncover the light caraway rye dough and add half of the starter (52 grams), mixing it by scooping your hand under the dough and folding it into the center until the sourdough is thoroughly mixed in. Re-cover the container and set aside. Uncover the pumpernickel dough and do the same thing, adding the remaining sourdough starter (52 grams) and folding the starter into the dough by hand. Re-cover the container. Let both doughs rest for 30 minutes.

Add the salt and caraway (both doughs)

• Uncover the light caraway rye dough. Add the salt, half of the ground caraway (4 grams), and half of the toasted caraway seeds (6 grams) to the dough, scooping under the dough with a wet hand and folding the dough into the center until it is homogeneous. Re-cover the container and set aside. Uncover the dark caraway rye dough and do the same thing, adding the salt, the remaining ground caraway (4 grams), and the toasted caraway seeds (6 grams) and mixing them in by hand. Re-cover the container and set aside. Let both doughs rest for 30 minutes.

Make 3 stretch and folds

• Uncover the light caraway rye dough. With wet hands, scoop underneath the top edge of the dough, stretch it out, and fold it down two-thirds of the way toward the bottom edge. Stretch out and fold the bottom edge up to meet the top edge, as if you were folding a letter, pressing on the dough just enough to get it to stay in place. Do the same with the two sides, stretching and folding the right edge two-thirds of the way toward the left edge, and stretching and folding the left edge to meet the right edge. Then flip the dough upside down. Re-cover the container. Repeat the stretching and folding for the pumpernickel dough and re-cover the container. Set both doughs aside for 30 minutes.

· Repeat the stretching and folding for both doughs a second time for a second fold. Re-cover and set the doughs aside for 30 minutes.

· Repeat the stretching and folding for both doughs a final time for a third fold. Re-cover and set the doughs aside for 1 hour.

Laminate the two doughs together

· Lightly spread a tablespoon or two of water over a large work surface. Use wet hands to scoop under the light caraway rye dough and place it on the work surface gently. Stretch the dough into a 12-inch square by scooping the dough from underneath, wetting your hands as needed, and pulling it gently out.

· Using wet hands, scoop under the pumpernickel dough and lift it out of the container, placing it directly on top of the light caraway rye dough. Pull the pumpernickel dough until it covers the surface of the light caraway dough.

· To fold the combined doughs together, scoop underneath the top edge of the two doughs and fold them two-thirds of the way toward the bottom edge. Fold the bottom edge up to meet the top edge, as if you were folding a letter, pressing on the dough just enough to get it to stay in place. Do the same with the sides, folding the right edge two-thirds of the way toward the left edge, and folding the left edge to meet the right edge. Then flip the dough upside down and place it back into one of the containers. Re-cover the container and set the dough aside for 1 hour.

Make a final stretch and fold

· Remove the cover from the container. With wet hands, scoop underneath the top edge of the dough and stretch and fold it down two-thirds of the way toward the bottom edge. Stretch out and fold the bottom edge up to meet the top edge, as if you were folding a letter, pressing on the dough just enough to get it to stay in place. Do the same with the two sides, stretching and folding the right edge two-thirds of the way toward the left edge, and stretching and folding the left edge to meet the right edge. Then flip the dough upside down. Re-cover the container and set the dough aside for 30 minutes for a total fermentation time of 4½ hours.

Shape and retard the loaf

· Line a 3-quart bowl with a lightweight kitchen towel (or use a linen-lined banneton) and dust with brown rice flour. Set aside.

· Dust a large work surface with bread flour. Use a plastic dough scraper or rubber spatula to scoop the dough onto the floured surface. Gently coax the dough into a rough squarish shape.

· First, to create tautness: Begin at the top right corner of the dough and fold the corner two-thirds of the way across the top. Fold the top left corner to meet the right edge. Repeat the folding from right to left and then from left

Laminating the two doughs together

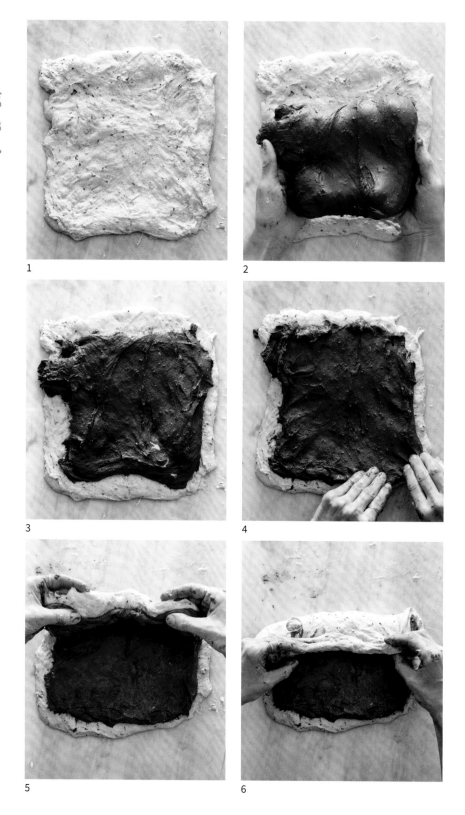

1

2

3

4

5

6

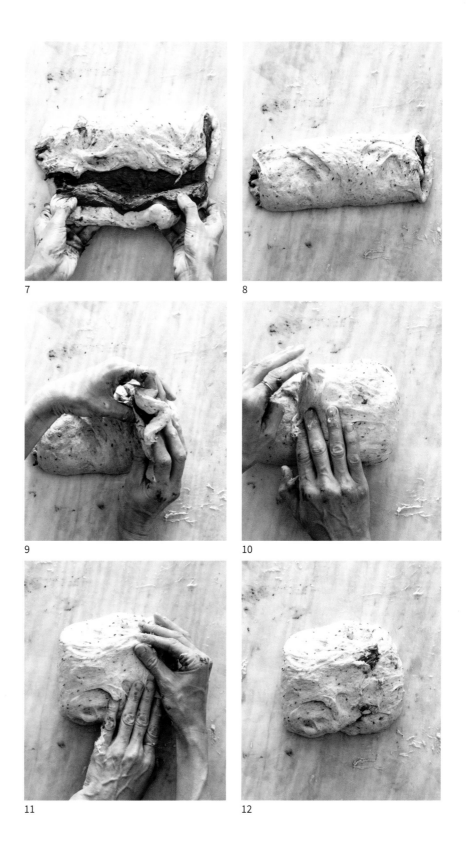

7

8

9

10

11

12

to right, working your way down the loaf until you reach the bottom closest to you. This should be accomplished in three to four complete folds.

· Then fold the loaf like a letter, folding the top edge two-thirds of the way down and folding the bottom edge to meet the top pressing on the dough just enough to get it to stay in place. Pick the dough up and place it seam-side up in the lined bowl.

· Wrap the bowl in plastic wrap and place it in the refrigerator to proof overnight, or for at least 8 hours.

Score and bake the bread

· Thirty minutes before you plan to bake, arrange an oven rack in the center position with no racks above it. Place a 5-quart Dutch oven on the rack and preheat the oven to 500°F.

· Take the dough out of the refrigerator and remove the plastic. Dust the top of the loaf with brown rice flour. Open the oven and carefully slide the oven rack out partway. Remove the Dutch oven lid. Use the towel to flip the ball of dough into the palm of your free hand. Place the dough seam-side down into the Dutch oven. Score the bread decoratively with a lame or small, sharp serrated knife. Replace the lid and slide the oven rack back into the oven.

· Bake the bread for 25 minutes. Reduce the oven temperature to 450°F and carefully remove the lid. Bake the bread for 20 to 25 minutes longer, until it has a deeply burnished crust.

Cool the bread

· Remove the Dutch oven from the oven. Slide a large metal spatula under the bread and, holding the bread with your other hand (protected by a clean kitchen towel), remove it from the Dutch oven. Place the bread on a cooling rack to cool completely.

Schedule for Marbled Rye

Making sourdough marbled rye involves a lot of steps, and it's easy to lose where you are in the process. This schedule will help you plan the steps out.

Day One
This day is about getting the starter ready and mixing the dough. At the end of the day, the dough is shaped and then retarded in the refrigerator overnight.

8:00 a.m. Mix the starter; prepare the caraway seeds.
10:00 a.m. Autolyse the water and the flours for both the light and dark rye doughs.
12:00 p.m. Add the sourdough starter to both doughs.
12:30 p.m. Add the salt and whole and ground caraway seeds to both doughs.
1:00 p.m. First stretch and fold for both doughs.
1:30 p.m. Second stretch and fold for both doughs.
2:00 p.m. Third stretch and fold for both doughs.
3:00 p.m. Laminate the light and dark doughs together.
4:00 p.m. Final stretch and fold.
4:30 p.m. Shape and retard the loaf overnight.

Day Two
This is the baking day. The loaf can be baked at any time throughout the day. I like to bake it early in the morning.

8:00 a.m. Preheat the oven.
8:30 a.m. Bake the marbled rye.
9:20 a.m. Remove the loaf from the oven and let it cool.

Caraway Rye Pullman

Makes one 9-inch Pullman loaf

I make this light caraway rye in a Pullman loaf pan so that it's the perfect size for triple-decker sandwiches (see Roast Beef Triple-Deckers, page 139). The sides of the pan are straight and the lid makes the top edge straight, too. This loaf is made from start to finish in one day.

Equipment A 9 × 4 × 4-inch Pullman loaf pan with lid

			Baker's %
Sourdough Starter			
Water (70°–75°F)	2 tablespoons + 2 teaspoons	40 grams	100
Mother sourdough starter	1 tablespoon	25 grams	62.5
Bread flour	⅓ cup	40 grams	100
For the dough			
Caraway seeds	2 tablespoons + 1½ teaspoons	20 grams	
Water (80°–90°F)	2 cups	470 grams	81
Bread flour	4 cups + more for dusting	480 grams	83
Rye flour	½ cup + ⅓ cup	100 grams	17
Sourdough Starter (above)	½ cup + 1 tablespoon	105 grams	18
Fine sea salt	2½ teaspoons	15 grams	2.6

Mix the starter

· Mix the sourdough starter 4 to 5 hours before adding it to the dough. Put the water in a 1-quart container with a lid and add 25 grams (1 tablespoon) of the ripened mother sourdough starter. Add the flour and stir with a metal spoon to combine. Cover the container and set the starter aside in a warm place (about 75°F) until it is ripe and passes the Float Test (page xxxi).

Prepare the caraway seeds

· In a medium skillet, toast the caraway seeds over medium-high heat for 2 to 3 minutes, shaking the pan frequently so they toast evenly and don't burn, until they are fragrant and begin popping. Pour the seeds out of the skillet into a medium bowl to cool to room temperature.

· Put 1 tablespoon (8 grams) of the seeds in a spice grinder and pulse to pulverize. Put the ground caraway back into the bowl with the remaining caraway seeds and set aside.

Autolyse the dough

· In a shallow 3- to 4-quart container, stir together the water, bread flour, and rye flour with a metal spoon to combine. Cover the container and set aside in a warm place (about 75°F) for 2 to 3 hours to autolyse.

For more information on why we are resting the dough before mixing the sourdough starter, salt, and caraway into the dough, see Autolyse (page 5).

Add the sourdough starter to the dough

- As soon as the starter is ripe, uncover the dough and add the starter, mixing it by scooping your hand under the dough and folding the dough into the center until the starter is thoroughly mixed in. Re-cover the container and let the dough rest for 30 minutes.

Add the salt and caraway to the dough

- Uncover the dough. Add the salt, ground caraway, and toasted caraway seeds and scoop under the dough with a wet hand and fold the dough into the center until it is homogeneous. Re-cover the container and let the dough rest for 30 minutes.

Make 4 stretch and folds

- Uncover the dough. With wet hands, scoop underneath the top edge of the dough, stretch it out, and fold it down two-thirds of the way toward the bottom edge. Stretch out and fold the bottom edge up to meet the top edge, as if you were folding a letter, pressing on the dough just enough to get it to stay in place. Do the same with the two sides, stretching and folding the right edge two-thirds of the way toward the left edge, and stretching and folding the left edge to meet the right edge. Then flip the dough upside down. This is your first fold. Re-cover the container and set the dough aside for 30 minutes.
- Repeat stretching and folding the dough a second time for a second fold. Re-cover and set the dough aside for 30 minutes.
- Repeat stretching and folding the dough a third time for a third fold. Re-cover and set the dough aside for 30 minutes.
- Repeat stretching and folding the dough one last time for a fourth fold. Re-cover and set the dough aside for 1 hour for a total fermentation time of 3½ hours.

Shape and proof the loaf

- Spray a 9 × 4-inch Pullman loaf pan and the inside of its lid with nonstick cooking spray. Set aside.
- Dust a large work surface with bread flour. Use a plastic dough scraper or rubber spatula to scoop the dough onto the floured surface.
- Gently pat the dough into a rectangle about the length of the pan, with a long side facing you. Use your hands to scoop underneath the top edge of the dough and fold it down about two-thirds of the way from the top like a letter. Scoop your hands under the bottom edge of the dough (the edge closest to you) and fold it up over the top so the bottom edge is even with the top edge. Lift the dough and flip it over into the pan so the seam is on the bottom. Pat the dough into the corners of the pan, evening out the surface of the dough. Slide the lid onto the pan, leaving it cracked open by 1 inch.
- Place the loaf in a warm place for 2 to 3 hours until the dough rises to ½ inch from the top of the pan. Close the lid completely.

Bake the bread	▪ Thirty minutes before you plan to bake, arrange an oven rack in the center position with no racks above it and preheat the oven to 500°F.
	▪ Bake the loaf for 25 minutes. Reduce the oven temperature to 450°F, rotate the pan from front to back, and bake for an additional 25 minutes. To check for doneness, using oven mitts or kitchen towels, remove the Pullman loaf lid and set aside, being careful of any steam that might rise when you open the pan. The loaf should emit a hollow sound when tapped on its top.
Cool the bread	▪ Invert the pan so the loaf falls onto a cooling rack. Let it cool completely.

Roast Beef Triple-Deckers

Makes 24 party-size squares

This recipe is inspired by the sloppy joe sandwiches from Town Hall Deli in Orange, New Jersey, and I like to think of it as the art of making a not-so-sloppy layered sandwich. You should have a Caraway Rye Pullman (page 136) ready. Rather than slicing into 4-inch squares, you slice the loaf lengthwise into 9 × 4-inch slices. An unsliced Pullman loaf from your local bakery can substitute. Part of the art of making layered sandwiches is getting everything to stick and not slip out. A liberal amount of butter helps to hold things together and make things tasty. The coleslaw is drained and then gets patted down, and the Russian dressing is absorbed into the coleslaw. The result is a neat, compact triple-decker sandwich that doesn't fall apart when it's sliced into small party-size squares. I like to think of these as the ne plus ultra of triple-decker sandwiches, and I'm happy to share my technique!

Caraway Rye Pullman (page 136)	1 loaf	
Unsalted butter, softened	9 tablespoons	126 grams
Roast beef, sliced	1½ pounds	680 grams
Coleslaw (recipe follows)	2 cups drained	
Russian Dressing (recipe follows)	12 tablespoons	
Swiss cheese, sliced	6 ounces	170 grams

- Use a serrated bread knife to slice the Pullman loaf lengthwise, first slicing off the end, and then slicing to yield 9 slices that are 9 × 4 inches and ⅜ inch thick. Discard the end (or toast and butter it for a snack). Place a slice in front of you and butter it with 1 tablespoon butter. Arrange 4 ounces (113 grams) roast beef neatly on the buttered bread, taking care not to let the meat hang over the edges. With an offset spatula, spread 5 tablespoons of drained coleslaw on top of the beef, patting it as tightly as possible. Drizzle 2 tablespoons of Russian dressing over the coleslaw and then layer 2 slices of Swiss cheese on top.
- Butter another slice of bread on both sides, using about ½ tablespoon butter per side, and place on top of the cheese. Repeat the layering with another 4 ounces roast beef, 5 tablespoons drained coleslaw, 2 tablespoons Russian dressing, and 2 slices Swiss cheese.
- Butter one side of a third slice of bread with about 1 tablespoon of butter and place it, butter-side down, on top of the cheese.
- Build two more sandwiches in the same way with the remaining bread and ingredients.
- To serve, cut each sandwich into party-size squares: Use a serrated bread knife to cut a sandwich in half lengthwise (using a gentle sawing motion to prevent it from falling apart). Then cut the sandwich crosswise into 4 equal sections, for a total of 8 squares per sandwich. Keep the sandwich squares refrigerated until ready serve. They are best the day they are made but can be held in the refrigerator for several days.

Coleslaw

Serves 8–10

Green cabbage	1 small head	908 grams
Carrots	3 medium	100 grams
Distilled white vinegar	½ cup	118 grams
Vegetable oil	¼ cup	55 grams
Granulated sugar	½ cup	100 grams
Mayonnaise	1 cup	208 grams
Lemon, juiced	1	
Fine sea salt	2 teaspoons	12 grams
Freshly ground black pepper	to taste	

• Place the cabbage on a cutting board and quarter it. Grate the quarters on the large holes of a box grater into a large bowl. Grate the carrots in the same way, adding them to the bowl with the cabbage.

• In a medium bowl, whisk together the vinegar, vegetable oil, sugar, mayonnaise, lemon juice, salt, and pepper. Pour the dressing over the grated cabbage and carrots and stir with a rubber spatula to combine. Transfer the cabbage to a covered container and refrigerate until ready to use or for up to 1 week.

Russian Dressing

Makes ¾ cup

Mayonnaise	½ cup	104 grams
Ketchup	¼ cup	68 grams
Worcestershire sauce	2 teaspoons	10 grams
Prepared horseradish	2 teaspoons	15 grams
Tabasco sauce	1 dash	
Freshly ground black pepper	to taste	

• In a medium bowl, whisk together the mayonnaise, ketchup, Worcestershire sauce, horseradish, Tabasco, and pepper. Transfer the dressing to a covered container and refrigerate until ready to use or for up to 1 week.

Toasted Sesame Durum Sourdough

Makes 1 loaf

This is one of my favorite breads to make. The toasted sesame seeds are mixed into the dough and also coat the outside of the loaf. And the crumb is faintly yellow from the durum flour, and tender from the combination of bread and durum flours. It toasts perfectly, too, and I love to slather it with salted butter. Durum flour is finely milled from durum wheat. Semolina also comes from durum wheat but is coarse and sandy in texture. Durum wheat grows in arid desert climates, and its berries are very hard, making it difficult to mill finely into durum flour. It is high in protein but not the kind of protein that forms gluten well. It is great to make into pasta but usually needs help from bread flour to make loaves of bread. To achieve an open crumb, it is used here in a much smaller proportion to the bread flour.

Sourdough Starter			Baker's %
Water (70°–75°F)	2 tablespoons + 2 teaspoons	40 grams	100
Mother sourdough starter	1 tablespoon	25 grams	62.5
Bread flour	⅓ cup	40 grams	100
For the dough			
Water (70°–75°F)	2⅓ cups + 1 tablespoon	563 grams	97
Bread flour	4 cups + more for dusting	480 grams	83
Durum flour	¾ cup	98 grams	17
Sourdough Starter (above)	½ cup + 2 tablespoons	105 grams	18
Fine sea salt	2½ teaspoons	15 grams	2.6
Toasted sesame seeds	2 cups	180 grams	16

Mix the starter

- Mix the sourdough starter 4 to 5 hours before adding it to the dough. Put the water in a 1-quart container with a lid and add 25 grams (1 tablespoon) of the ripened mother sourdough starter. Add the flour and stir with a metal spoon to combine. Cover the container and set the starter aside in a warm place (about 75°F) until it is ripe and passes the Float Test (page xxxi).

Autolyse the dough

- In a shallow 3- to 4-quart container, stir together the water, bread flour, and durum flour with a metal spoon to combine. Cover the container and set it aside in a warm place (about 75°F) for 2 to 3 hours to autolyse.

For more information on why we are resting the dough before mixing the sourdough starter, salt, and sesame seeds into the dough, see Autolyse (page 5).

Add the sourdough starter to the dough

- As soon as the starter is ripe, uncover the dough and add the starter, mixing it by scooping your hand under the dough and folding the dough into the center until the sourdough is thoroughly mixed in. Measure the temperature of the dough. It should be between 78° and 82°F. Re-cover the container and let the dough rest for 30 minutes.

Add the salt and sesame seeds to the dough

- Uncover the dough. Add the salt and 1 cup (90 grams) of the sesame seeds and scoop under the dough with a wet hand and fold the dough into the center until it is homogeneous. Re-cover the container and let the dough rest for 30 minutes.

Make 3 stretch and folds

- Uncover the dough. With wet hands, scoop underneath the top edge of the dough, stretch it out, and fold it down two-thirds of the way toward the bottom edge. Stretch out and fold the bottom edge up to meet the top edge, as if you were folding a letter, pressing on the dough just enough to get it to stay in place. Do the same with the two sides, stretching and folding the right edge two-thirds of the way toward the left edge, and stretching and folding the left edge to meet the right edge. Then flip the dough upside down. This is your first fold. Re-cover the container and set the dough aside for 30 minutes.
- Repeat stretching and folding the dough a second time for a second fold. Re-cover and set the dough aside for 30 minutes.
- Repeat stretching and folding the dough one last time for a third fold. Re-cover and set the dough aside for 1 hour for total fermentation time of 3 hours.

Shape and retard the loaf

- Line a 3-quart bowl with a lightweight kitchen towel (or use a linen-lined banneton). Set aside.
- Dust a large work surface with bread flour. Use a plastic dough scraper or rubber spatula to scoop the dough onto the floured surface. Gently coax the dough into a rough squarish shape.
- First, to create tautness: Begin at the top right corner of the dough and fold the corner two-thirds of the way across the top. Fold the top left corner to meet the right edge. Repeat the folding from right to left and then from left to right, working your way down the loaf until you reach the bottom closest to you. This should be accomplished in three to four complete folds.
- Then fold the dough like a letter, folding the top edge two-thirds of the way down and the bottom edge up to meet the top, pressing on the dough just enough to get it to stay in place.
- Spread the remaining 1 cup (90 grams) sesame seeds out onto a baking sheet. Place a damp kitchen towel on the work surface next to the loaf.
- Cradle the loaf with both hands and gently roll it on the damp towel to moisten the entire loaf. Roll the moistened loaf in the sesame seeds to coat it. Pick the loaf up and place it seam-side up into the prepared bowl.
- Wrap the bowl in plastic wrap and place it in the refrigerator to proof overnight, or for at least 8 hours.

Score and bake the bread

- Thirty minutes before you plan to bake, arrange an oven rack in the center position with no racks above it. Place a 5-quart Dutch oven on the rack and preheat the oven to 500°F.
- Take the dough out of the refrigerator and remove the plastic. Open the oven and carefully slide the oven rack out partway. Remove the Dutch oven lid. Use the towel to flip the ball of dough into the palm of your free hand. Place the dough seam-side down in the Dutch oven. Score the bread decoratively with a lame or small, sharp serrated knife. Replace the lid and slide the oven rack back into the oven.
- Bake the bread for 25 minutes. Reduce the oven temperature to 450°F and carefully remove the lid. Bake the bread for 20 to 25 minutes longer, until it has a deeply burnished crust.

Cool the bread

- Remove the Dutch oven from the oven. Slide a large metal spatula under the bread and, holding the bread with your other hand (protected by a clean kitchen towel), remove it from the Dutch oven. Place the bread on a cooling rack to cool completely.

Sourdough English Muffins

Makes 10 English muffins

Nooks and crannies are the name of the English muffin game. And there are a couple of tricks to achieve this. First the muffins need to be very proofed before they are griddled. This proofing helps the gluten network expand to produce larger air bubbles. The second is the temperature of the skillet. It needs to be low enough so that the muffins have time to puff up and grow as they cook. They also need time to cook all the way through. If the skillet is too hot, the tops and bottoms brown too quickly before the muffins are cooked all the way through, and the dough will set up too early, making for a tighter crumb. I like adding sourdough starter to my English muffins because they toast up crisper—more little crunchy crags. I also like to use ring molds when I griddle them. The rings make them perfectly round. You can easily forgo the rings if you prefer.

Plan ahead Mix your starter 12 hours before you plan to make the dough. I suggest you mix the starter in the evening, and then mix the dough the next morning.

Equipment Three 4-inch English muffin rings

Sourdough Starter			Baker's %
Water (70°–75°F)	⅓ cup	79 grams	99
Mother sourdough starter	1 tablespoon	25 grams	31
Bread flour	⅔ cup	80 grams	100
For the dough			
Water (75°–80°F)	1⅓ cups	313 grams	61
Instant yeast	2¼ teaspoons	7 grams	1.4
Sourdough Starter (above)	1 heaping cup	184 grams	36
Extra-virgin olive oil	1 tablespoon	13 grams	2.5
Bread flour	3 cups + more for dusting	360 grams	71
Whole wheat bread flour	1¼ cups	150 grams	29
Granulated sugar	2 tablespoons + 2 teaspoons	35 grams	7
Fine sea salt	2½ teaspoons	15 grams	2.9
For proofing and cooking			
Cornmeal	½ cup	70 grams	
Unsalted butter, melted	2 tablespoons	28 grams	

Mix the starter

· Mix the sourdough starter the evening (or at least 12 hours) before you plan to make the English muffin dough. Put the water in a 1-quart container with a lid and add 25 grams (1 tablespoon) of the ripened mother sourdough starter. Add the flour and stir with a metal spoon to combine. Cover the container and set aside in a warm place (about 75°F).

Mix the dough

· Put the water in the bowl of a stand mixer. Sprinkle the yeast on top and let rest for 5 minutes to help dissolve the yeast. Then whisk the yeast into the water. Add the sourdough starter, olive oil, bread flour, whole wheat bread flour, sugar, and salt. Fit the mixer with the dough hook and mix on low speed for 3 minutes. Increase the speed to medium-high and mix for 5 minutes.

Ferment and stretch and fold the dough

· Remove the dough hook and wipe it clean with a wet hand. Cover the bowl with plastic wrap. Set the dough in a warm place in your kitchen and let it ferment for 1 hour.

· Uncover the bowl and turn the dough, using a wet hand to fold the top edge down two-thirds and fold the bottom edge to meet it, so the dough is folded like a letter. Fold the sides inward in the same way to form a sort of ball, then flip the ball upside down and re-cover the bowl. Let the dough ferment for 1 more hour.

Shape and retard the muffins

· Line a baking sheet with parchment paper and spray the paper with nonstick cooking spray. Sprinkle the entire surface with ¼ cup (35 grams) cornmeal. Save the remaining cornmeal for later.

· Lightly dust your work surface with flour. Using a plastic bowl scraper, scoop the dough onto the floured surface. Dust the top of the dough with flour and use a bench knife to divide it into 10 (100-gram) pieces. Put one piece of dough in front of you and dust your hands lightly with flour. Gently rest your palm on the dough and roll it into a tight round ball. Put the ball on the prepared baking sheet. Repeat the process with the remaining pieces of dough, leaving about 2 inches between the balls on the baking sheet.

· Spray a sheet of plastic wrap with nonstick cooking spray and place it, sprayed-side down, over the baking sheet. Place the baking sheet in the refrigerator to retard the muffins overnight, or for a minimum of 8 hours.

Proof the muffins

· Remove the baking sheet from the refrigerator and uncover it. Sprinkle the remaining cornmeal on the tops of the muffins and let them warm up to room temperature, 1 to 1½ hours, to finish proofing until they have grown 1½ times in size.

Griddle the muffins

· Place a 12-inch skillet over medium heat. Brush the insides of the three English muffin rings with the melted butter and place the rings in the skillet. Heat the skillet for about 5 minutes until it is hot. Gently pick up an English muffin with both hands and place it in the center of one of the muffin rings. Repeat with 2 more muffins, filling the rings in the skillet. Griddle for 3 minutes, or until the tops of the muffins have puffed up and the bottoms are lightly browned. Lift and remove the rings with a pair of tongs and flip the muffins over with a metal spatula. Cook for 3 to 5 minutes, until the bottoms are browned and the muffins are cooked through. Transfer the muffins to a cooling rack. Butter the ring molds again before placing them back in the skillet and continue griddling the remaining muffins.

Einkorn Pan Bread

Makes one 9-inch Pullman loaf

Danish rugbrød is a Danish rye bread that is baked in a pan and is densely loaded with seeds and grains. The dough holding the seeds and grains together is so wet that it seems more like a batter. This einkorn pan bread is similar in style. Einkorn flour is used instead of the rye flour, and einkorn berries are sprouted and folded into the dough along with toasted sesame seeds, pumpkin seeds, and flaxseeds. Einkorn is an ancient variety of wheat that originated in the Fertile Crescent. It disappeared for over five thousand years, and as a result, it is the only type of wheat that has never been hybridized ("crossing two genetically different individuals to result in a third individual with a different set of traits").

Plan ahead It takes 2 days to sprout the einkorn plus one day to mix the dough before retarding it overnight. If you want to have your loaf ready on Sunday, plan to begin sprouting the berries on Thursday.

Equipment A 9 × 4 × 4-inch Pullman loaf pan with a lid

			Baker's %
For the sprouted einkorn			
Einkorn berries	1 cup	190 grams	
Water (70°–75°F)	2 cups	470 grams	
Sourdough Starter			
Water (70°–75°F)	¼ cup	59 grams	98
Mother sourdough starter	2 tablespoons	50 grams	83
Bread flour	½ cup	60 grams	100
For the dough			
Golden flaxseeds	¾ cup	109 grams	39
Sesame seeds	⅔ cup	60 grams	21
Sunflower seeds	3 tablespoons	30 grams	11
Pumpkin seeds	3 tablespoons	33 grams	12
Buttermilk, cold	½ cup	125 grams	45
Lager beer, room temperature (70°–75°F)	⅓ cup	79 grams	28
Water (95°–100°F)	1 cup	235 grams	85
Barley malt syrup	3 tablespoons	60 grams	21
Sourdough Starter (above)	1 cup	169 grams	69
Einkorn flour	2⅓ cups	280 grams	100
Sprouted einkorn berries (above)	2 cups	300 grams	1.1
Fine sea salt	1 tablespoon	18 grams	6.4

Sprout the einkorn berries

- Place the einkorn berries in a large bowl, cover them with the water, and soak for 8 hours. Drain in a mesh sieve and return to the bowl. Cover the bowl with plastic wrap and let the berries rest at room temperature overnight, or for at least 8 hours.
- The next morning, to keep the berries moist, uncover the bowl and cover the berries with room temperature water (70°–75°F). Immediately drain in a

mesh sieve. Return all the berries to the bowl. Re-cover the bowl and let the berries rest at room temperature for 12 hours.

· Repeat this rinsing process in the evening, uncovering the bowl, covering the berries with water, draining the water immediately, and re-covering the bowl. Let the berries rest at room temperature overnight.

· Once sprouts begin to grow, refrigerate the sprouted einkorn in a covered container. The sprouted grain can stay refrigerated for up to 1 week before using. (Alternatively, they can be frozen and then thawed overnight in the refrigerator before using.)

Mix the starter

· Mix the sourdough starter 4 to 5 hours before adding it to the dough. Put the water in a 1-quart container with a lid and add 50 grams (2 tablespoons) of the ripened mother sourdough starter. Add the flour and stir with a metal spoon to combine. Cover the container and set the starter aside in a warm place (about 75°F) until it is ripe and passes the Float Test (page xxxi).

Toast the seeds

· Arrange an oven rack in the center position and preheat the oven to 300°F.
· Spread the flaxseeds, sesame seeds, sunflower seeds, and pumpkin seeds on a baking sheet and toast them for about 20 minutes, or until they are golden brown and fragrant. Remove them from the oven and set aside to cool to room temperature.

Mix and ferment the dough

· In a large bowl, whisk together the buttermilk, beer, water, barley malt syrup, and sourdough starter. Then whisk in the einkorn flour. The dough will resemble a loose batter. Cover the bowl with plastic wrap and let rest in a warm place for 30 minutes.
· Uncover the bowl and add the toasted seeds, sprouted einkorn, and salt and stir the dough well with a rubber spatula to evenly distribute the ingredients. Re-cover the bowl and set it aside in a warm place to ferment for 45 minutes.

Make 3 stretch and folds

· Uncover the dough. With wet hands, scoop underneath the top edge of the dough and fold it two-thirds of the way toward the bottom edge. Fold the bottom edge to meet the top edge, as if you were folding a letter, pressing on the dough just enough to get it to stay in place. Do the same with the two sides, folding the right edge two-thirds of the way toward the left edge, and folding the left edge to meet the right edge. This is the first fold. Re-cover the bowl with the plastic wrap and set the dough aside for 45 minutes.
· Repeat stretching and folding the dough a second time for a second fold. Re-cover and set the dough aside for 45 minutes.
· Repeat stretching and folding the dough one last time for a third fold. Re-cover and set the dough aside for 45 minutes for a total fermentation time of 3½ hours.

As the dough ferments, gluten forms and the seeds absorb water, both of which make the batter-like dough thicker.

Retard the loaf

- Spray a 9 × 4-inch Pullman loaf pan and the inside of its lid with nonstick cooking spray.
- Using a plastic bowl scraper, scoop all of the dough into the pan. Wet your hands and use them to even out the surface of the dough. Slide the lid onto the pan, leaving it cracked open by 1 inch.
- Place the loaf in a warm place for about 2 hours until the dough rises to ½ inch from the top of the pan. Close the lid completely and refrigerate the loaf overnight.

Bake the bread

- Thirty minutes before you plan to bake, arrange an oven rack in the center position with no racks above it and preheat the oven to 425°F.
- Move the loaf from the refrigerator directly into the oven and bake the loaf for about 1 hour 25 minutes, or until the temperature at the center of the loaf measures 210°F. (To check the temperature, carefully slide the oven rack out and slide the lid of the pan open partway before inserting the thermometer.) Remove the loaf from the oven.
- Using oven mitts, immediately slide the lid off the pan. Invert the pan directly onto a cooling rack. Let the loaf cool completely before slicing.

Yellow Grits Porridge Pullman Loaf

Makes one 9-inch Pullman loaf

Breadmakers add grains to bread in a variety of ways. Most commonly the grains are soaked overnight and then drained and added to the dough during mixing the next day. Another way to add grain to the dough is to cook it in advance. You cook the grain with water to make a porridge. Bread for which the grains are cooked in advance is called porridge bread. When the grain is cooked with water, the starches gelatinize and form bonds that hold the water. The water doesn't leak out and is held stably. This means more dough hydration without the dough feeling sloppy wet. Popular Japanese milk breads work the same way, cooking a roux that gets added to the dough for extreme hydration.

Equipment A 9 × 4 × 4-inch Pullman loaf pan with a lid

Sourdough Starter			Baker's %
Water (70°–75°F)	2 tablespoons + 2 teaspoons	40 grams	100
Mother sourdough starter	1 tablespoon	25 grams	67
Bread flour	⅓ cup	40 grams	100
For the dough			
Water for the grits	2 cups	470 grams	
Yellow corn grits	1 cup	155 grams	
Water (80°–90°F)	1⅔ cups	392 grams	73
Bread flour	4 cups + more for dusting	480 grams	89
Whole wheat bread flour	½ cup	60 grams	11
Sourdough Starter (above)	½ cup + 1 tablespoon	105 grams	19
Fine sea salt	2½ teaspoons	15 grams	2.8

Mix the starter

- Mix the sourdough starter 4 to 5 hours before adding it to the dough. Put the water in a ½-quart container with a lid and add 12 grams (1½ teaspoons) of ripened mother sourdough starter. Add the flour and stir with a metal spoon to combine. Cover the container and set the starter aside in a warm place (about 75°F) until it is ripe and passes the Float Test (page xxxi).

Cook the grits

- Line a baking sheet with parchment paper and set aside.
- In a medium saucepan, bring 2 cups (470 grams) water to a boil. Add the grits, reduce the heat to maintain a gentle simmer, and cook, stirring constantly with a wooden spoon, for 5 minutes.
- Remove the saucepan from the heat and spread the grits out on a plate to cool to room temperature.

Autolyse the dough

- In a shallow 3- to 4-quart container, stir together 1⅔ cups (392 grams) water, bread flour, and whole wheat bread flour with a metal spoon to combine. Cover the container and set aside in a warm place (about 75°F) for 2 to 3 hours to autolyse.

For more information on why we are resting the dough before mixing the sourdough starter, salt, and grits into the dough, see Autolyse (page 5).

Add the sourdough starter to the dough

- As soon as the starter is ripe, uncover the dough and add the starter, mixing it by scooping your hand under the dough and folding it into the center until the sourdough is thoroughly mixed in. Re-cover the container and let the dough rest for 30 minutes.

Add the salt and cooled grits

- Uncover the dough. Add the salt and cooled grits, scooping under the dough with a wet hand and folding the dough into the center until it is homogeneous. Re-cover the container and let the dough rest for 30 minutes.

Make 4 stretch and folds

- Uncover the dough. With wet hands, scoop underneath the top edge of the dough, stretch it out, and fold it down two-thirds of the way toward the bottom edge. Stretch out and fold the bottom edge up to meet the top edge, as if you were folding a letter, pressing on the dough just enough to get it to stay in place. Do the same with the two sides, stretching and folding the right edge two-thirds of the way toward the left edge, and stretching and folding the left edge to meet the right edge. Then flip the dough upside down. This is your first fold. Re-cover the container and set the dough aside for 30 minutes.
- Repeat the stretching and folding a second time for a second fold. Re-cover and set the dough aside for 30 minutes.
- Repeat the stretching and folding a third time for a third fold. Re-cover and set the dough aside for 30 minutes.
- Repeat the stretching and folding one final time for a fourth fold. Re-cover and set the dough aside for 1 hour for a total fermentation time of 3½ hours.

Shape, proof, and bake the loaf

- Lightly spray a 9 × 4-inch Pullman loaf pan and the inside of its lid with nonstick cooking spray.
- Dust a large flat work surface heavily with bread flour. Uncover the dough and use a plastic dough scraper to scoop it onto the floured surface. Gently pat the dough into a rectangle about the length of the pan, with the long edge parallel to you. Use your hands to get underneath the top edge of the dough and fold it down about two-thirds of the way from the top like a letter. Scoop your hands under the bottom edge of the dough (the edge closest to you) and fold it up over the top so the bottom edge is even with the top edge. Lift the dough and flip it over into the pan so the seam is on the bottom. Use your hands to pat the dough into the corners and even out the surface of the dough. Slide the lid on the pan, leaving it cracked open by 1 inch.
- Place the loaf in a warm place for about 2 hours until the dough reaches ½ inch from the top of the pan. Close the lid completely.

- While the dough is proofing, arrange the oven racks so one is in the center position. Preheat the oven to 450°F.
- Place the loaf on the center rack of the oven to bake for about 50 minutes, until the top is golden brown, rotating the pan from front to back halfway through. (To check for doneness, using oven mitts or kitchen towels, slide the Pullman lid open enough to see the color, being careful of any steam when you open the pan.) Remove the loaf from the oven.
- Using oven mitts or kitchen towels, immediately slide the lid off the loaf pan. Invert the pan directly onto a cooling rack. Let the loaf cool completely and slice as desired.

Strawberry Rhubarb Mountain Pies

Makes 11 to 12 mountain pies

While I was growing up, my family made mountain pies every summer when camping—two slices of white bread and some canned pie filling, pressed in a mountain pie maker and toasted over a fire. My mom would also bring along tomato sauce and sliced cheese for a pizza version, which was my brother's favorite. A mountain pie maker, also called a pie iron, is made of two pieces of cast iron mounted on rods that are hinged at one end and press your filled pie or sandwich together. The fun is slowly roasting them over the campfire. Mountain pies are common in the Midwest and in Pennsylvania where I grew up.

When I was invited to the Charleston Wine + Food Festival, I was asked to participate in the Corkscrews + Campfires event, and I immediately wanted to make mountain pies. I created this one: a Pullman loaf of yellow grits porridge bread filled with strawberry rhubarb pie filling. The yellow grits that I use to make the sourdough bread (see Yellow Grits Porridge Pullman Loaf, page 151) come from Anson Mills, an heirloom grain grower and miller in Columbia, South Carolina. This special Pullman loaf toasts beautifully both in and out of a cast-iron pie iron. Of course, you can use any square bread slices, but I do prefer this one or another sourdough Pullman. Not everyone has even heard of a mountain pie or has a mountain pie maker handy. If you don't have one, you can easily crimp the edges of the buttered bread slices together with a fork and bake the pies at 350°F on a parchment-lined baking sheet for about 20 minutes.

Equipment One or several mountain pie makers

For the filling		
Strawberries	1½ pounds	681 grams
Rhubarb	1 pound	454 grams
Granulated sugar	2 cups	400 grams
Orange	1	
Vanilla bean	1	
Arrowroot powder	¼ cup + 2 tablespoons	44 grams
Fine sea salt	1 teaspoon	6 grams
For assembling the pies		
Yellow Grits Porridge Pullman Loaf (page 151)	1 loaf	
Unsalted butter, softened	8 tablespoons	113 grams

Make the filling

• Arrange an oven rack in the center position and preheat the oven to 375°F. Hull the strawberries and cut them into ½-inch pieces. Put the strawberries in a large bowl. Wipe the rhubarb with a damp paper towel. Cut off and discard the ends of the stalks and cut the rhubarb crosswise into ½-inch-thick slices. Put the rhubarb in the bowl with the strawberries.

- Place the granulated sugar in a medium bowl and use a fine Microplane to grate the orange zest over the sugar. Split the vanilla bean down the middle with a small sharp knife and use the knife to scrape out seeds into the bowl of sugar and zest. Work the sugar between your fingertips to disperse the zest and vanilla seeds throughout. Add the arrowroot and salt and whisk to combine. Add to the bowl with the strawberries and rhubarb and gently toss with a rubber spatula to coat the fruit with the sugar.
- Scoop the filling into an 8 × 12-inch baking dish. Transfer to the oven and bake, uncovered, for 20 minutes, stirring halfway through the baking time, until the filling is thick and bubbling. Remove the filling from the oven and set aside to cool slightly.
- Transfer the strawberry rhubarb filling to a small container and refrigerate until it has completely cooled or for up to 3 days.

Assemble and cook the mountain pies

- On a cutting board, use a bread knife to slice off and discard both ends of the loaf of bread. Slice the loaf crosswise into ½-inch-thick slices; you should get 22 to 24.
- Generously butter one side of 2 slices of the bread. Open the mountain pie maker and place one slice of bread, buttered-side down, into one of the cavities. Spoon ¼ cup strawberry rhubarb filling onto the bread and place the second slice, buttered-side up, on top of the filling. Close the mountain pie maker and trim off any crust that is sticking out on the outside.
- Place the pie maker into a hot campfire and cook for 3 to 6 minutes, turning occasionally, until the bread is golden and toasted. Remove the pie maker from the fire and carefully open it. Use a small paring knife to loosen the edges of the pie. Tilt the pie maker and let the pie fall out onto a plate.
- Repeat with the remaining bread, butter, and pie filling.

Cherry Pecan Anadama

Makes 1 loaf

Traditionally anadama is a sweet yeasted bread made from cornmeal and molasses. In this version, I replace the commercial yeast with sourdough starter and cook the grits before adding them to the dough. Doing both adds a complexity of flavor and texture to the loaf, which I find appealing.

			Baker's %
Sourdough Starter			
Water (70°–75°F)	2 tablespoons	30 grams	98
Mother sourdough starter	1½ teaspoons	12 grams	83
Bread flour	¼ cup	30 grams	100
For the dough			
Pecans	¾ cup	83 grams	23
Water for grits	1 cup	235 grams	
Yellow corn grits	½ cup	78 grams	53*
Dried cherries	½ cup	75 grams	21
Water (90°–95°F)	1 cup + 1 tablespoon	250 grams	69
Bread flour	2 cups	240 grams	67
Whole wheat bread flour	1 cup	120 grams	33
Sourdough Starter (above)	⅓ cup	72 grams	18
Molasses	1½ tablespoons	32 grams	9.0
Salt	2½ teaspoons	15 grams	4
For dusting the towel-lined bowl			
Brown rice flour	4 tablespoons		

* The baker's percentage for the grits is the weight of the grits after they have been cooked.

Mix the starter

· Mix the sourdough starter 4 to 5 hours before adding it to the dough. Put the water in a 1-quart container with a lid and add 12 grams (1½ teaspoons) of ripened mother sourdough starter. Add the flour and stir with a metal spoon to combine. Cover the container and set the starter aside in a warm place (about 75°F) until it is ripe and passes the Float Test (page xxxi).

Toast the pecans, cook the grits, and soak the cherries

· Arrange an oven rack in the center position and preheat the oven to 300°F.
· Spread the pecans on a baking sheet and toast for 20 to 22 minutes, shaking the pan once during that time for even toasting, until the nuts are golden brown and fragrant. Remove the baking sheet from the oven and set aside to cool the nuts to room temperature.
· In a medium saucepan, bring 1 cup (235 grams) water to a boil. Add the grits, reduce the heat to maintain a gentle simmer, and cook, stirring constantly with a wooden spoon, for 5 minutes. Remove the saucepan from the heat and spread the grits out on a plate to cool to room temperature.
· Place the cherries in a small bowl, cover with hot water, and soak for 5 minutes. Drain the cherries in a fine-mesh sieve and let them sit in the sieve so they continue to drain until you're ready to use them.

Autolyse the dough	• In a shallow 3- to 4-quart container, stir together 1 cup + 1 tablespoon (250 grams) water, the bread flour, and the whole wheat bread flour with a metal spoon to combine. Cover the container and set aside in a warm place (about 75°F) for 2 to 3 hours to autolyse.
	For more information on why we are resting the dough before mixing the sourdough starter, salt, and remaining ingredients into the dough, see Autolyse (page 5).
Add the sourdough starter to the dough	• As soon as the starter is ripe, uncover the dough and add the starter, mixing it by scooping your hand under the dough and folding the dough into the center until the starter is thoroughly mixed in. Measure the temperature of the dough. It should be between 78° and 82°F. Re-cover the container and let the dough rest for 30 minutes.
Add the remaining ingredients to the dough	• Uncover the dough. Add the molasses, salt, toasted pecans, cooked grits, and soaked cherries, scooping under the dough with a wet hand and folding the dough into the center until it is homogeneous. Measure the temperature of the dough. It should be between 80° and 82°F. Re-cover the container and let the dough rest for 30 minutes.
Make 1 stretch and fold	• Uncover the dough. With wet hands, scoop underneath the top edge of the dough, stretch it out, and fold it down two-thirds of the way toward the bottom edge. Stretch out and fold the bottom edge up to meet the top edge, as if you were folding a letter, pressing on the dough just enough to get it to stay in place. Do the same with the two sides, stretching and folding the right edge two-thirds of the way toward the left edge, and stretching and folding the left edge to meet the right edge. Then flip the dough upside down. Re-cover the container and set the dough aside in a warm place for 4 hours until the dough has doubled in volume for a total fermentation time of 5 hours.
Shape and retard the loaf	• Line a 3-quart bowl with a lightweight kitchen towel (or use a linen-lined banneton) and dust with brown rice flour. Set aside. • Dust a large work surface with bread flour. Use a plastic dough scraper or rubber spatula to scoop the dough onto the floured surface. Gently coax the dough into a rough squarish shape. • First, to create tautness: Begin at the top right corner and fold the corner two-thirds of the way across the top. Fold the top left corner to meet the right edge. Repeat the folding from right to left and then from left to right, working your way down the loaf until you reach the bottom closest to you. This should be accomplished in three to four complete folds.

- Then fold the loaf like a letter, folding the top edge of the loaf two-thirds of the way down and folding the bottom edge up to meet it, pressing on the dough just enough to get it to stay in place. Pick the loaf up and place it into the prepared bowl.
- Wrap the bowl in plastic wrap and place it in the refrigerator to proof overnight, or for at least 8 hours.

This sourdough loaf bakes at 450°F throughout its bake. Unlike the other loaves in this chapter, the extra sugar in the dough from the molasses causes the bread to brown very quickly, hence the lower baking temperature to start.

Score and bake the bread

- Thirty minutes before you plan to bake, arrange an oven rack in the center position with no racks above it. Place a 5-quart Dutch oven on the rack and preheat the oven to 450°F.
- Take the dough out of the refrigerator and remove the plastic. Dust the top of the loaf with brown rice flour. Open the oven and carefully slide the rack out partway. Remove the Dutch oven lid. Use the towel to flip the ball of dough into the palm of your free hand. Place the dough seam-side down into the Dutch oven. Score the bread decoratively with a lame or a small, sharp serrated knife. Replace the lid and slide the oven rack back into the oven.
- Bake the bread for 25 minutes. Carefully remove the lid and bake the bread for 20 to 25 minutes longer, until it has a deeply burnished crust.

Cool the bread

- Remove the Dutch oven from the oven. Slide a large metal spatula under the bread and, holding the bread with your other hand (protected by a clean kitchen towel), remove it from the Dutch oven. Place the bread on a cooling rack to cool completely.

Petits
Pains

At Per Se, where I worked as head baker

from 2008 to 2010, I was responsible for creating all the miniature breads for dinner service. There was a hot roll to start the meal, then a breadbasket filled with a half dozen miniature breads that was brought to each table and the breads were served with silver tongs and salted butter. Long, thin ficelles of fruit and nut bread were thinly sliced and offered with the cheese course. Each miniature bread was different—a different shape and style, temperature, flavor—but all were the same size. There were baguettes and ciabatta, rye rolls, fantails, and sourdough. It was a challenge to create a new roll that complemented the other rolls but had its own personality.

In French, *petit pain* means "small bread." The breads in this chapter are my favorite petits pains. They include my greatest hits at Per Se and more recent creations. They vary in style and technique but are all small. Some are made with laminated dough: a block of dough composed of many layers of dough and butter. Laminated dough is most often associated with sweet pastries like croissants. I focused an entire chapter in my book *A Good Bake* on laminated pastries. The laminated breads in this chapter are savory.

Some petits pains use only sourdough starter to leaven the dough. This is special because bread bakers often use a combination of sourdough starter and commercial yeast particularly for small breads, rolls, and baguettes, where the starter is used solely for flavor and commercial yeast does the heavy lifting in raising the dough. A more traditional baker will say that using only sourdough starter will make rolls that are too chewy and not light enough. (An example of a light roll is the classic Parker House roll.) When only sourdough starter is used, the dough will ferment more slowly because the natural yeasts grow at a slower rate than robust commercial yeast. A slower fermentation produces more flavor in the bread and it also gives the bread a thicker, chewier crust. I like some rolls to be deeply chewy and rustic, and others, like the Parker House rolls, to be light and airy. Combining those different rolls in one breadbasket is the ne plus ultra to me.

At the end of the day, or at the end of a great meal, I am super content to skip the dessert and go for a cheese plate with a beautiful selection of rolls, and maybe some sliced baguette.

Master Class
A Step-by-Step Tutorial to Laminated Dough

Successful lamination is all about evenness: creating and maintaining perfectly even layers of butter and dough that are consistent all the way across the dough. The steps that we take during the lamination process are all working toward this goal.

The two most familiar types of laminated dough are croissant dough and puff pastry, both of which you can find in my book *A Good Bake*. But in fact you can laminate many types of dough, including savory dough. In this chapter, I laminate brioche dough to make Brioche Feuilleté (page 171) and another similarly enriched dough to make Black Truffle Fantails (page 181).

Make and chill the dough

After making the dough you are going to be laminating, you will chill it until you're ready to roll it out in the following steps.

Make the butter packet

A butter packet is a term I use to refer to what is technically called a *beurrage*, which is a sheet of solid butter that is placed on a sheet of dough to begin the lamination process. For my professional kitchens, I purchase the *beurrage*, which comes as a 1-kilogram ½-inch-thick sheet of unsalted French Normandy butter. When the baker goes to laminate their dough, they simply unwrap the prepared sheet of butter and place it on the sheet of dough. It's very convenient and efficient.

However, that is not practical for the home cook, so here I have essentially replicated this experience for the home baker, creating a butter packet that is the size that suits an amount of dough suitable for the scale of home baking. The butter packet is the most effective way to ensure even layers in your lamination. Many recipes for home bakers call for you to smear the butter onto the dough, which is not a good alternative. Making a butter packet ensures that you create a really smooth, even layer. In my opinion, it is a must for anyone trying to make professional-looking laminated pastries at home. The packet also gives you total control over the temperature of the butter. I like to make butter packets in advance. I keep a stack in my refrigerator so they're ready to go when I want to make laminated dough.

Butter Packet

To make a butter packet:

Place a 12 × 15- or 16-inch piece of parchment paper on a work surface with a long side facing you. Fold the sides inward and the top and bottom inward to create a 10 × 6-inch rectangle, creasing the paper to mark out the rectangle.

Cut the butter lengthwise into slices ¼ inch thick.

Open the paper packet and lay the butter slices in a single layer like tiles in the rectangle you created by folding the paper. Fold the sides and top and bottom in to enclose the butter and flip the packet so the seam is facing down. Let the butter packet rest at room temperature for 30 to 45 minutes, until the butter is very soft but not greasy.

Roll a rolling pin over the packet to distribute the butter in an even layer all the way to the edges and into the corners of the packet with no spaces between the tiles.

Put the butter packet in the refrigerator to chill until it is firm, about 20 minutes. (It will keep for up to 2 weeks.)

Temper the butter

Once you have your dough resting in the refrigerator and you have made and chilled your butter packet, it's time to start the lamination. But first you need to temper the butter, or soften it so it is the same degree of malleability as the dough. This is very important because next you are going to encase the butter in a sheet of dough and then begin the process of rolling the dough with the butter inside.

If the butter is colder and stiffer than the enclosing dough, when you put pressure on the dough, the butter will splinter or shatter under the pressure. This results in a "broken" lamination. You will be able to see the shattered butter throughout the dough, and the dough will feel bumpy. The result of a broken lamination is uneven layers in your baked goods, and dough that does not bake as high.

If the butter is too warm and softer than the dough, when you apply the necessary pressure to roll out the dough, the butter will ooze out of the dough that encases it. This, too, results in an uneven lamination, and it also means you are going to lose some of your butter.

The doughs in this chapter are fairly soft, so to get the butter at the correct temperature, remove it from the refrigerator and set it out at room temperature until it is soft and bendy. There is no temperature gauge I can give you to help you; you have to do it based on feel. I suggest that, after the butter has sat on your counter for about 5 minutes, you take the dough out of the refrigerator and give it a gentle squeeze or bend. Then do the same with the butter. When you feel that the butter has the same amount of bendiness as the dough, that's when you should move on to the next step of locking in the butter.

Lock in the butter

Locking in the butter refers to the process of encasing the butter packet in a sheet of dough. Think of it as wrapping a present; the present is the butter packet, and the wrapping paper is a rolled-out sheet of dough. I give exact measurements for rolling out the dough for the butter lock-in, but what is important to learn about this step is not the precise dimension, but that the dough be rolled out to a size that can be wrapped around the butter packet. Just as you would cut a sheet of paper to fit around a gift you are wrapping, you want to roll out the dough to dimensions that are big enough to reach around the butter it will encase. I use my butter packet as my measuring device. I keep the packet next to me when I'm rolling out the dough, and as the dough begins to reach the correct size, I put the packet on top and eyeball it to see if the dough will reach around it. If not, I keep rolling. Use whichever system—measuring or eyeballing—works better for you.

Traditionally, butter is locked in by placing the butter in the center of a square of dough and folding the corners inward over the block of butter, like an envelope. I prefer to do it differently: I lay the butter packet on a long sheet of dough and fold the sides of the dough over the butter. I think it's easier this way.

Roll out and fold the dough

Folding refers to the process of folding the dough with the butter locked inside to create layers of butter. You go straight into folding the dough after locking in the butter, without chilling the dough first. This is the reason the butter has to be tempered to the correct temperature to begin with.

The folding step actually consists of three smaller steps: rolling out the dough, trimming the edges, and making the fold.

Roll the dough The first step in folding dough is to roll it out into a long sheet. When I am laminating dough, I always roll so that the dough stretches out away from me. You want to work as quickly as you can when rolling dough for laminating, so the butter doesn't get too soft in the process.

Trim the dough To make perfect laminated dough, you must trim the edges of the dough before each fold. Use a pastry wheel (a bench knife or long sharp knife will also work) to trim the top and bottom edges of the dough. You lose some dough in the process, but trimming the edges between folds creates a clean, even lamination layer, ensuring that the baked good is going to be perfect. The idea is to trim the edges just enough to expose the butter layer; this will usually be about 1 inch toward the center. If you do not trim the dough, there will be pockets of dough that do not contain any or contain very few butter layers and you end up with an uneven lamination. The baked good made from that dough will not be as flaky, because there are not as many distinct layers. Discard the trimmings or bake them separately for a tasty treat.

Fold the dough Now that your dough has been rolled out and trimmed, it is ready to be folded. There are different types of folds. The first type of fold is a letter fold, where the dough is folded into thirds, like a letter. The second type of fold is a book fold, or a fold within a fold. First, the top and bottom edges are folded toward each other; then the bottom edge is folded to meet the top, like a book, the spine of which is facing you. A book fold creates 4 layers of butter and dough. The recipes in this chapter use letter folds. A letter fold produces 3 layers of butter and dough. The number of layers produced by a fold increase exponentially; for example, 2 letter folds produce 9 layers of butter and dough.

Stop fermentation

After laminating dough made with yeast, I put the block of dough in the freezer for 1 hour to quickly stop the fermentation process. The block gets warm during the rolling, and warmth encourages fermentation. If you put the block directly in the refrigerator, it won't cool down quickly enough and will continue to rise. You will open your refrigerator the next day to find your blocks of dough have expanded to look like little balloons. If this were to happen with dough that is not laminated, it would not be a big deal. But since lamination is dependent on all the layers being even, having the dough expand after it has been layered with butter is a laminating disaster. It breaks the lamination. The extreme cold of the freezer stops the fermentation process. After an hour in the freezer, you will transfer the dough to the refrigerator to let it rest overnight.

Temper and roll out the dough

Now that the dough is laminated, the most important thing is that you bring it to the correct temperature before you roll, cut, and shape it. Even if you have laminated the dough perfectly, if you do not temper it properly, the butter between the layers will shatter when you apply pressure on the dough, resulting in a broken lamination. A broken lamination will yield uneven layers, and also cause the butter to leak out of the pastry when baked. To temper a laminated block of dough, pull it out of the refrigerator and let it rest at room temperature until it is just bendy enough that you can roll it without applying too much pressure. This usually takes 5 to 10 minutes, but it is important that you judge by feel, not by time. Rest the dough for a few minutes before you begin cutting the shapes. This will help keep your shapes from shrinking.

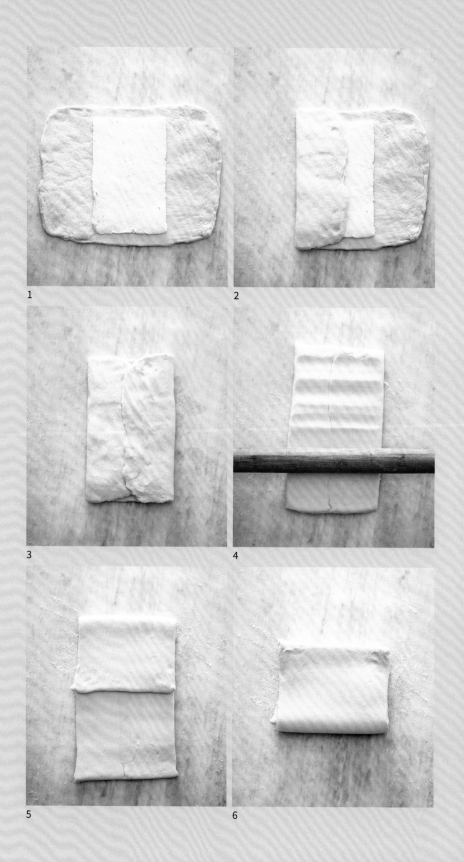

7

8

9

10

Brioche Feuilleté

Makes 15 brioche

Laminating brioche might seem counterintuitive at first. There is already a lot of butter in brioche dough, and then you add more butter through lamination. But layering butter into enriched doughs, like brioche, creates a tender, rich, flaky pastry. It is one of my favorite applications for brioche dough. The recipe for Salted Caramel Sticky Buns in my book *A Good Bake* is based on laminated brioche. And here it is a savory spiral, which is perfect as an opener to an elegant meal. When I first began to laminate brioche, I had difficulties because the butter sheet would break in the dough, and I would see small chunks of butter throughout. I kept tweaking my work and found that when the butter was closer to room temperature it broke less. I also tried different combinations of folds to see how that affected the laminating butter. I began with a standard three letter folds and eventually found that two letter folds worked best. It kept the layers separate and the butter broke less.

Plan ahead Make your butter packet in advance, or while the dough is in the refrigerator. Place the packet in the refrigerator to chill until you're ready to laminate the dough, then remove it from the refrigerator to soften it slightly when called to do so in the recipe.

Equipment Three 6-cup jumbo muffin tins (see Note)

Note 1 If you do not have 3 jumbo muffin tins or do not want to bake all of the brioche feuilleté at once, you can keep them in the refrigerator as long as overnight and bake as desired.

Note 2 The dough gets trimmed three times, and you can either discard the trimmings or save them all up and bake them together in a muffin tin for a baker's treat.

For the dough			Baker's %
All-purpose flour	4 cups	480 grams	100
Granulated sugar	¼ cup	50 grams	10
Instant yeast	1 tablespoon	9 grams	1.9
Fine sea salt	2 teaspoons	12 grams	2.5
Whole milk	1 cup	240 grams	50
Egg, large	1	50 grams	10
Egg yolk, large	1	17 grams	3.5
Unsalted butter, cubed and softened	10 tablespoons	140 grams	29
1 Butter Packet (page 165), chilled	12 tablespoons	170 grams	
Nonstick cooking spray			
For finishing			
Unsalted butter, melted	2 tablespoons	28 grams	
Flaky sea salt	1 tablespoon	13 grams	

Make the dough

- In a medium bowl, stir together the flour, sugar, yeast, and salt.
- To a stand mixer fitted with the dough hook, add the milk, whole egg, and egg yolk. Add the dry ingredients and cubed butter on top. Mix on low speed for 2 minutes. Increase the speed to medium and mix for 5 minutes.

Ferment the dough

· Scrape the dough off the hook with a wet hand. Place a clean kitchen towel or plastic wrap over the bowl and set aside at room temperature to let the dough ferment for 1 hour.

Retard the détrempe

· Line a baking sheet with parchment paper and spray the parchment with nonstick cooking spray.

· Use a plastic bowl scraper to scrape the dough out of the bowl and onto the prepared baking sheet. Using wet hands, pat and form the dough gently into an 8-inch square. Refrigerate the dough for at least 1 hour or up to 8 hours. If you are refrigerating the dough for longer than 1 hour, remove it from the refrigerator after 1 hour, wrap it in plastic wrap, and return it to the refrigerator.

Détrempe is a term for the dough before adding the layering butter. The layering butter is also called beurrage.

Laminate the Dough

Lock in the butter

· Remove the butter packet from the refrigerator and set it on the counter to soften until it is bendy but still cool. You want the butter to be softer and more malleable than the dough but not so soft that it will ooze out of the dough. This may take anywhere from 5 to 20 minutes, depending on how cold the butter packet is.

· Lightly dust a large work surface with flour. Remove the dough from the refrigerator, unwrap it, and place it on the floured surface. Lightly dust the top of the dough and a rolling pin with flour and roll the dough out into a roughly 14 × 11-inch rectangle, dusting the work surface, rolling pin, and the top of the dough lightly with flour as you roll the dough so it doesn't stick.

· Set the rectangle of dough with a long side facing you. Open the parchment packet to expose the butter and flip the packet over to place the butter on the dough, centering the butter packet on the dough. Peel off and discard the parchment paper. Fold the left and right sides of the dough over the butter so they meet in the middle and pinch the two edges of dough together with your fingers. Gently press the top and bottom edges of the dough together to seal the packet closed and lock in the butter.

Make 2 letter folds

· Lightly dust your work surface with flour. Lightly dust the top of the dough and the rolling pin with flour and roll the dough until it is 18 inches from top to bottom, dusting the work surface, rolling pin, and the top of the dough lightly with flour as you roll the dough so it doesn't stick. Using a pastry wheel or a bench knife, trim the top and bottom edges of the dough (see Note on previous page) just enough to expose the layer of butter in the center of the dough. Fold the top edge down two-thirds and fold the bottom edge to meet the top edge, so the dough is folded into thirds, like a letter.

· Rotate the dough 90 degrees so the closed edges are facing left and right and one of the open edges (with the visible layers) is facing you. Lightly dust the work surface, dough, and rolling pin with flour and roll out the dough until it is roughly 18 inches from top to bottom, dusting with flour as needed. Trim the top and bottom edges (see Notes) to expose the butter layers. Fold the top edge down and the bottom edge up to make a second letter fold.

Retard the dough

· Wrap the laminated block of dough in plastic wrap and place it in the freezer to chill for 1 hour. Move the dough from the freezer to the refrigerator for at least 8 hours and up to 12 hours to retard the dough.

Form and proof the rolls

· Remove the laminated block of dough from the refrigerator and set it on the counter to rest for 20 to 30 minutes, until you can feel that the butter layers inside the dough are just becoming malleable (but not soft) when you bend the block slightly.

· Spray three 6-cup jumbo muffin tins with nonstick cooking spray.

· Lightly dust your work surface with flour. Unwrap the dough and place it on the floured surface. Lightly dust the top of the dough and rolling pin with flour and roll the dough out to 18 inches from top to bottom and 13 inches from left to right. Using a straightedge and pastry wheel, or a long knife, trim the edges (see Notes) to get an even rectangle that is 16 inches top to bottom and 12 inches left to right.

· Score the dough 1¼ inches from the bottom edge on the right and left sides. Using the straightedge as a guide, cut from one mark to another to cut the first strip. Work your way from the bottom to the top edge of dough, scoring the dough every 1¼ inches and cutting it as you go until you have cut 15 strips that are 1¼ inches wide.

· Pick up 1 strip and roll it into a spiral. Lay the spiral facing up in one of the prepared muffin cups. Repeat, rolling the remaining strips and putting them in the prepared muffin cups.

· Cover the muffin tins with a lightweight kitchen towel and set them aside in a warm place (about 80°F) to proof until they start to puff up and expand, 1½ to 2 hours.

Brioche Feuilleté continues

Bake the rolls
- Arrange oven racks in the top third and the bottom third of the oven and preheat the oven to 350°F.
- Place one muffin tin on one rack and the other tins on the second rack of the oven. Bake the rolls for 25 to 30 minutes, until the tops are deep golden brown, switching racks and rotating the muffin tins from front to back halfway through the baking time so the rolls brown evenly.
- Remove the tins from the oven. Immediately brush the rolls with the melted butter and sprinkle each roll with a generous pinch of flaky sea salt. Set the tins on a cooling rack and let the rolls cool in the pan for 5 to 10 minutes. Remove the rolls and serve them warm or at room temperature.

Chapeau Rolls

Makes 34 rolls

I first made these rolls when I worked as the head baker at Per Se restaurant in New York City. They are small sourdough dinner rolls, with crunchy trompe l'oeil hats, hence the French name. These are not fluffy, light-as-air rolls; they are toothsome, which is very much to my liking. And they are divine with salted French butter.

They are chewy and not fluffy for a couple of scientific reasons: First, they are lower in hydration than many of the other bread recipes in this book. And second, they are leavened only with sourdough starter and receive a long, overnight fermentation, which improves their flavor and gives them a noticeable crust when baked. If commercial yeast was added to this dough, the fermentation time would shorten and the rolls would be your average sourdough dinner roll companions.

The hydration on these rolls is less than many of the other bread recipes that require an autolyse. For that reason, this autolyse is best done using a mixer with a dough hook attachment to combine the water and flours.

Equipment: You will need a linen cloth and a spray bottle filled with water.

			Baker's %
Sourdough Starter			
Water (70°–75°F)	⅓ cup	78 grams	100
Mother sourdough starter	2 tablespoons	50 grams	62.5
Bread flour	⅔ cup	80 grams	100
For the dough			
Water (80°–90°F)	2½ cups	588 grams	67
Bread flour	7 cups + more for dusting	840 grams	95
Whole wheat bread flour	⅓ cup	40 grams	5.0
Sourdough Starter (above)	1 cup + 2 tablespoons	208 grams	24
Fine sea salt	3½ teaspoons	21 grams	2.4
Rye flour	½ cup for dusting	60 grams	

Mix the starter

▪ Two hours before autolysing the water and flour, put the water in a 1-pint container with a lid. Add 50 grams (2 tablespoons) of the ripened mother sourdough starter to the container. Add the flour and stir with a metal spoon to combine. Cover the container and set the starter aside in a warm place (about 75°F) for 4 to 5 hours.

Autolyse the dough

▪ In a stand mixer fitted with the dough hook, combine the water, bread flour, and whole wheat bread flour. Mix on low speed for 2 to 3 minutes to combine the water and flours into a dough. Turn off the mixer, leaving the hook in place, and cover with a kitchen towel. Set the bowl in a warm place (about 75°F) for about 2 hours to autolyse.

For more information on why we are resting the dough before mixing the sourdough starter and salt into the dough, see Autolyse (page 5).

Add the sourdough starter to the dough

• As soon as the starter is ripe, add it to the dough, mixing it on low speed with the dough hook for 2 to 3 minutes. Let the dough rest for 30 minutes.

Add the salt to the dough

• Add the salt and mix on low speed for 2 to 3 minutes. Remove the dough hook and wipe it clean with a wet hand. Cover the bowl with a kitchen towel and let the dough rest for 2 hours.

Make 2 stretch and folds

• Uncover the dough. With wet hands, scoop underneath the top edge of the dough, stretch it out, and fold it down two-thirds of the way toward the bottom edge. Stretch out and fold the bottom edge up to meet the top edge, as if you were folding a letter, pressing on the dough just enough to get it to stay in place. Then fold the right edge of the dough two-thirds of the way toward the left edge, and stretch and fold the left edge to meet the right. Then flip the dough upside down. This is your first fold. Re-cover the bowl and set the dough aside for 2 hours for a total of 4½ hours fermentation.
• Repeat stretching and folding the dough a second time for a second fold.

Retard the dough

• Re-cover the bowl with plastic wrap and place it in the refrigerator for 8 hours or overnight.

Shape and proof the rolls

• Remove the bowl from the refrigerator and let it sit out at room temperature for 1 hour before proceeding.
• Dust a large work surface with bread flour. Use a plastic bowl scraper to scoop the dough out of the bowl onto the floured work surface. Dust the top of the dough lightly with more flour. Use a bench knife to cut off a 1-pound (454-gram) piece of dough and set this piece aside. Divide the remaining dough into 34 (35-gram) pieces.
• Put one piece of dough in front of you on the work surface. Dust your hand lightly with flour. Gently rest your palm on the dough and roll it into a tight round ball. Place the ball on a lightly flour-dusted corner of your work surface, away from where you are rolling, and continue rolling the remaining pieces of dough into balls and moving them aside to rest. (If you don't have enough space on your counter, place the balls on a flour-dusted baking sheet instead.)
• Dust the work surface heavily with some of the rye flour and place the reserved 1-pound piece of dough on the flour. Heavily dust the top of the dough with more rye flour. With a rolling pin, roll out the dough until it is ⅜ inch thick, dusting both underneath and on top of the dough with more rye flour if the dough gets sticky. Let all the dough rest for 15 minutes.

- While the dough is resting, prepare a proofing board. Flip a baking sheet upside down and place a linen cloth on top. Heavily dust the linen with the remaining rye flour, about ¼ cup.
- Using a 1⅜-inch cookie cutter, cut out 34 discs from the dough rolled in rye flour. Dust your hands with bread flour and pick up one of the balls of dough that you set aside. If it sticks to the work surface, use a bench knife to scrape underneath and release it. Flip the ball upside down and onto one of the cut-out discs. Dust your index finger with more flour and push down through the center of the ball to adhere the disc to the ball. Transfer the roll onto the dusted proofing linen, leaving the roll with the disc on the bottom to proof. Continue attaching the balls to their discs and moving them onto the proofing linen, spacing the rolls 1 inch apart. When all the rolls are formed, cover them with a light kitchen towel and proof for 2 hours at room temperature, until they are swollen and do not spring back readily when poked on their sides.

Bake the rolls

- Thirty minutes before you plan to bake, arrange oven racks in the top third and bottom third of the oven and preheat the oven to 450°F.
- Line two baking sheets with parchment paper.
- Uncover the rolls. Use a bench knife to scoop under a roll and place it disc-side up on one of the baking sheets. Continue to transfer the rolls to the baking sheets in this way, spacing them apart by 2 inches.
- Place one baking sheet on each oven rack, spritz the rolls with water, and bake for 20 to 25 minutes, until they are golden brown and emit a hollow sound when you tap on the bottom of one with your finger, switching racks and rotating the baking sheets from front to back halfway through the baking time.

Cool the rolls

- Remove the rolls from the oven and use a spatula or offset spatula to transfer them to a cooling rack to cool.

Classic Parker House Rolls

These Parker House rolls follow the classic folded-over shape. They are a bit more sophisticated than pull-apart rolls and are an elegant addition to a bread basket.

Makes 2 dozen rolls

			Baker's %
Sourdough Starter			
Water (70°–75°F)	4 teaspoons	20 grams	100
Mother sourdough starter	1½ teaspoons	12 grams	62.5
Bread flour	2½ tablespoons	20 grams	100
For the dough			
Whole milk	1 cup	240 grams	57
Instant yeast	1½ teaspoons	4.5 grams	1.1
Sourdough Starter (above)	¼ cup + 1 tablespoon	52 grams	12
Egg, large	1	50 grams	12
Bread flour	3½ cups	420 grams	100
Granulated sugar	2 tablespoons	26 grams	6
Fine sea salt	2 teaspoons	12 grams	2.9
Unsalted butter, cubed and softened	12 tablespoons	170 grams	40
For baking the rolls			
Unsalted butter, melted and cooled slightly	3 tablespoons	42 grams	
Flaky salt	1 tablespoon	10 grams	

Mix the starter

- Mix the sourdough starter 4 to 6 hours before adding it to the dough. Put the water in a 1-pint container with a lid. Add 25 grams (1 tablespoon) of the ripened mother sourdough starter to the container. Add the flour and stir with a metal spoon to combine. Cover the container and set aside in a warm place (about 75°F) until it is ripe and passes the Float Test (page xxxi).

Mix and ferment the dough

- Pour the milk into the bowl of a stand mixer. Sprinkle the instant yeast on top of the milk and let it rest for 5 minutes to begin to dissolve. Then whisk the yeast into the milk.
- Add the sourdough starter and egg, followed by the flour, sugar, and salt. Fit the mixer with the dough hook and mix on low speed for 2 minutes. Increase the mixer speed to medium and mix the dough for about 5 minutes, until it is smooth and no longer sticky. Add the cubed butter and mix on low speed until there are no chunks of butter remaining, 5 to 10 minutes, stopping to scrape down the sides of the bowl if the butter is sticking.
- Remove the dough hook and wipe it clean with a wet hand. Cover the bowl with a clean kitchen towel or plastic wrap and set in a warm place to allow the dough to ferment for 1 hour.

Stretch and fold the dough

- Uncover the bowl and use a wet hand to stretch and fold the top edge down two-thirds and stretch and fold the bottom edge up to meet the top edge, so the dough is folded like a letter. Fold the sides inward in the same way to form a sort of ball. Re-cover the bowl and set aside to ferment for 1 hour.
- While the dough is fermenting, line a baking sheet with parchment paper and spray the paper with nonstick cooking spray.
- Transfer the dough, to the baking sheet and spread it out. Put it in the refrigerator for 1 hour, until it's chilled and no longer sticky, or up to overnight. (The colder the dough, the easier it will be to handle.)

Shape and proof the rolls

- Lightly dust a large work surface with flour and use a plastic bowl scraper to scoop the dough up from the baking sheet onto the floured surface. Flip the parchment paper over onto the baking sheet with the clean side facing up and spray the paper with nonstick cooking spray.
- Lightly dust the top of the dough with flour and use a bench knife to divide it into 24 (40-gram) pieces.
- Put one piece of dough in front of you on the work surface. Dust your hands lightly with flour. Gently rest your palm on the dough and roll it into a tight round ball. Put the ball back on the baking sheet and repeat with the remaining pieces of dough. Place the baking sheet back into the refrigerator and chill the balls for 30 minutes.
- Line two baking sheets with parchment paper and lightly spray with nonstick cooking spray.
- Lightly dust your work surface with additional flour. Remove the baking sheet with the dough balls from the refrigerator. Pick up one ball and place it in front of you on the work surface. Flatten it into a disc with the palm of your hand. Take a ¼-inch wooden dowel (or alternatively a chopstick) and press through the center of the disc to create an indentation. Fold the disc in half along the indentation line. The top should not quite line up with the bottom but should be a little offset. Place the roll upside down on the prepared baking sheets.
- Repeat, shaping the remaining balls the same way, leaving 1½ to 2 inches between them on the baking sheets. When all the rolls are shaped, cover them with damp cloths and proof in a warm place (about 75°F) for 2 hours.

Bake the rolls

- While the rolls are proofing, arrange oven racks in the top third and bottom third of the oven and preheat the oven to 350°F.
- Using a bench knife, gently flip the rolls right-side up. Gently brush the tops of the rolls with the half the melted butter. Reserve the remaining butter.
- Bake the rolls for 20 to 25 minutes, until they are light golden brown.
- Remove the rolls from the oven and brush with the remaining melted butter. Sprinkle a generous pinch of flaky sea salt on top of each roll. Serve warm.

Black Truffle Fantails

Makes 12 fantails

These small breads are perfect for a special occasion or when you are feeling luxurious. Black truffle is grated into the dough and the flavor of the dough is augmented with black truffle oil. I have found that preserved black truffle works well in the dough, and it keeps it from becoming exorbitant. I do not skimp on the black truffle oil, though. I use truffle oil that is prepared by infusing fresh black truffles into high-quality extra-virgin olive oil. The quality of the oil makes all the difference. My favorite brand to use is Regalis.

Fantails are a laminated bread; the name refers to their shape. They are made by cutting dough into squares, turning the squares on their sides and baking them in muffin cups. When the dough expands during baking, the squares open up in the individual cups like a fan.

Plan ahead Make your butter packet in advance, or while the dough is in the refrigerator. Place the packet in the refrigerator to chill until you're ready to laminate the dough, then remove it from the refrigerator to soften it slightly when called to do so in the recipe.

Equipment A standard 12-cup muffin tin

Note The dough gets trimmed several times, and you can either discard the trimmings or save them all up and bake them together in a muffin tin for a baker's treat.

			Baker's %
For the dough			
Whole milk	1 cup	240 grams	50
Instant yeast	1 tablespoon	9 grams	1.9
Egg, large	1	50 grams	10
Egg yolk, large	1	17 grams	4
Black truffle oil	1 tablespoon	14 grams	3
Bread flour	4 cups + more for dusting	480 grams	100
Granulated sugar	¼ cup	50 grams	10
Fine sea salt	2 teaspoons	12 grams	2.5
Unsalted butter, cubed and softened	10 tablespoons	140 grams	29
Black truffle	1 ounce	28 grams	6
1 Butter Packet (page 165), chilled	12 tablespoons	170 grams	
Nonstick cooking spray			
For finishing			
Black truffle oil	3 tablespoons	42 grams	
Flaky sea salt	1 tablespoon	10 grams	

Mix and ferment the dough

· Put the milk in the bowl of a stand mixer. Sprinkle the yeast on top and let it rest for 5 minutes to help the yeast to dissolve. Then whisk the yeast into the milk. Add the whole egg, egg yolk, and black truffle oil, followed by the flour, sugar, salt, and butter. Use a Microplane to grate the truffle into the bowl.

- Fit the mixer with the dough hook and mix on low speed for 2 minutes. Increase the speed to medium and mix for 5 minutes. Scrape the dough off the hook with a wet hand. Place a clean kitchen towel or plastic wrap over the bowl and set the dough aside at room temperature to ferment for 1 hour.

Retard the détrempe

- Line a baking sheet with parchment paper and spray the parchment with nonstick cooking spray. Use a plastic bowl scraper to scrape the dough onto the prepared baking sheet. Using wet hands, pat and form the dough gently into an 8-inch square. Refrigerate the dough for at least 1 hour or up to 8 hours. If you are refrigerating the dough for longer than 1 hour, remove it from the refrigerator after 1 hour, wrap it in plastic wrap, and return it to the refrigerator.

Détrempe is a term for the dough before adding the layering butter. The layering butter is also called beurrage.

Laminate the Dough

Lock in the butter

- Remove the butter packet from the refrigerator and set it on the counter to soften until it is bendy but still cool. You want the butter to be slightly softer and more malleable than the dough but not so soft that it will ooze out of the dough. This could take anywhere from 5 to 20 minutes, depending on how cold the butter is.
- Lightly dust a large flat work surface with flour. Remove the dough from the refrigerator, unwrap the dough, and place it on the floured surface. Lightly dust the top of the dough and the rolling pin with flour and roll the dough out into a roughly 14 × 11-inch rectangle, dusting the work surface, the rolling pin, and the top of the dough lightly with flour as you roll the dough so it doesn't stick.
- Set the rectangle of dough with a long side facing you. Open the parchment packet to expose the butter and flip the packet over to place the butter on the dough, centering the butter packet on the dough. Peel off and discard the parchment paper. Fold the left and right sides of the dough over the butter so they meet in the middle and pinch the two edges of dough together with your fingers. Gently press the top and bottom edges of the dough together to seal the packet closed and lock in the butter.

Make 2 letter folds

- Lightly dust your work surface with flour. Dust the top of the dough and the rolling pin with flour and roll the dough until it is 18 inches from top to bottom, dusting the work surface, rolling pin, and the top of the dough lightly with flour as you roll the dough so it doesn't stick. Using a pastry wheel or a bench knife, trim the top and bottom edges of the dough just enough to expose the layer of butter in the center of the dough (see Note on page 181). Fold the top edge down two-thirds and fold the bottom edge to meet the top edge, so the dough is folded into thirds, like a letter.

· Rotate the dough 90 degrees so the closed edges are facing left and right and one of the open edges (with the visible layers) is facing you. Lightly dust the work surface, dough, and rolling pin with flour and roll out the dough until it is roughly 18 inches from top to bottom, dusting with flour as needed. Trim the top and bottom edges (see Note) to expose the butter layers. Fold the top edge down and the bottom edge up to make a second letter fold.

Retard the dough

· Wrap the laminated block of dough in plastic wrap and place it in the freezer to chill for 1 hour. Move the dough from the freezer to the refrigerator for at least 8 hours and up to 12 hours to retard the dough.

Cut the fantails

· Remove the laminated block of dough from the refrigerator and set it on the counter to rest for 20 to 30 minutes, until you can feel that the butter layers inside the dough are just becoming malleable (but not soft) when you bend the block slightly.

· Spray 12 cups of a standard muffin tin with nonstick cooking spray.

· Lightly dust your work surface with flour. Unwrap the dough and place it on the floured surface with a long side facing you. Lightly dust the top of the dough. If the dough is smaller than a 7½-inch square, roll the dough out to those dimensions.

· Cut the dough into 1½-inch squares with a pastry wheel or a large chef's knife.

· Turn the fantail cubes on their sides and place 2 pieces in each muffin cup. Cover the muffin tin with a damp lightweight kitchen towel and set aside in a warm place for about 1 hour to proof the fantails until they just start to puff up.

Bake the fantails

· Arrange an oven rack in the center position and preheat the oven to 350°F.

· Bake the fantails for 25 to 30 minutes, until the tops are deep golden brown, rotating the muffin tin from front to back halfway through the baking time so the pastries brown evenly.

· Remove the muffin tin from the oven. Immediately brush the fantails with the truffle oil and sprinkle each with a generous pinch of flaky sea salt. Set the muffin tin on a cooling rack and let the fantails cool in the pan for 5 to 10 minutes. Remove the fantails and serve them warm or at room temperature.

Petits Pains de Seigle aux Raisins

Makes 24 rolls

These petite rye rolls dotted with raisins are the rolls that I crave when I want to slather on some soft or runny cheese. They are very French, and my favorites come from Poilâne bakery in Paris. I like them so much that I will have them with cheese in the evening, and then save what's left for the morning to slice and toast and spread with salted butter and jam.

Sourdough Starter			Baker's %
Water (70°–75°F)	2 tablespoons + 2 teaspoons	40 grams	100
Mother sourdough starter	1 tablespoon	25 grams	69
Bread flour	2 tablespoons	18 grams	50
Rye flour	2 tablespoons	18 grams	50
For the dough			
Water (80°–90°F)	1¾ cups + 2 tablespoons	439 grams	81
Bread flour	1¾ cups	210 grams	39
Whole wheat bread flour	½ cup	60 grams	11
Rye flour	2¼ cups	270 grams	50
Sourdough Starter (above)	½ cup + 2 tablespoons	108 grams	20
Raisins	1 cup	150 grams	28
Fine sea salt	2 teaspoons	12 grams	2.2
For dusting the rolls			
Rye flour	3 tablespoons		

Mix the starter

· Mix the sourdough starter 4 to 5 hours before adding it to the dough. Put the water in a 1-quart container with a lid. Add 25 grams (1 tablespoon) of the ripened mother sourdough starter to the container. Add the bread flour and rye flour and stir with a metal spoon to combine. Cover the container and set the starter aside in a warm place (about 75°F) until it is ripe and passes the Float Test (page xxxi).

Autolyse the dough

· In a shallow 3- to 4-quart container, stir together the water, bread flour, whole wheat bread flour, and rye flour with a metal spoon to combine. Cover the container and set it aside in a warm place (about 75°F) for 2 to 3 hours to autolyse.

For more information on why we are resting the dough before mixing the sourdough starter, salt, and raisins into the dough, see Autolyse (page 5).

Add the sourdough starter to the dough

· As soon as the starter is ripe, uncover the dough and add the starter, mixing it by scooping your hand under the dough and folding the dough into the center until the starter is thoroughly mixed in. Re-cover the container and let the dough rest for 30 minutes.

Soak the raisins

- Place the raisins in a small bowl, cover with hot tap water, and set aside to soak for 10 minutes. Drain the raisins in a sieve and let them sit in the sieve to continue to drain.

Add the salt and raisins to the dough

- Uncover the dough. Add the salt and rehydrated raisins and scoop under the dough with a wet hand and fold the dough into the center until it is homogeneous. Re-cover the container and let the dough rest for 30 minutes.

Make 5 stretch and folds and retard the dough

- Uncover the dough. With wet hands, scoop underneath the top edge of the dough, stretch it out, and fold it down two-thirds of the way toward the bottom edge. Stretch out and fold the bottom edge up to meet the top edge, as if you were folding a letter, pressing on the dough just enough to get it to stay in place. Do the same with the two sides, stretching and folding the right edge two-thirds of the way toward the left edge, and stretching and folding the left edge to meet the right edge. Then flip the dough upside down. This is your first fold. Re-cover the container and set the dough aside for 30 minutes.
- Repeat stretching and folding the dough a second time for a second fold. Re-cover and set the dough aside for 30 minutes.
- Repeat stretching and folding the dough a third time for a third fold. Re-cover and set the dough aside for 1 hour.
- Repeat stretching and folding a fourth time for a fourth fold. Re-cover and set the dough aside for 1 hour.
- Repeat stretching and folding the dough one last time for a fifth fold. Re-cover the container and place it in the refrigerator to retard overnight, or for at least 8 hours.

Shape and proof the rolls

- Remove the container of dough from the refrigerator and let it sit out at room temperature for 1 hour before proceeding.
- Lightly dust a large work surface with flour and use a plastic bowl scraper to scrape the dough onto the floured surface. Lightly dust the top of the dough with flour and use a bench knife to divide the dough into 24 (50-gram) pieces.
- Line two baking sheets with parchment paper. Use a fine mesh sieve to lightly dust rye flour over the parchment paper. Put one piece of dough in front of you on the work surface. Dust your hands lightly with flour. Gently rest your palm on the dough and roll the dough into a tight round ball. Put the ball on one of the prepared baking sheets. Repeat the process with the remaining pieces of dough, spacing the balls out evenly between the two baking sheets.
- Cover the balls with two damp lightweight kitchen towels. Set aside in a warm place to proof the rolls for 2½ to 3 hours, until the rolls are swollen looking and one and a half times their original size.

Bake the rolls
- Thirty minutes before you plan to bake, arrange oven racks in the top third and bottom third of the oven and preheat the oven to 450°F.
- Uncover the rolls and dust their tops using the sieve with rye flour. Place a baking sheet on each oven rack. Bake the rolls for 20 to 25 minutes, until they are golden brown and emit a hollow sound when you tap on the bottom of one with your finger, switching racks and rotating the baking sheets from front to back halfway through the baking time.

Cool the rolls
- Remove the rolls from the oven and use a spatula or offset spatula to transfer them to a cooling rack to cool.

Schedule for Petits Pains de Seigle

These rolls take time and many steps. This schedule will help you plan the steps out.

Day One

This day is about getting the starter ready and mixing the dough. At the end of the day, the dough is retarded in bulk in the refrigerator overnight.

8:00 a.m. Mix the starter.

10:00 a.m. Autolyse the water and the flours.

12:00 p.m. Add the sourdough starter to the dough.

12:15 p.m. Soak and drain the raisins.

12:30 p.m. Add the salt and raisins to the dough.

1:00 p.m. First stretch and fold.

1:30 p.m. Second stretch and fold.

2:00 p.m. Third stretch and fold.

3:00 p.m. Fourth stretch and fold.

4:00 p.m. Final stretch and fold. Retard the dough overnight.

Day Two

This is the shaping, proofing, and baking day. It is important to let the dough sit out at room temperature for about 1 hour before beginning to divide and shape it.

8:00 a.m. Remove the dough from the refrigerator.

9:00 a.m. Divide and round the rolls. Begin their proofing.

11:30 a.m. Preheat the oven.

12:00 p.m. Bake the rolls.

12:30 p.m. Remove the rolls from the oven and let them cool.

Chocolate Brandied Cherry Rolls

Makes 15 rolls

These rolls are the opposite of unassuming, and they are addictive. They are overstuffed with dried and brandied cherries and milk and bittersweet chocolate. The hardest part about making them is incorporating all the cherries and chocolate into the dough. Folding the cherries and chocolate into the dough takes some time. At first it will seem like the dough will not come together, but then it does. So persevere.

			Baker's %
Dried cherries	1 cup	155 grams	40
Water (65°–70°F)	1 cup	235 grams	60
Instant yeast	2 teaspoons	6 grams	1.5
Extra-virgin olive oil	1 tablespoon + more for coating	14 grams	4.0
Bread flour	2¾ cups + more for dusting	330 grams	85
Rye flour	½ cup	60 grams	15
Fine sea salt	2 teaspoons	12 grams	3.1
Bittersweet chocolate bar, chopped, or chips	4½-ounce bar or ¾ cup chips	127 grams	33
Milk chocolate, bar or chips	4½-ounce bar or ¾ cup chips	127 grams	33
Brandied cherries, pitted	1 cup	155 grams	40
Nonstick cooking spray			
For baking the rolls			
Extra-virgin olive oil	2 tablespoons	30 grams	

Soak the dried cherries

· Place the dried cherries in a small bowl, cover with hot tap water, and set aside to soak for 10 minutes. Drain the cherries in a sieve and let them sit in the sieve to continue to drain.

Mix and ferment the dough

· Put the water in the bowl of a stand mixer. Sprinkle the yeast on top and let it rest for 5 minutes to help it dissolve. Then whisk the yeast into the water. Add the olive oil, bread flour, rye flour, and salt. Fit the mixer with the dough hook and mix on low speed for 3 minutes. Increase the speed to medium and mix for 5 minutes to develop the gluten. Turn off the mixer and add the rehydrated cherries and bittersweet and milk chocolates. Mix on low speed for 3 minutes to incorporate. Remove the bowl from the stand, remove the dough hook, and wipe it clean with a wet hand. Add the brandied cherries and mix in by scooping under the dough bowl and set aside. Let the dough rest for 1 hour.

Stretch and fold the dough

· Uncover the dough. With wet hands, scoop underneath the top edge of the dough and stretch and fold the top edge down two-thirds and stretch and fold the bottom edge to meet the top edge, so the dough is folded like a letter. Fold the sides inward in the same way to form a sort of ball. Flip the ball upside down. Re-cover the bowl and let the dough rest for 1 hour.

Shape and retard the rolls

• Line two baking sheets with parchment paper and spray the parchment paper lightly with nonstick spray.

• Lightly dust a large flat work surface with flour and use a plastic bowl scraper to scrape the dough onto the floured surface. Lightly dust the top of the dough with flour and use a bench knife to divide the dough into 15 (80-gram) pieces.

• Put one piece of dough in front of you on the work surface. Dust your hands lightly with flour. Gently rest your palm on the dough and roll the dough into a tight round ball. Put the ball on one of the prepared baking sheets. Repeat the process with the remaining pieces of dough, spacing the balls out evenly between the two baking sheets.

• Wrap both baking sheets with plastic wrap, spraying the plastic wrap with nonstick cooking spray to prevent the rolls from sticking to it. Place them in your refrigerator to proof overnight, or a minimum of 8 hours.

Bake the rolls

• Thirty minutes before you plan to bake, arrange oven racks in the top third and bottom third of the oven and preheat the oven to 425°F.

• Pour the olive oil into a small bowl. Remove the plastic from the rolls and gently brush their tops with the olive oil.

• Place a baking sheet on each oven rack and bake the rolls for 25 to 30 minutes, until they are golden brown and emit a hollow sound when you tap on the bottom of one with your finger, switching racks and rotating the baking sheets from front to back halfway through the baking time.

Cool the rolls

• Remove the rolls from the oven and use a spatula to transfer them to a cooling rack to cool.

Sandwich Buns
and Rolls

I love making rolls and buns for sandwiches, and that is what this short and sweet chapter is. It has three recipes, which distinguish themselves from the petits pains one finds in a bread basket or at the end of a meal. Although these are delicious by themselves, I encourage you to fill them up for savory bites!

Green Olive Rolls

Makes 12 rolls

I first made theses rolls when I was a beginning baker at Sullivan Street Bakery, and I have loved them ever since. There is intentionally no salt in this dough because the salt comes from the olives. I love the contrast of unsalted dough with salty olives. Because salt normally controls the growth of the yeast, I have reduced the amount of yeast so that the rolls don't grow rampant.

			Baker's %
For the dough			
Water (70°–80°F)	1⅔ cups	392 grams	89
Instant yeast	½ teaspoon	1.5 grams	0.3
Bread flour	3⅓ cups + more for dusting	400 grams	91
Whole wheat bread flour	⅓ cup	40 grams	9.0
Pitted Castelvetrano olives, drained	1½ cups	200 grams	45
Nonstick cooking spray			
For baking the rolls			
Extra-virgin olive oil	2 tablespoons	30 grams	

Mix and ferment the dough

▪ Put the water in shallow 3- to 4-quart container. Sprinkle the yeast on top and let rest for 5 minutes to begin to dissolve. Then whisk the yeast into the water. Add the bread flour and whole wheat bread flour and use a metal spoon to stir the dough until it becomes a lumpy mass. Cover the container and set it aside in a warm place (about 75°F) for 30 minutes.

Add the olives to the dough

▪ Uncover the dough and add the olives, mixing them in by scooping under the dough with a wet hand and folding it into the center until the dough is homogeneous. Re-cover the container and let the dough rest for 30 minutes.

Make 2 stretch and folds

▪ Uncover the dough. With wet hands, scoop underneath the top edge of the dough, stretch it out, and fold it down two-thirds of the way toward the bottom edge. Stretch and fold the bottom edge to meet the top edge, as if you were folding a letter, pressing on the dough just enough to get it to stay in place. Do the same with the two sides, stretching and folding the right edge two-thirds of the way toward the left edge, and stretching and folding the left edge to meet the right edge. Then flip the dough upside down. This is your first fold. Re-cover the container and set the dough aside for 1 hour.
▪ Repeat stretching and folding the dough a second time for a second fold. Re-cover and set aside for 1 hour.

Shape and proof the rolls

▪ Line two baking sheets with parchment paper and spray the parchment paper lightly with nonstick spray.

- Lightly dust a large flat work surface with flour and use a plastic bowl scraper to scrape the dough onto the floured surface. Lightly dust the top of the dough with flour and use a bench knife to divide the dough into 12 (80-gram) pieces.
- Put one piece of dough in front of you on the work surface. Dust your hands lightly with flour. Gently rest your palm on the dough and roll the dough into a tight round ball. Put the ball on one of the prepared baking sheets. Repeat the process with the remaining portions of dough, spacing the balls out evenly between the two baking sheets.
- Cover the balls with two damp lightweight kitchen towels. Set aside in a warm place to proof the rolls for 2½ to 3 hours, until the rolls are swollen looking and touching each other.

Bake the rolls

- Thirty minutes before you plan to bake, arrange oven racks in the top third and bottom third of the oven and preheat the oven to 425°F.
- Pour the olive oil into a small bowl. Uncover the rolls and gently brush the tops with the olive oil.
- Place a baking sheet on each oven rack and bake the rolls for 25 to 30 minutes, until they are golden brown and emit a hollow sound when you tap on the bottom of one with your finger, switching racks and rotating the baking sheets from front to back halfway through the baking time.

Cool the rolls

- Remove the rolls from the oven and use a spatula to transfer them to a cooling rack to cool.

Seeded Hoagie Rolls

Makes 7 rolls

I'm from Pennsylvania, and I grew up calling a 6-inch-long sandwich roll filled with deli meats a hoagie. I knew that it could also be called a sub or hero, but I didn't realize that very few people outside of Pennsylvania had ever even heard the word hoagie. Regardless of what they're called, these are the best long rolls for sandwiches. I like to use buttermilk in the dough; its acidity tenderizes the dough and makes a nice soft squishy roll.

For the dough			Baker's %
Whole milk	1 cup	240 grams	30
Instant yeast	1 tablespoon	9 grams	1.1
Buttermilk	1 cup	250 grams	31
Eggs, large	2	100 grams	12
Bread flour	6¾ cups	810 grams	100
Granulated sugar	2 tablespoons	26 grams	3.0
Fine sea salt	1 tablespoon	18 grams	2.2
Nonstick cooking spray			
Sesame seeds	1 cup	90 grams	

Mix and ferment the dough

- Pour the milk into the bowl of a stand mixer. Sprinkle the yeast on top and let rest for 5 minutes to help dissolve the yeast. Then whisk the yeast into the milk.
- Add the buttermilk, eggs, flour, sugar, and salt to the bowl. Fit the mixer with the dough hook and mix on low speed for 3 minutes. Increase the speed to medium and mix for 5 minutes to develop the gluten. Remove the dough hook and wipe it clean with a wet hand. Cover the bowl with a clean kitchen towel or plastic wrap and set the dough in a warm place (about 75°F) to ferment for 1 hour.

Make 2 stretch and folds and retard the dough

- Uncover the dough. With wet hands, scoop underneath the top edge of the dough, stretch it out, and fold it down two-thirds of the way toward the bottom edge. Stretch and fold the bottom edge to meet the top edge, as if you were folding a letter, pressing on the dough just enough to get it to stay in place. Do the same with the two sides, stretching and folding the right edge two-thirds of the way toward the left edge, and stretching and folding the left edge to meet the right edge. Then flip the dough upside down. This is your first fold. Re-cover the container and set the dough aside for 1 hour.
- Repeat stretching and folding the dough a second time for a second fold. Place the dough in the refrigerator overnight to retard the dough.

Preshape the rolls

- Remove the dough from the refrigerator. Lightly dust a large flat work surface with flour and use a plastic bowl scraper to scrape the dough out of the bowl and onto the floured surface. Dust the top of the dough with flour and use a bench knife to divide it into 7 (150-gram) pieces.
- Put one piece of dough in front of you on the work surface. Dust your hands lightly with flour. Gently rest your palm on the dough and roll the dough into a tight round ball. Place the ball off to the side of the work surface and continue rolling the rest of the pieces of dough into balls, moving them off to the side as you do. Let the balls rest for 15 minutes.

Shape and proof the rolls

- Line two baking sheets with parchment paper and spray the parchment paper lightly with nonstick spray.
- Lightly dust your hands with flour and place one ball of dough on your work surface in front of you. Gently press on it with the palm of your hand to flatten it into a thick pancake. Using both hands, pick up the top edge of the round and fold it down by one-quarter, pinching it into the dough log with the tips of your fingers. Repeat, moving the top edge toward the center and pinching it into the dough, two or three more times until you reach the bottom of the log. Re-dust your work surface and hands with flour and use your hands to roll the log until it is 6 inches long.
- Arrange the log so that the seam is on the bottom and push down on the dough with the palm of one hand to flatten the log. Set the roll to the side and repeat, shaping the remaining balls of dough in the same way.

To evenly coat the rolls with sesame seeds, roll them first on a wet towel to moisten their surface and then roll them in the seeds.

- To coat the rolls with sesame seeds, spread the sesame seeds on a dinner plate. Saturate a kitchen towel with water and wring dry. Fold the towel in half and place it on your work surface in front of you. Pick up one roll and press it down on the wet towel. Flip it over and press it down on its other side. Then move the roll to the plate of seeds and coat its top and bottom with seeds. Place the roll, seam-side down, on one of the prepared baking sheets. Repeat the process with the remaining rolls, spacing them evenly apart on the two baking sheets.
- Cover the baking sheets with damp lightweight kitchen towels and set them aside in a warm place to proof for 2¾ to 3 hours, until they have doubled in size; the dough will not spring back when poked in the center.

Bake the rolls
- Thirty minutes before you plan to bake, arrange oven racks in the top third and bottom third of the oven and preheat the oven to 375°F.
- Place a baking sheet on each oven rack and bake for 30 minutes, until the tops of the rolls are golden brown, switching racks and rotating the baking sheets from front to back halfway through the baking time.

Cool the rolls
- Remove the rolls from the oven and use a spatula to transfer them to a cooling rack to cool.

Italian Combo Sandwiches

Makes 2 sandwiches

When I worked at Roberta's in Brooklyn, I would bake seeded hoagie rolls and send them to a pizzeria that would make fantastical Italian combo sandwiches with them. Those sandwiches stayed in my memory because all of the ingredients were balanced—the textures of the different meats, salt, fat, acid from the vinaigrette, and more texture from the chopped romaine. This recipe is how I remember those sandwiches.

Seeded Hoagie Rolls (page 199)	2	
Garlic Mayonnaise (recipe follows)	2 tablespoons	50 grams
Provolone cheese, sliced	2 ounces	57 grams
Mortadella, thinly sliced	2½ ounces	71 grams
Fennel salami, thinly sliced	2½ ounces	71 grams
Hot coppa, thinly sliced	2½ ounces	71 grams
Pepperoncini, stemmed and thinly sliced	3 to 4 peppers (1 ounce)	28 grams
Iceberg lettuce, shredded	¼ head	
Oregano Vinaigrette (recipe follows)	⅓ cup	80 grams

▪ Split the seeded hoagie rolls in half horizontally. Spread 1 tablespoon of garlic mayonnaise over the bottom half of each roll. Dividing evenly, layer each sandwich with the provolone, mortadella, salami, and coppa. Sprinkle the pepperoncini on top. Pile on the shredded lettuce and drizzle generously with oregano vinaigrette. Cover with the top halves of the rolls.

Garlic Mayonnaise

Makes 1¼ cups

I use this garlic mayonnaise at home for all sorts of things. Large fat homemade French fries with this mayonnaise are gone in seconds at my home. The best tip I can give you for this recipe is to let the mayonnaise rest overnight in the refrigerator for the garlic to meld.

Ingredient	Amount	Weight
Egg yolks, large	2	34 grams
Garlic, minced	2 large	
Lemon juice	1 tablespoon	17 grams
Dijon mustard	1 teaspoon	7 grams
Fine sea salt	¾ teaspoon	4.5 grams
Canola oil	¾ cup	165 grams
Extra-virgin olive oil	¼ cup	55 grams

▪ In a food processor, combine the egg yolks, minced garlic, lemon juice, mustard, and salt in the bowl of a food processor fitted with a metal blade and pulse for about 30 seconds to break up the garlic and combine the ingredients. With the food processor running, add a few drops of the canola oil. Continue adding the canola oil and then the olive oil in a slow drizzle until all of the oil has been added. Turn the machine off. Refrigerate the mayonnaise overnight and for up to 3 days.

Oregano Vinaigrette

This classic vinaigrette provides a good amount of acid, perfect to balance meat and cheese sandwiches like the Italian combo. It is also great on simple salads, roasted vegetables, and fish.

Makes ½ cup

Shallot, finely diced	1 large	80 grams
Garlic, finely diced	1 clove	
Red wine vinegar	3 tablespoons	45 grams
Fine sea salt	½ teaspoon	3 grams
Dried oregano	1 tablespoon	1 gram
Freshly ground black pepper	Several twists	
Extra-virgin olive oil	¼ cup	55 grams

▪ In a medium bowl, combine the shallot, garlic, vinegar, salt, oregano, and black pepper, whisking to combine. Add the olive oil in a slow, thin stream, whisking constantly to emulsify. Use the vinaigrette right away or store in an airtight container in the refrigerator for up to 3 days.

Enriched Breads

There should always be an aspect of fun in breadmaking, and the breads I include in this chapter reflect that. These breads use commercial yeast, or a combination of commercial yeast and sourdough starter, which makes them easier to achieve success with, and more forgiving. And they are also enriched breads, which means they have something *in* them, such as sugar, eggs, or butter. These are breads that I have fun making at home over and over again, and that I want to share with you.

Whole Wheat Olive Oil Brioche

Makes one 13-inch Pullman loaf

Butter is traditionally used to enrich brioche dough. In the South of France, in Provence, there's a brioche called pompe à l'huile that uses olive oil instead. Pompe à l'huile is traditionally shaped like a fougasse, which also comes from the South of France. Fougasse is a flat bread shaped and slashed to resemble a sheaf of wheat. I like the flavor the olive oil imparts to the dough and created my own version. Please note that the brioche dough here is wet and needs to be baked in a pan.

Equipment A 13 × 4 × 4-inch Pullman loaf pan with a lid

Sourdough Starter			Baker's %
Water (70°–75°F)	⅓ cup	78 grams	100
Mother sourdough starter	1 tablespoon	25 grams	62.5
Bread flour	⅔ cup	80 grams	100
For the dough			
Whole milk	½ cup	118 grams	30
Instant yeast	4 teaspoons	12 grams	3.0
Sourdough Starter (above)	1 cup + 1 tablespoon	183 grams	46
Eggs, large	4	200 grams	50
Bread flour	1½ cups	180 grams	45
Whole wheat bread flour	2½ cups	220 grams	55
Honey	3 tablespoons	63 grams	16
Fine sea salt	2 teaspoons	12 grams	3.0
Extra-virgin olive oil	1 cup	220 grams	55
Nonstick cooking spray			

Mix the starter

· Mix the sourdough starter 8 to 12 hours before you plan to add it to the dough. Put the water in a 1-quart container with a lid. Add 25 grams (1 tablespoon) of the ripened mother sourdough starter to the container. Add the flour and stir with a metal spoon to combine. Cover the container and set aside in a warm place (about 75°F) until the starter is ripe and passes the Float Test (page xxxi).

Mix the dough

· As soon as the starter is ripe, pour the milk in the bowl of a stand mixer. Sprinkle the instant yeast on top of the milk and let it rest for 5 minutes to dissolve. Then whisk the yeast into the milk.

· Add all the ripened starter (183 grams), the eggs, bread flour, whole wheat bread flour, honey, and salt to the bowl. Fit the mixer with the dough hook and mix the ingredients on low speed for 2 minutes. Increase the speed to medium and mix for 5 minutes to develop the gluten. Turn the mixer speed down to low and trickle in a couple of tablespoons of the extra-virgin olive oil. Mix on low until the olive oil is mostly absorbed and then trickle in a couple more tablespoons. Continue to mix on low, adding the oil slowly until it is completely absorbed.

Ferment and fold the dough

· Remove the dough hook and wipe it clean with a wet hand. Cover the bowl with a clean kitchen towel or plastic wrap and set the dough aside in a warm place (about 75°F) to ferment for 1 hour.

· Uncover the dough. With wet hands, scoop underneath the top edge of the dough, stretch it out, and fold it down two-thirds of the way toward the bottom edge. Stretch and fold the bottom edge to meet the top edge, as if you were folding a letter, pressing on the dough just enough to get it to stay in place. Do the same with the two sides, stretching and folding the right edge two-thirds of the way toward the left edge, and stretching and folding the left edge to meet the right edge. Then flip the dough upside down. Re-cover the bowl and place it in the refrigerator to retard overnight, or for at least 8 hours.

Form and proof the loaf

· Lightly spray the insides and the underside of the lid of a 13 × 4-inch Pullman loaf pan with nonstick cooking spray.

· Dust a large work surface with bread flour. Using a plastic bowl scraper, scrape the dough onto the floured surface. Lightly flour the top of the dough and pat it into a rectangle about the length of the pan you will be baking it in, with a long side facing you. Use your hands to get underneath the top edge of the dough and fold it down about two-thirds of the way from the top like a letter. Scoop your hands under the bottom edge of the dough (the edge closest to you) and fold it up over the top so the bottom edge is even with the top edge. Lift the dough and flip it over into the pan so the seam is on the bottom. Use your hands to pat the dough into the corners of the pan and even out the surface of the dough. Slide the lid closed on the pan, leaving it cracked open by 1 inch.

· Place the loaf in a warm place (about 75°F) for 2 to 3 hours to proof the dough, until the dough begins to peek out of the opening in the lid. Close the lid completely and discard any dough that gets pinched off by closing the lid.

Bake the bread

· Thirty minutes before you plan to bake, arrange a oven rack in the center position and preheat the oven to 375°F.

· Bake the loaf for 45 to 50 minutes, until the top is dark golden brown. (To check for doneness, using oven mitts or kitchen towels, slide the Pullman loaf lid open enough to see the color, being careful of any steam that might rise when you open the pan.) Remove the loaf from the oven.

Cool the loaf

· Using oven mitts or kitchen towels to protect your hands, immediately slide off the lid of the loaf pan. Invert the pan so the bread falls onto a cooling rack. Let the loaf cool completely and slice as desired.

Cinnamon Swirl Pumpkin Challah

Makes one 13-inch loaf

This loaf reminds me of autumn. It's great for French toast or perfect on its own. The cinnamon sugar in the swirl is just enough to create the swirl. Too much cinnamon sugar will melt and create an undesirable gap in the swirl.

Equipment A 13 × 4 × 4-inch Pullman loaf pan

			Baker's %
Water (75°F)	¾ cup	176 grams	23
Instant yeast	1 tablespoon	9 grams	1.2
Canned pumpkin puree	1¼ cups	281 grams	37
Egg, large	1	50 grams	7.0
Egg yolks, large	3	51 grams	7.0
Canola or vegetable oil	½ cup + 1 tablespoon	124 grams	17
Mild-flavored honey, such as wildflower or clover	3 tablespoons	60 grams	8.0
Bread flour	4 cups + more for dusting	750 grams	100
Fine sea salt	1 tablespoon	18 grams	2.4
Ground cinnamon	1½ teaspoons	3 grams	< 1
Ground ginger	½ teaspoon	1 gram	< 1
Ground allspice	¼ teaspoon	< 1 gram	< 1
Ground nutmeg	¼ teaspoon	< 1 gram	< 1
Nonstick cooking spray			
For the cinnamon swirl			
Ground cinnamon	1 tablespoon	6 grams	
Granulated sugar	1 tablespoon	13 grams	
For baking the loaf			
Egg, large	1	50 grams	
Fine sea salt	big pinch		

Mix the dough

- Put the water in the bowl of a stand mixer. Sprinkle the yeast on top and let stand for 5 minutes to help dissolve the yeast. Then whisk the yeast into the water.
- Stir in the pumpkin puree, egg, yolks, oil, and honey. Add the flour, salt, cinnamon, ginger, allspice, and nutmeg. Fit the mixer with the dough hook and mix on low speed for 2 minutes. Hold on to the bowl to steady it and increase the speed to medium. Mix on medium for 5 minutes to develop the gluten, holding on to the mixer the entire time; the dough is stiff and can cause it to jump around.

Ferment the dough

- Use a wet hand to clean the dough off the hook. Cover the bowl with a clean kitchen towel or plastic wrap and set aside in a warm place to ferment for 1 hour.

Stretch and fold the dough	· Uncover the dough. With wet hands, scoop underneath the top edge of the dough, stretch it out, and fold it down two-thirds of the way toward the bottom edge. Stretch and fold the bottom edge to meet the top edge, as if you were folding a letter, pressing on the dough just enough to get it to stay in place. Do the same with the two sides, stretching and folding the right edge two-thirds of the way toward the left edge, and stretching and folding the left edge to meet the right edge. Then flip the dough upside down. Re-cover the bowl and let ferment for 1 hour.
Make the cinnamon swirl	· In a small bowl, stir together the cinnamon and granulated sugar for the swirl and set aside.
Shape and proof the loaf	· Lightly spray the insides of a 13 × 4-inch Pullman loaf pan with nonstick cooking spray. · Lightly dust your work surface with flour. Using a plastic bowl scraper, scoop the dough onto the work surface. Lightly dust the top of the dough with flour and pat it into a rectangle that is 12 × 14 inches, dusting with flour as needed. · Set the rectangle with a short side facing you. Brush the surface of the dough lightly with water. Sprinkle the cinnamon sugar over the surface of the dough, leaving 1 inch at the top free of cinnamon sugar. · Beginning with the edge closest to you, make one small, tight roll away from you. Continue to roll the dough away from you as tightly as you can until you've rolled it into a tight log. Adjust the log so the seam is on the bottom. Scoop the log up and place it with the seam on the bottom into the prepared pan. Use your hands to pat the loaf into the corners of the pan and even out the surface of the dough. · Whisk the egg with a pinch of salt to make an egg wash. Brush the top of the loaf with the egg wash. Set the remaining egg wash aside. · Cover the dough with a damp lightweight kitchen towel and set aside in a warm place to proof for about 2 hours, until the dough has risen and is about ¼ inch from the top rim of the pan.
Bake the loaf	· Thirty minutes before you plan to bake, arrange an oven rack in the center position and preheat the oven to 375°F. · Brush the top of the loaf a second time with the egg wash. · Bake for about 45 minutes, until the top is a mahogany brown, rotating the pan from front to back halfway through.
Cool the loaf	· Remove the loaf from the oven. Invert the pan so the loaf falls onto a cooling rack. Turn the loaf right-side up and let it cool completely.

Main de Nice

Makes 5 small loaves

Literally "hand of Nice," this bread comes from the Côte d'Azur and is perfumed with olive oil and lemon zest. There is an iconic photograph, by the photographer Robert Doisneau, of Pablo Picasso at a breakfast table with these breads.

			Baker's %
For the dough			
Water (75°F)	1½ cups	352 grams	62
Instant yeast	1½ teaspoons	4.5 grams	0.8
Bread flour	4¾ cups + more for dusting	570 grams	100
Fine sea salt	2½ teaspoons	15 grams	2.6
Extra-virgin olive oil	3 tablespoons	42 grams	7
Lemon	1		
Nonstick cooking spray			
For finishing			
Extra-virgin olive oil	1 tablespoon	14 grams	

Mix the dough

· Put the water in the bowl of a stand mixer. Sprinkle the yeast on top and let rest for 5 minutes to help dissolve the yeast. Then whisk the yeast into the water.

· Add the flour, salt, and olive oil. Use a fine Microplane to grate the lemon zest into the mixer bowl. Fit the mixer with the dough hook and mix on low speed for 3 minutes to combine the ingredients. Increase the mixer speed to medium and mix for 3 minutes to develop the gluten.

Ferment the dough

· Scrape off the hook with a wet hand. Cover the bowl with plastic wrap or a linen kitchen towel and set the dough aside at room temperature (about 70°F) to ferment for 1 hour.

Preshape and retard the dough

· Line a baking sheet with parchment paper and generously spray with nonstick cooking spray.

· Lightly dust a large work surface with flour. Transfer the dough to the floured work surface and use a bench knife to divide it into 5 (200-gram) pieces.

· Put a piece of dough on the work surface in front of you. Using both hands, shape the dough into a log by picking up the top edge and folding it a quarter of the way toward the bottom edge, pinching the top edge into the log with the tips of your fingers to create tension. Repeat, folding the top edge down by a quarter toward the center and pinching it into the dough. Do this two or three more times, until you reach the bottom of the log. Repeat with the other pieces of dough. Place the logs on the prepared baking sheet, spacing them evenly apart.

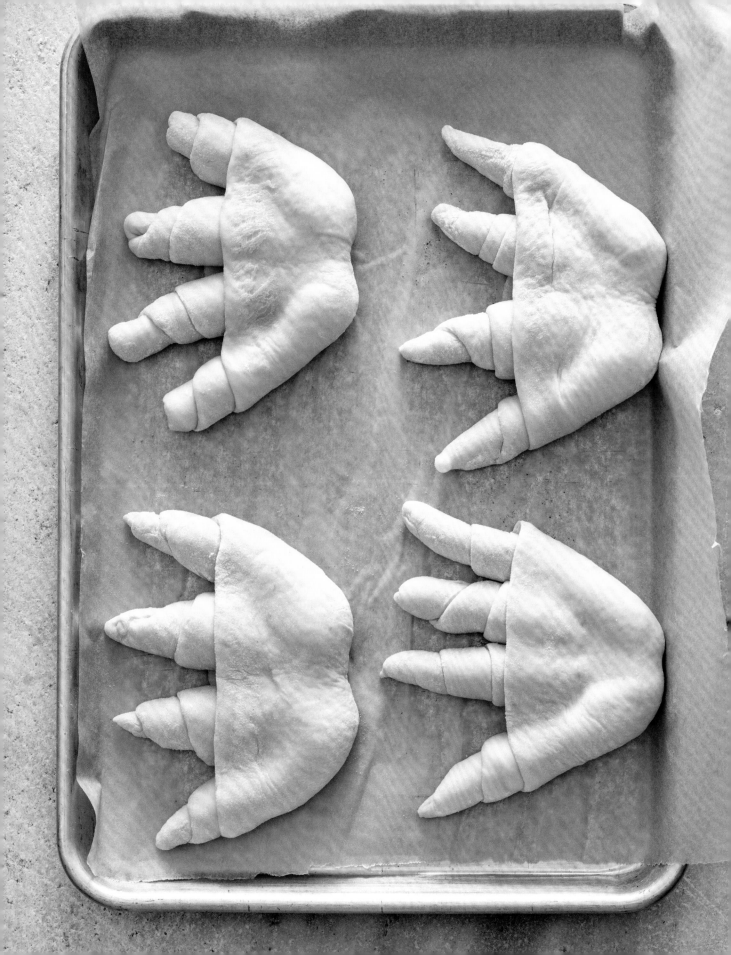

Retarding the dough relaxes the gluten and makes it easier to roll out and shape the bread.

- Spray a sheet of plastic wrap with nonstick cooking spray and place it sprayed-side down over the baking sheet to prevent the logs from developing a skin. Put the baking sheet in the refrigerator to chill the dough for at least 2 hours, or preferably overnight.

Shape and proof the breads

- Line two baking sheets with parchment paper.
- Lightly dust a large work surface with flour. Remove one piece of dough from the refrigerator and place it on the floured surface. Dust the top of the dough and a rolling pin with flour. Roll the dough into an 18 × 4-inch rectangle, rotating the dough and dusting the work surface, the dough, and the rolling pin with flour as needed to prevent the dough from sticking.
- Make a 1-inch-long, perpendicular cut in the center of each short side. Fold the small flaps of dough created by the cuts outward like you are shaping a croissant. Working from one short side at a time, roll the dough toward the center, using the palms of your hands, rolling until both sides meet in the middle.
- Fold the dough in half so that all of the "fingers" created from the rolling are on the same side, arranging the fingers so that bottom ones are in the middle and the top ones are on each end. Place the main de Nice on one of the prepared baking sheets. Continue to form the rest of the mains de Nice in the same way, arranging them on the two baking sheets.
- Lightly spray two sheets of plastic wrap with cooking spray and lay each one, sprayed-side down, over the baking sheets. Set the sheets in a warm place (about 75°F) to proof for about 1½ hours, until the breads appear puffy around the edges and do not spring back when pressed with a finger.

Bake the breads

- Thirty minutes before you plan to bake, arrange oven racks in the top third and bottom third of the oven and preheat the oven to 450°F.
- Pour about a tablespoon of water into a small bowl. Uncover the mains de Nice and gently brush them with the water.
- Place a baking sheet on each oven rack and bake for 20 to 25 minutes, until the mains de Nice are golden brown and emit a hollow sound when you tap on the bottom with a finger, switching racks and rotating the baking sheets from front to back halfway through the baking time.

Cool the breads

- Remove them from the oven and brush them all over with olive oil. Use a spatula or offset spatula to transfer them to a cooling rack to cool.

Pain au Lait Pullman

Makes one 13-inch Pullman loaf

Pain au lait, or "milk bread," has a tight crumb, and is enriched primarily with milk. This is a straightforward recipe, and I think it is on the easier side to make. There are no preferments, and the liquid and fat content are relatively low, making this dough very easy to handle.

Equipment A 13 × 4-inch Pullman loaf pan with a lid

			Baker's %
Milk	2 cups	480 grams	73
Instant yeast	2 teaspoons	6 grams	0.9
Bread flour	5½ cups + more for dusting	660 grams	100
Honey	1 tablespoon	20 grams	3.0
Fine sea salt	2½ teaspoons	15 grams	2.3
Unsalted butter, softened	6 tablespoons	84 grams	13

Mix the dough

- Pour the milk into the bowl of a stand mixer. Sprinkle the instant yeast on top of the milk and let rest for 5 minutes to help dissolve the yeast. Then whisk the yeast into the milk.
- Add the bread flour, honey, salt, and butter to the bowl. Fit the mixer with the dough hook and mix the ingredients on low speed for 2 minutes. Increase the speed to medium and mix for 5 minutes to develop the gluten.

Ferment the dough

- Remove the dough hook and wipe it clean with a wet hand. Cover the bowl with a clean kitchen towel or plastic wrap and set aside in a warm place to ferment the dough for 1 hour.

Stretch and fold the dough

- Uncover the dough. With wet hands, scoop underneath the top edge of the dough, stretch it out, and fold it down two-thirds of the way toward the bottom edge. Stretch and fold the bottom edge to meet the top edge, as if you were folding a letter, pressing on the dough just enough to get it to stay in place. Do the same with the two sides, stretching and folding the right edge two-thirds of the way toward the left edge, and stretching and folding the left edge to meet the right edge. Then flip the dough upside down. Re-cover the bowl and ferment for 1 hour.

Folding the dough halfway through the fermentation helps to develop the gluten and distribute the yeast.

Form and proof the loaf

- Lightly spray the insides and the underside of the lid of a 13-inch Pullman loaf pan with nonstick cooking spray.

• Dust a large work surface with bread flour. Using a plastic bowl scraper, scrape the dough onto the floured surface. Gently pat the dough into a rectangle about the length of the pan with a long side facing you. Use your hands to get underneath the top edge of the dough and fold it down about two-thirds of the way from the top like a letter. Scoop your hands under the bottom edge of the dough (the edge closest to you) and fold it up over the top so the bottom edge is even with the top edge. Lift the dough and flip it over into the pan so the seam is on the bottom. Use your hands to pat the dough into the corners of the pan and even out the surface of the dough. Slide the lid closed on the pan, leaving it cracked open by 1 inch.

• Place the loaf in a warm place (75°F) for 2 to 3 hours to proof the dough, until it begins to peek out of the opening in the lid. Close the lid completely and discard any dough that has been pinched off by closing the lid.

Bake the bread

• Thirty minutes before you plan to bake, arrange an oven rack in the center position and preheat the oven to 375°F.

• Bake for 45 to 50 minutes, until the top is dark golden brown. (To check for doneness, using oven mitts or kitchen towels, slide the Pullman loaf lid open enough to see the color, being careful of any steam when you open the pan.)

Cool the loaf

• Remove the loaf from the oven. Using oven mitts or kitchen towels to protect your hands, immediately slide off the lid of the loaf pan. Invert the pan so the bread falls onto a cooling rack. Let the loaf cool completely and slice as desired.

Coronation Chicken Salad

Coronation chicken was originally created to celebrate Queen Elizabeth II's coronation. I love it as a sandwich filling between slices of pain au lait. Be sure to use good-quality curry powder and mango chutney.

Makes 4 to 6 servings

Kosher salt	¼ cup	34 grams
Water (90°F)	4 cups	940 grams
Boneless, skinless chicken breasts	2 pounds	908 grams
Unsalted butter	3 tablespoons	42 grams
Onion, finely diced	1 medium (6 to 7 ounces)	200 grams
Tomato puree	½ cup	130 grams
Mango chutney	5 tablespoons	100 grams
Curry powder	2 tablespoons	10 grams
Red wine vinegar	1 tablespoon	15 grams
Fine sea salt	½ teaspoon + more to taste	3 grams
Mayonnaise	½ cup	110 grams
Whole-milk Greek yogurt	¼ cup	58 grams
Dried apricots, finely chopped	2 ounces	57 grams
Lemon juice	2 tablespoons	30 grams
Freshly ground black pepper	to taste	

• In a large bowl, whisk together the kosher salt and warm water. Submerge the chicken breasts in the brine for 30 minutes. Remove from the brine and pat dry.

• Meanwhile, arrange an oven rack in the center position with no racks above it and preheat the oven to 375°F.

• Rub 1 tablespoon of the butter over the bottom of a 9 × 13-inch baking dish. Place the chicken in the dish, cover with aluminum foil, and bake for 25 to 30 minutes, removing the foil after 20 minutes, until the chicken reaches an internal temperature of 165°F. Remove from the oven and let cool while you prepare the dressing.

• In a large saucepan, melt the remaining 2 tablespoons butter over medium heat. Add the onion and sauté for about 5 minutes, until translucent and just beginning to brown. Add the tomato puree, mango chutney, curry powder, vinegar, and salt. Bring to a simmer and cook for 5 to 7 minutes, stirring frequently to prevent scorching, until the sauce becomes a thick paste.

• Transfer the sauce to a large bowl and add the mayonnaise, yogurt, apricots, and lemon juice. Set aside.

• Shred or dice the chicken into bite-size pieces. Stir the chicken into the dressing and season to taste with salt and pepper. Refrigerate until ready to eat or use. The chicken salad will keep for 2 to 3 days refrigerated.

Fondue Brioches à Tête

Makes 11 brioches à tête

I love fondue. It picks me up in the gray days of January and February. It's warm and comforting and always reminds me of sitting near a fire when it's cold outside. And of course, it pairs perfectly with bread! One winter I toasted cubes of my sesame durum sourdough loaf to dip, and I thought that nothing could be more perfect until Meredith Erickson's *Alpine Cooking* came along. It's one of my favorite cookbooks, and this is my adaptation of her recipe. Essentially, you make a fondue, chill it down, roll it into balls, and then wrap brioche around them. Proof, bake, and rip open and eat while warm!

Plan ahead Make the brioche dough and the fondue the evening before you plan to bake. The brioche retards overnight in the refrigerator, which gives it more flavor and makes shaping the next day easier. The fondue will also chill overnight and will be easier to round into balls.

Equipment Two 6-cup jumbo muffin tins

For the dough			Baker's %
Whole milk	¼ cup	60 grams	14
Instant yeast	1 tablespoon + 1 teaspoon	15 grams	3.4
Eggs, large	4	200 grams	45
Bread flour	3⅔ cups + more for dusting	440 grams	100
Granulated sugar	¼ cup	50 grams	11
Fine sea salt	2 teaspoons	12 grams	2.7
Unsalted butter, cubed and softened	16 tablespoons	226 grams	51
Nonstick cooking spray			
For the fondue filling			
Gruyère cheese, grated	2½ cups	288 grams	
All-purpose flour	⅓ cup	40 grams	
Dry white wine	1 cup	235 grams	
Unsalted butter	3 tablespoons	42 grams	
Egg yolk, large	1	17 grams	
For baking the brioches			
Egg, large	1	50 grams	
Fine sea salt	big pinch		

Mix the dough

· Pour the milk into the bowl of a stand mixer. Sprinkle the yeast on top of the milk and let rest for 5 minutes to help dissolve the yeast. Then whisk the yeast into the milk.

· Add the eggs and put the flour, sugar, and salt on top. Fit the mixer with the dough hook and mix on low speed for 3 minutes. Turn the mixer speed up a couple of notches to medium and mix for 5 minutes to develop the gluten and create a homogeneous dough. Reduce the mixer speed to low and add the butter all at once. Continue to mix on low until the butter is incorporated into

the dough, stopping to scrape down the hook and the bowl once or twice with a plastic bowl scraper while you are incorporating the butter. Depending on how soft the butter is, this will take between 10 and 15 minutes.

Ferment the dough
· Scrape off the hook with a wet hand. Place a clean dish towel or plastic wrap over the bowl and set the dough aside at room temperature for 1 hour to ferment.

Retard the dough
· Line a baking sheet with parchment paper and spray it with nonstick cooking spray. Use a bowl scraper to scrape the dough onto the prepared baking sheet. Refrigerate the dough for at least 1 hour or up to 8 hours. If you are refrigerating the dough for longer than 1 hour, remove the baking sheet from the refrigerator after 1 hour, wrap it in plastic wrap, and return it to the refrigerator.

Make the fondue filling
· In a large bowl, toss together the Gruyère and flour and set aside. Line a baking sheet with plastic wrap and set aside.
· In a medium saucepan, combine the wine and butter and bring to a simmer over high heat. Add the cheese and flour mixture and reduce the heat to medium. Stir with a wooden spoon until the cheese is melted.
· Remove from the heat and stir the egg yolk into the cheese. Pour the fondue onto the lined baking sheet, using a silicone spatula to scrape it all out of the pan. Cover the fondue with another sheet of plastic wrap. Chill overnight in the refrigerator.

Shape and proof the brioches
· Lightly flour a large work surface. Remove the dough from the refrigerator, unwrap it if it is wrapped, and peel it from the parchment paper using a plastic scraper. Place the dough on the floured surface. Use a bench knife to cut into 11 (70-gram) pieces and 11 (10-gram) pieces.
· Put one piece of dough on the work surface closest to you. Dust your hands lightly with flour. Gently rest your palm on the dough and roll it into a tight round ball. Place the ball back onto the parchment-lined baking sheet. Continue rolling the remaining pieces, both big and small, into balls and moving them onto the baking sheet. Refrigerate for 30 to 45 minutes.
· Spray two 6-cup jumbo muffin tins with nonstick cooking spray.
· Remove the fondue from the refrigerator, discard the top sheet of plastic wrap, and use a plastic scraper to divide it, right on the baking sheet, into 11 (50-gram) pieces. Round the pieces between the palms of your hands into balls and set aside on the work surface.
· Lightly dust your work surface with more flour. Remove the baking sheet with the brioche balls from the refrigerator. Take one of the large (70-gram) balls and place it on the flour-dusted surface. Flatten the ball with the palm

of your hand into a pancake and, using a rolling pin, roll it out into a round 4½ inches in diameter. Place one of the fondue balls onto the center of the brioche round. Pull up the edges of the brioche around the fondue to cover it and gather and pinch together like you are forming a dumpling. Flip the brioche upside down so that the gathered edge is on the bottom. Take a smaller (10-gram) ball and place it on top, pinching its edges together with the large ball to seal the two balls together. Place the brioche à tête into one of the cups of the muffin tins. Continue shaping the rest of the brioches in this way until all 11 are formed.

- Cover each muffin tin with a damp lightweight kitchen towel and set aside in a warm place (75°F) for the brioches to proof for about 2 hours, until they have started to grow and fill out the muffin cups; the small têtes on top will hold an indentation when gently pressed.

Bake the brioches à tête

- Thirty minutes before you plan to bake, arrange an oven rack in the center position and preheat the oven to 350°F.
- In a small bowl, whisk the egg and salt together to make an egg wash. Uncover the brioches and lightly brush them with the egg wash (you may not use it all).
- Place both muffin tins on the oven rack and bake the brioches for 25 to 30 minutes, until they are a deep golden brown.
- Remove the tins from the oven and let the brioches cool for a few minutes. Use a small offset spatula to transfer the brioches to a cooling rack. Serve warm while the fondue is gooey. As the brioches cool down, the melted fondue will absorb into the dough. I store leftover brioches in a zippered plastic bag in my refrigerator. To reheat, place the brioches on a baking sheet in a preheated 350°F oven and toast for about 5 minutes.

Baguettes
and Ciabatta

Why are the baguettes and ciabatta in the same chapter together? Baguettes are French and ciabatta is Italian! Both are modern breads created in the twentieth century using commercial yeast. They both follow a similar fermentation schedule—traditionally they are mixed, undergo a bulk fermentation of 2 hours, are divided, shaped, and then proofed for 1 hour or so, and then baked. In a professional bakery, a daily schedule of mixing, fermenting, shaping, proofing, and baking is made that includes all the breads to be made for the day. Because of their similar fermentation schedules, baguettes and ciabatta are typically made at the same time.

In a bakery, a traditional baguette is about 26 inches long. The baguettes in this chapter are closer in size to demi baguettes (half baguettes) so that they can fit into a home oven. In France a bread decree was passed in 1993 that codified a traditional baguette (baguette de tradition). The law said that a baguette can be made only from wheat flour, water, salt and leavened by baker's yeast and/or sourdough starter. It also said that the baguette must be made in-house, from mixing through fermentation and shaping to baking. Bakers shape their baguettes with pointy ends as a way to show that they were made by hand in house. This is how I like to shape my baguettes. And I am happy to share this in the baguette recipes in this chapter.

Ciabatta is a newer bread than the baguette. It was created in 1982 in the Veneto region of Italy as a response to the number of sandwiches made in Italy using baguettes. When I worked as a baker at Sullivan Street Bakery, we made two different sizes of ciabatta—an individual size and a larger "party" size. They proofed upside down, and we would flip them over and stretch them out before baking them. Once they had cooled down, they were packed and delivered to cafes and restaurants all over New York City.

Master Class
Baguette Guide

Shaping

Baguettes are notoriously one of the most difficult breads to shape. There must be enough tension in the dough so that the baguette holds its shape and doesn't go slack, and the baguette must be even, and the dough should not tear when you are rolling it out to its long shape. Follow these tips when shaping baguettes:

- Make the preshape as even and uniform as possible. This will help make the final shape uniform. If the preshape is uneven, it can be adjusted and reshaped to make it more even.
- Aim to create tension on the surface of the dough through its contact with the work surface. At the same time, try not to deflate the bubbles created from the fermentation.
- Use enough flour on your hands and underneath the dough so it does not stick to the work surface but does not slide around either. It is better to use less bench flour than you think necessary and add more as you go, than to start out with too much flour.
- If you have too much bench flour on your work surface and your baguette is slipping around, use a bench knife to scrape some of the flour away.
- If the baguette is sticking to the work surface, pick it up and dip its bottom into a little pile of bench flour and continue shaping.

Linen couche

A baguette is proofed on a stiff, flour-dusted linen called a couche. The French verb *coucher* means "to sleep." The baguettes "sleep" on the linen as the yeast works to inflate them. In a professional bakery, the couche is 26 inches wide and about 6 feet long. The fabric is very stiff when it is new and becomes softer as it is used. The couche is placed on an 18 × 26-inch wooden bread proofing board, dusted with flour, and pulled into folds to create "walls" that cradle the baguettes as they proof.

It is important to use thick linen because it absorbs moisture from the dough, particularly for long overnight proofs in the refrigerator, and it aids in the release of the bread when it is time to be baked. If you don't have a linen couche or linen towel, thick cotton towels can also work.

Here is what to do to use the couche at home:

- Fold the couche in half lengthwise so that it is 13 inches wide (this is for making the shorter baguettes in this book) and cut it to 3 feet long. This works particularly well on an inverted baking sheet in place of the wooden proofing board.

- Roll the folded couche up very tightly.
- Place the roll on the board or baking sheet and unwind it by about 12 inches. Roll the free end in toward the main roll, forming a second smaller roll that will act as a support "wall" for the outer baguette. Dust the unrolled, flat linen between the two rolls heavily with a rice-rye flour mix.
- Place a shaped baguette seam-side down on the dusted linen so that one side of the baguette is supported by the "wall." Unwind some more of the roll and fold the linen up next to the baguette to form a second wall to cradle the loaf. Dust more of the unrolled linen and repeat, placing the second baguette down and forming a fold with the linen to cradle the second baguette. Repeat until all the baguettes are supported by the couche.
- Once the bread is removed to be baked, the damp linen must be dried completely before reusing it or rolling it back up.

Scoring   Here are my tips for successful baguette scoring:

- During baking the baguette expands along the cuts created from scoring. As a cut opens up, an edge is formed resembling an ear that pops up and away from the loaf. There are many styles of lames, which can all be used to score baguettes. I have found that a double-edged razor blade inserted into a lame handle with the blade curved up works best to create a baguette "ear."
- Hold the lame at a 45-degree angle.
- Dough with higher hydration is more difficult to score than a drier dough. Cold dough scores more easily (baguettes straight from the refrigerator) than room-temperature dough.
- The direction of the scores should be nearly parallel with the length of the baguette. Each score should be just slightly curved.
- The scores should overlap each other by about 1 inch.
- The more proofed the baguette, the less oven spring (see The Twelve Steps of Breadmaking, page 5) there will be and the shallower the score should be. Likewise, if the baguette is underproofed, the scoring should be deeper.

Sourdough Baguettes

Makes four 275-gram baguettes

This recipe uses both a sourdough starter and a poolish, and it requires a long, cold bulk fermentation and cold overnight proofing. If you make your preferments (for more detail on preferments, see Yeast Tutorial, page xxv) on Wednesday evening, you will have baguettes on Saturday morning. This might sound crazy to you, but I promise that the time spent slowly fermenting the dough and slowly proofing the baguettes produces incredibly delicious baguettes. And the actual amount of time that you will be working with the dough each day is minimal. The poolish in the recipe is used to give the dough extensibility, that stretch that is needed to elongate baguettes. (Spelt flour, which is an extremely extensible flour, is also used to help with the overall extensibility of the dough.) And the small amount of sourdough starter reduces the amount of instant yeast and allows for a long fermentation. (More sourdough starter would just speed up the fermentation.) A cold fermentation slows down the yeast, and that gives the enzymes in the flour more time to break starches into sugars, which means more flavor. The same thing happens once the baguettes are shaped. The retardation slows things down again and contributes to the flavor and texture of the baguettes.

Equipment 1 linen couche (about 26 × 35 inches), 20 × 13½-inch baking stone, 18 × 13½-inch rectangular roasting pan lid (or spray bottle of water), 12 x 12-inch oven peel (or an inverted sheet pan), flipping board (or 12 × 3-inch piece of stiff cardboard)

			Baker's %
Poolish			
Water (70°–75°F)	½ cup	118 grams	98
Instant yeast	¹⁄₁₆ teaspoon	0.15 gram	0.13
Bread flour	1 cup	120 grams	100
Sourdough Starter			
Water (70°–75°F)	4 teaspoons	20 grams	100
Mother sourdough starter	1½ teaspoons	12 grams	62.5
Bread flour	2½ tablespoons	20 grams	100
For the dough			
Water (65°–75°F)	1½ cups	353 grams	69
Bread flour	3¾ cups + more for dusting	450 grams	88
Spelt flour	½ cup	60 grams	12
Poolish (above)	1½ cups	238 grams	47
Sourdough Starter (above)	¼ cup + 1 tablespoon	52 grams	10
Instant yeast	½ teaspoon	1.5 grams	0.29
Fine sea salt	2½ teaspoons	15 grams	2.9
For dusting the couche			
Rye flour	4 tablespoons		
Brown rice flour	4 tablespoons		

Mix the poolish	▪ The evening before you plan to mix the baguette dough, pour the water into a 1-quart container (ideally one with a lid). Sprinkle the yeast on top of the water and sprinkle the bread flour on top of that. Mix with a spoon until no flour is visible, cover with the lid, and set the poolish aside at room temperature to ferment for 12 to 18 hours, until it passes the Float Test (page xxxi), checking it at 12 hours, though it could go as long as 6 additional hours. (If you find that it is taking too long, set it in a warmer place, such as near the stove.) ▪ If your poolish is ready before you are ready to use it, place it in the refrigerator. If your poolish is cold when you use it, bring your water to 80°F instead of 70° to 75°F when mixing the baguette dough.
Mix the starter	▪ Put the water in a 1-pint container with a lid. Add 25 grams (1 tablespoon) of the ripened mother sourdough starter to the container. Add the flour and stir with a metal spoon to combine. Cover the container and set aside in a warm place (about 75°F) for 4 to 6 hours, or until the starter is ripe and passes the Float Test (page xxxi).
Autolyse the dough	▪ In a stand mixer fitted with the dough hook, combine the water, bread flour, and spelt flour. Mix on low speed for 2 to 3 minutes, until no flour is visible and very few lumps remain. Remove the bowl from the stand, but leave the dough hook in the bowl. Cover the bowl with plastic or a linen kitchen towel and place it in a warm place (about 75°F) for 2 to 3 hours to autolyse. **For more information on why we are resting the dough before mixing the poolish, sourdough starter, yeast, and salt into the dough, see Autolyse (page 5).**
Add the poolish and sourdough starter to the dough	▪ As soon as both the poolish and sourdough starter are ripe (if one is ripe before the other, let it rest at room temperature until both are ripe), uncover the dough and add the poolish and starter, mixing on low speed for 3 to 5 minutes to incorporate. Turn off the mixer, leave the hook in the bowl, re-cover the dough, and let it rest for 30 minutes.
Mix the yeast and salt into the dough and ferment	▪ Uncover the dough and sprinkle the yeast and salt on the top. Return the bowl to the stand and mix with the dough hook for 2 minutes on low speed. Increase the speed to medium and mix for 4 minutes to develop the gluten. ▪ Remove the dough hook and wipe it clean with a wet hand. Use a plastic bowl scraper to scrape the dough into a shallow 3- to 4-quart container. Cover the container and set the dough in a warm place (about 75°F) for 30 minutes to ferment.
Stretch and fold the dough	▪ Uncover the container and use a wet hand to stretch and fold the top edge down two-thirds and stretch and fold the bottom edge to meet the top edge, so the dough is folded like a letter. Stretch and fold the sides inward in the same way. Re-cover the container and set aside in a warm place for 30 minutes.

Retard the dough

· Place the container of dough in the refrigerator overnight or for at least 8 hours to retard the dough.

Divide and preshape the baguettes

· Lightly dust a large work surface with flour. Remove the dough from the refrigerator and uncover it. Use a plastic bowl scraper to scrape it onto the work surface. Lightly dust the top of the dough with flour and use a bench knife to cut the dough into 4 (270-gram) pieces.

· Place one piece of dough in front of you. Dust your hands lightly with flour and gently tuck the edges of the dough inward to form a football-shaped log with a fatter middle and narrowing ends. Set aside. Repeat, forming football shapes with the remaining pieces and setting them to the side. Let the preshaped baguettes rest for 15 to 20 minutes to allow the gluten to relax.

Dusting the linen couche with a rye–rice flour mix prevents the baguettes from sticking to the couche. Rice flour is gluten-free, and rye flour is low in gluten-forming protein, which makes both ideal flours to use to dust bannetons and a couche because they are not absorbed into the dough.

Shape the baguettes

· In a small bowl, stir the rye and rice flours together, and set aside to dust the couche. Flip a baking sheet upside down and place the rolled linen couche on it. Unroll the couche by about 12 inches and dust it with some of the rye-rice flour. Set the baking sheet with the prepared couche to one side. (For more details on using the couche, see Baguette Guide, page 230.)

· Dust the work surface with more flour. Use a bench knife to scoop up one of the preshaped baguettes and place it with a long side facing you. Dust your hands lightly with flour and gently press on the baguette with the palm of your hand to flatten the dough to form it into a small oval. Pick up the long edge on the side away from you with both hands and bring your hands to the center of the dough, pushing down slightly. Repeat, folding the top edge down to the center until the top meets the bottom edge of the dough.

· Dust your hands with more flour and place them on top of the dough. Applying good pressure, rock the dough back and forth to elongate it as you move your hands apart to taper the dough into pointed ends. Continue to elongate the baguette until it reaches about 12 inches after it springs back. Place the baguette seam-side down on the floured couche. Unwind some more of the couche and fold the linen up to form a wall to cradle the baguette. Dust more of the unrolled linen with the rye–rice flour mix. Repeat shaping the remaining baguettes in the same way.

Retard the loaves

· Unwind the remaining length of couche and fold it over the shaped baguettes to cover them. Gently wrap the baking sheet of shaped baguettes with plastic wrap and refrigerate the baguettes overnight.

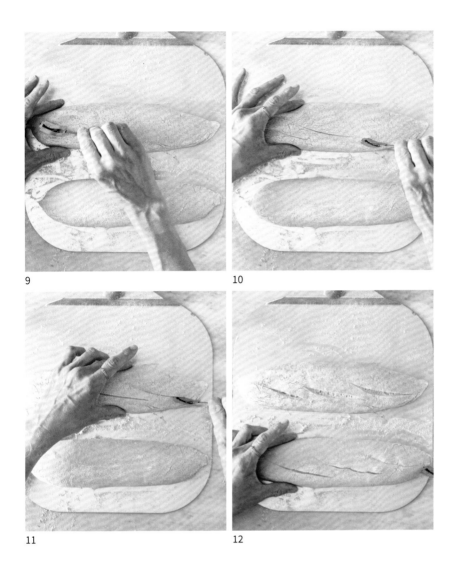

9

10

11

12

Bake the baguettes
- Thirty minutes before you plan to bake, arrange an oven rack in the center position with no racks above it. Place the baking stone on the rack and place the rectangular roaster lid on the stone (if you don't have a roaster lid, you'll use a spray bottle later). Preheat the oven to 500°F.
- Place an oven peel on a flat work surface and lightly dust it with flour. Remove the baguettes from the refrigerator and uncover them. Holding a flipping board in your right hand, with your left hand unfold the couche supporting the first baguette, pick up the couche, and flip the baguette onto the flipping board seam-side up. Flip the baguette onto the peel so that now it is seam-side down. Repeat, flipping the second baguette onto the peel. Re-cover the remaining two baguettes and return them to the refrigerator. With a razor blade held by a lame, at a 45-degree angle, or a sharp, serrated knife, score the baguettes down the center, making 3 cuts about 4 inches long and ½ inch deep. (For more detail, see Baguette Guide, page 230.)
- Open the oven and remove the roasting pan lid. Place the edge of the peel toward the back of the stone, and with a series of quick jerks, shake the baguettes off the peel and onto the stone. With oven mitts, place the roasting pan lid over the dough to cover it. (Alternatively, fill a spray bottle with water and heavily spritz the baguettes.) Close the oven door.
- Bake the baguettes for 15 minutes. Remove the roasting pan lid from the oven and bake the baguettes for 5 more minutes, until the crust is light to amber brown.

Cool the baguettes
- Slide the oven peel under the baguettes and remove them to a cooling rack to cool. Repeat baking the remaining baguettes the same way.

Schedule for Sourdough Baguettes

Here is a schedule to help you plan all of the steps to make these baguettes. Nothing is terribly difficult, but having a schedule will help you to succeed!

Day One

This day is about getting the poolish and starter ready. If your mother starter is in the refrigerator, pull it out in the morning and feed it. Otherwise, feed your mother starter in the evening at the same time you mix your poolish.

8:00 p.m. Mix the poolish and feed the mother starter.

Day Two

This is a mixing day. You will refresh the starter for the baguette dough and mix and retard the dough.

8:00 a.m. Mix the starter.
12:00 p.m. Autolyse the water and the flours for the dough.
1:30 p.m. Add the poolish, starter, salt, and yeast to the dough and ferment the dough.
2:00 p.m. Stretch and fold the dough.
2:30 p.m. Retard the dough in bulk.

Day Three

Today the dough is divided and shaped and the baguettes are retarded overnight.

8:00 a.m. Divide and preshape the baguettes.
8:30 a.m. Shape the baguettes and retard overnight.

Day Four

Baking day! (Finally!)

8:00 a.m. Preheat the oven.
8:30 a.m. Bake the baguettes.

Buckwheat Baguettes

Makes four 250-gram baguettes

I first tasted a buckwheat baguette in Paris when I was in my twenties, and I clearly remember being struck by the beautiful crumb and deep, earthy flavor. When I got home, I began to think about how to create one myself. I've tinkered with the recipe over the years, and here is the result—a sourdough baguette, with a generous proportion of buckwheat flour. Bread flour is used for structure, and both the sourdough starter and buckwheat flour are used for flavor.

Equipment 1 linen couche (about 26 × 35 inches), 20 × 13½-inch baking stone, 18 × 13½-inch rectangular roasting pan lid (or a spray bottle of water), 12 x 12-inch oven peel (or inverted sheet pan), flipping board (or 12 × 3-inch piece of stiff cardboard)

			Baker's %
Sourdough Starter			
Water (70°–75°F)	2 tablespoons + 2 teaspoons	40 grams	100
Mother sourdough starter	1 tablespoon	25 grams	62.5
Bread flour	⅓ cup	40 grams	100
For the dough			
Water (65°–75°F)	1⅔ cups	392 grams	73
Bread flour	3¾ cups + more for dusting	450 grams	83
Buckwheat flour	¾ cup	90 grams	17
Sourdough Starter (above)	½ cup + 2 tablespoons	105 grams	19
Instant yeast	½ teaspoon	1.5 grams	0.28
Fine sea salt	2 teaspoons	12 grams	2.2
For dusting the couche			
Rye flour	4 tablespoons		
Brown rice flour	4 tablespoons		

Mix the starter

· Put the water in a 1-pint container with a lid. Add 25 grams (1 tablespoon) of the ripened mother sourdough starter to the container. Add the flour and stir with a metal spoon to combine. Cover the container and set aside in a warm place (about 75°F) for 4 to 6 hours, or until the starter is ripe and passes the Float Test (page xxxi).

Autolyse the dough

· In a stand mixer fitted with the dough hook, combine the water, bread flour, and buckwheat flour. Mix on low speed for 2 to 3 minutes, until no flour is visible and very few lumps remain. Remove the dough hook, wipe it clean with a wet hand, and set it aside for later. Cover the bowl and set the dough aside in a warm place (about 75°F) to rest for 2 to 3 hours to autolyse.

For more information on why we are resting the dough before mixing the sourdough starter, yeast, and salt into the dough, see Autolyse (page 5).

Add the sourdough starter to the dough

- As soon as the sourdough starter is ripe, uncover the dough and add it, mixing on low speed for 3 to 5 minutes to incorporate. Turn off the mixer, leave the hook in the bowl, re-cover the dough, and let it rest for 30 minutes.

Mix the yeast and salt into the dough and ferment

- Uncover the dough and sprinkle the yeast and salt on the top. Return the bowl to the stand and mix with the dough hook for 2 minutes on low speed. Increase the speed to medium and mix for 4 minutes to develop the gluten.
- Remove the dough hook and wipe it clean with a wet hand. Use a plastic bowl scraper to scrape the dough into a shallow 3- to 4-quart container. Cover the container and set the dough in a warm place (about 75°F) for 30 minutes to ferment.

Stretch and fold the dough

- Uncover the container and use a wet hand to stretch and fold the top edge down two-thirds and stretch and fold the bottom edge to meet the top edge, so the dough is folded like a letter. Stretch and fold the sides inward in the same way. Re-cover the container and set aside in a warm place for 30 minutes.

Retard the dough

- Place the container of dough in the refrigerator overnight or for at least 8 hours to retard the dough.

Divide and preshape the baguettes

- Lightly dust a large work surface with flour. Remove the dough from the refrigerator and uncover it. Use a plastic bowl scraper to scrape it onto the work surface. Lightly dust the top of the dough with flour and use a bench knife to cut the dough into 4 (250-gram) pieces.
- Place one piece of dough in front of you. Dust your hands lightly with flour and gently tuck the edges of the dough inward to form a football-shaped log with a fatter middle and narrowing ends. Set aside. Repeat forming loose football shapes with the remaining pieces and setting them to the side. Let the preshaped baguettes rest for 15 to 20 minutes to allow the gluten to relax.

Dusting the linen couche with a rye–rice flour mix prevents the baguettes from sticking to the couche. Rice flour is gluten-free, and rye flour is low in gluten-forming protein, which makes both ideal flours to use to dust bannetons and couche because they are not absorbed into the dough.

Shape the baguettes and proof

- In a small bowl, stir the rye and rice flours together and set aside to dust the couche. Flip a baking sheet upside down and place the rolled linen couche on it. Unroll the couche by about 12 inches and dust it with some of the rye-rice flour. Set the baking sheet with the prepared couche to one side. (For more details on using the couche, see Baguette Guide, page 230.)
- Dust the work surface with more flour. Use a bench knife to scoop up one of the preshaped baguettes and place it with the long side facing you. Dust your

hands lightly with flour and gently press on the baguette with the palm of your hand to flatten the dough into a small oval. Pick up the long edge on the side away from you with both hands and bring your hands to the center of the dough, pushing down slightly. Repeat, folding the top down to the center until the top meets the bottom edge of the dough.

• Dust your hands with more flour and place them on top of the dough. Applying good pressure, rock the dough back and forth to elongate it as you move your hands apart to taper the dough into pointed ends. Continue to elongate the baguette until it reaches about 12 inches after it springs back. Place the baguette seam-side down on the floured couche. Unwind some more of the couche and fold the linen up to form a wall to cradle the baguette. Dust more of the unrolled linen with the rye–rice flour mix. Repeat shaping the remaining dough in the same way.

• Unwind the remaining couche and fold it over the shaped baguettes to cover them. Set the baguettes aside in a warm place (about 75°F) to proof for 1 hour.

Bake the baguettes

• About 30 minutes before the baguettes are done proofing, arrange an oven rack in the center position with no racks above it. Place the baking stone on the center rack and place the rectangular roaster lid on the stone (if you don't have a roaster lid, you'll use a spray bottle later). Preheat the oven to 500°F.

• Place an oven peel on a flat work surface and lightly dust it with flour. Uncover the baguettes. Holding a flipping board in your right hand, with your left hand unfold the couche supporting the first baguette, pick up the couche, and flip the baguette onto the flipping board seam-side up. Flip the baguette onto the peel so that now it is seam-side down. Repeat, flipping the second baguette onto the peel. Re-cover the remaining two baguettes and place them in the refrigerator to halt their proofing. With a razor blade held by a lame, at a 45-degree angle, or a sharp, serrated knife, score the baguettes down the center, making 3 cuts, about 4 inches long and ½ inch deep. (For more detail, see Baguette Guide, page 230.)

• Open the oven and remove the roasting pan lid. Place the edge of the peel toward the back of the stone, and with a series of quick jerks, shake the baguettes off the peel and onto the stone. With oven mitts, place the roasting pan lid over the dough to cover it. (Alternatively, fill a spray bottle with water and heavily spritz the baguettes.) Close the oven door.

• Bake the baguettes for 15 minutes. Remove the roasting pan lid from the oven and bake the baguettes for 5 more minutes, until the crust is light to amber brown.

Cool the baguettes

• Slide the oven peel under the baguettes and remove them to a cooling rack to cool. Repeat baking the remaining baguettes the same way.

Per Se Baguettes

Makes four 300-gram baguettes

This is the baguette recipe I used when I was head baker at Per Se restaurant. It is a classic recipe for baguettes, using only poolish for its preferment (for more detail on preferments, see Yeast Tutorial, page xxv). Poolish makes baguette dough extensible so it can be stretched and shaped without tearing. When water is added to flour, protease, an enzyme found in flour and yeast, goes to work and breaks the protein into smaller pieces. This makes the dough flow. Poolish has relatively high protease activity, and adding it to baguette dough helps to make shaping easier. And poolish is relatively easy to make and does not need to be maintained like sourdough starter. That is why a poolish baguette is considered a classic baguette, and it has become my go-to when I need to make baguettes but do not have enough time for a long fermentation.

Equipment 1 linen couche (about 26 × 35 inches), 20 × 13½-inch baking stone, 18 × 13½-inch rectangular roasting pan lid (or spray bottle of water), 12 x 12-inch oven peel (or inverted baking sheet), flipping board (or 12 × 3-inch piece of stiff cardboard)

Poolish			Baker's %
Water (70°–75°F)	½ cup	118 grams	98
Instant yeast	1/16 teaspoon	0.15 gram	0.13
Bread flour	1 cup	120 grams	100
For the dough			
Water (65°–75°F)	1½ cups	353 grams	73
Bread flour	4 cups + more for dusting	480 grams	100
Poolish (above)	1½ cups	238 grams	50
Instant yeast	½ teaspoon	1.5 grams	0.31
Fine sea salt	2 teaspoons	12 grams	2.5
For dusting the couche			
Rye flour	4 tablespoons		
Brown rice flour	4 tablespoons		

Make the poolish

• The evening before you plan to make the baguettes (12 hours before you plan to mix the dough), pour the water into a 1-quart container (ideally one with a lid). Sprinkle the yeast on top of the water and sprinkle the bread flour on top of that. Mix with a spoon until no flour is visible, cover with the lid, and set the poolish aside at room temperature to ferment for 12 to 18 hours, until it passes the Float Test (page xxxi), checking it at 12 hours, though it could go as long as 6 additional hours. (If you find that it is taking too long, set it in a warmer place, such as near the stove.)

• If your poolish is ready before you are ready to use it, place it in the refrigerator. If using refrigerated poolish, bring your water to 80°F instead of 70° to 75°F when mixing the baguette dough.

Autolyse the dough

• In a stand mixer fitted with the dough hook, combine the water and bread flour and mix on low speed for 2 to 3 minutes, until no flour is visible and very few lumps remain. Remove the bowl from the stand, but leave the dough hook in the bowl. Cover the bowl with plastic or a linen kitchen towel and place it in a warm place (about 75°F) for about 90 minutes to autolyse.

For more information on why we are resting the dough before mixing the poolish, salt, and yeast into the dough, see Autolyse (page 5).

Add the poolish to the dough

· As soon as the poolish is ripe, uncover the dough and add the poolish, mixing on low speed for 3 to 5 minutes to incorporate. Turn off the mixer, leave the hook in the bowl, re-cover the dough, and let it rest for 30 minutes.

Mix the yeast and salt into the dough and ferment

· Uncover the dough and sprinkle the yeast and salt on the top. Return the bowl to the stand and mix with the dough hook for 2 minutes on low speed. Increase the speed to medium and mix for 4 minutes to develop the gluten.
· Remove the dough hook and wipe it clean with a wet hand. Cover the bowl and set the dough in a warm place (about 75°F) for 1 hour to ferment.

Stretch and fold the dough

· Uncover the bowl and use a wet hand to stretch and fold the top edge down two-thirds and stretch and fold the bottom edge to meet the top edge, so the dough is folded like a letter. Stretch and fold the sides inward in the same way. Re-cover the bowl and set aside for 1 hour to ferment.

Divide and preshape the baguettes

· Lightly dust a large work surface with flour. Uncover the dough and use a plastic bowl scraper to scrape the dough onto the work surface. Lightly dust the top of the dough with flour and use a bench knife to cut the dough into 4 (300-gram) pieces.
· Place one piece of dough in front of you on the work surface. Dust your hands lightly with flour and gently tuck the edges of the dough inward and form a football-shaped log with a fatter middle and narrowing ends. Set aside. Repeat forming football shapes with the remaining pieces and setting them to the side. Let the preshaped baguettes rest for 15 to 20 minutes to allow the gluten to relax.

Dusting the linen couche with a rye–rice flour mix prevents the baguettes from sticking to the couche. Rice flour is gluten-free, and rye flour is low in gluten-forming protein, which makes both ideal flours to use to dust bannetons and couche because they are not absorbed into the dough.

Shape the baguettes and proof

· In a small bowl, stir the rye and rice flours together and set aside to dust the couche. Flip a baking sheet upside down and place the rolled linen couche on it. Unroll the edge of the couche by about 12 inches and dust it with some of the rye-rice flour. Set the baking sheet with the prepared couche to one side. (For more details on using the couche, see Baguette Guide, page 230.)

- Dust the work surface with more flour. Use a bench knife to scoop up one of the preshaped baguettes and place it with the long side facing you. Dust your hands lightly with flour and gently press on the baguette with the palm of your hand to flatten the dough into a small oval. Pick up the long edge on the side away from you with both hands and bring your hands to the center of the dough, pushing down slightly. Repeat, folding the top edge down to the center until the top meets the bottom edge of the dough.
- Dust your hands with more flour and place them on top of the dough. Applying good pressure, rock the dough back and forth to elongate it as you move your hands apart to taper the dough into pointed ends. Continue to elongate the baguette until it reaches about 12 inches after it springs back. Place the baguette seam-side down on the floured couche. Unwind some more of the couche and fold the linen up to form a wall to cradle the baguette. Dust more of the unrolled linen with the rye–rice flour mix. Repeat shaping the remaining dough in the same way.
- Unwind the remaining couche and fold it over the shaped baguettes to cover them. Proof the baguettes for 1 hour.

Bake the baguettes

- About 30 minutes before the baguettes are done proofing, arrange an oven rack in the center position with no oven racks above it. Place a baking stone on the center rack and place the rectangular roaster lid on the stone (if you don't have a roaster lid, you'll use a spray bottle later). Preheat the oven to 500°F.
- Place an oven peel on a flat work surface and lightly dust it with flour. Remove the baguettes from the refrigerator and uncover them. Holding a flipping board in your right hand, with your left hand unfold the couche supporting the first baguette, pick up the couche, and flip the baguette onto the flipping board seam-side up. Flip the baguette onto the peel so that now it is seam-side down. Repeat, flipping the second baguette onto the peel. Re-cover the remaining two baguettes and return them to the refrigerator. With a razor blade held by a lame, at a 45-degree angle, or a sharp, serrated knife, score the baguettes down the center making 3 cuts, about 4 inches long and ½ inch deep. (For more detail, see Baguette Guide, page 230.)
- Open the oven and remove the roasting pan lid. Place the edge of the peel toward the back of the stone, and with a series of quick jerks, shake the baguettes off the peel and onto the stone. With oven mitts, place the roasting pan lid over the dough to cover it. (Alternatively, fill a spray bottle with water and heavily spritz the baguettes.) Close the oven door.
- Bake the baguettes for 15 minutes. Remove the roasting pan lid from the oven and bake the baguettes for 5 more minutes, until the crust is light to amber brown.

Cool the baguettes

- Slide the oven peel under the baguettes and remove them to a cooling rack to cool. Repeat baking the remaining baguettes the same way.

Spelt Ciabatta

Makes two 500-gram ciabatta

Ciabatta—the Italian word for "slipper"—is so named because of its flattened, rectangular shape. It is Italy's answer to the baguette. One of its most desirable qualities is its large holes, which is where the spelt flour in this recipe comes into play. The air bubbles in the bread will inflate better if the cell walls of the alveoli (the gas bubbles or pockets of air) are extensible, and spelt flour has superior extensibility properties.

Equipment A 20 × 13½-inch baking stone, 18 × 13½-inch rectangular roasting pan lid, 12-inch oven peel

Poolish			Baker's %
Water (70°–75°F)	½ cup	118 grams	98
Instant yeast	¹⁄₁₆ teaspoon	0.15 gram	0.13
Bread flour	½ cup	60 grams	50
Spelt flour	½ cup	60 grams	50
For the dough			
Water (70°–75°F)	1⅓ cups	313 grams	70
Bread flour	2½ cups + more for dusting	300 grams	67
Spelt flour	1¼ cups	150 grams	33
Poolish (above)	2 cups	238 grams	53
Instant yeast	1 teaspoon	3 grams	0.67
Fine sea salt	2 teaspoons	12 grams	2.7

Make the poolish

· The evening before you plan to make the ciabatta (12 hours before you plan to mix the dough), pour the water into a 1-quart container (ideally one with a lid). Sprinkle the yeast on top of the water and sprinkle the bread flour and spelt flour on top of that. Mix with a spoon until no flour is visible, cover with a lid (or plastic wrap), and set the poolish aside at room temperature to ferment for 12 to 18 hours, until it passes the Float Test (page xxxi), checking it at 12 hours, though it could go as long as 6 additional hours. (If you find that it is taking too long, set it in a warmer place, such as near the stove.)

· If your poolish is ready before you are ready to use it, place it in the refrigerator. If using refrigerated poolish, bring your water to 80°F instead of 70°F when mixing the ciabatta dough.

Autolyse the dough

· In a stand mixer fitted with the dough hook, combine the water, bread flour, and spelt flour. Mix on low speed for 2 to 3 minutes, until no flour is visible and very few lumps remain. Remove the bowl from the stand, but leave the dough hook in the bowl. Set the dough aside to rest in a warm place (about 75°F) for 1 hour.

For more information on why we are resting the dough before mixing the poolish, salt, and yeast into the dough, see Autolyse (page 5).

Add the poolish, yeast, and salt to the dough

· Scoop the poolish out of its container and onto the top of the dough and place the yeast and salt on the top of the poolish. Return the bowl to the stand and mix with the dough hook for about 2 minutes on low speed. Increase the speed to medium and mix for 5 minutes to develop the gluten.

Ferment the dough

· Remove the dough hook and wipe it clean with a wet hand. Cover the bowl with plastic or a linen kitchen towel and set the dough in a warm place (about 75°F) for 1 hour to ferment.

Stretch and fold the dough

· Uncover the bowl and use a wet hand to stretch and fold the top edge down two-thirds and stretch and fold the bottom edge to meet the top edge, so the dough is folded like a letter. Stretch and fold the sides inward in the same way. Re-cover the bowl and set aside for 1 hour to ferment.

Shape and proof the ciabatta

· Uncover the bowl. Heavily dust a work surface with flour. Use a plastic bowl scraper to scrape the dough onto the floured work surface. Dust the top of the dough with more flour. With a bench knife, cut the dough in half. Separate the two halves and gently coax each into an 8-inch square. Cover the two loaves with a lightweight kitchen towel and proof for 1 hour at room temperature, until they appear puffy around the edges and the sides do not spring back when pressed with a finger.

As the ciabatta proofs on the floured surface, it will absorb some of the flour. Using an ample amount of flour on the work surface prevents the ciabatta from sticking.

Bake the ciabatta

· About 30 minutes before the ciabatta is done proofing, arrange an oven rack in the center position with no oven racks above it. Place the baking stone on the center rack and place the rectangular roaster lid on the stone. Preheat the oven to 500°F.
· Place an oven peel on a flat work surface and lightly dust it with flour. Uncover the dough and use the bench knife to scoop under one of the pieces of dough. Use your free hand and bench knife to cradle the dough and flip it upside down, transferring it onto the edge of the peel. Re-cover the remaining piece of dough with the kitchen towel.
· Open the oven and remove the roaster pan lid from the oven. Place the edge of the peel toward the back of the stone, and with a series of quick jerks, shake the ciabatta off the peel and onto the stone. With oven mitts, place the roasting pan lid over the dough to cover it. Close the oven door.
· Bake the ciabatta for 15 minutes. Remove the roasting pan lid from the oven and reduce the oven temperature to 450°F. Bake the ciabatta for 5 to 10 minutes more, until it has a nicely burnished crust.

Cool the bread

· Slide the oven peel under the bread and place the bread on a cooling rack to cool. Repeat, baking the second loaf the same way.

Schedule for Spelt Ciabatta

Day One

This day is about getting the poolish ready.

8:00 p.m. Mix the poolish.

Day Two

Today you will mix, ferment, shape, proof, and bake the ciabatta.

8:00 a.m. Autolyse the water and the flours for the dough.
9:00 a.m. Add the poolish, salt, and yeast to the dough and mix the dough.
10:00 a.m. Stretch and fold the dough.
11:00 a.m. Divide the dough and begin to proof the two loaves.
12:00 p.m. Bake the first loaf.
12:30 p.m. Bake the second loaf.

Pan Bagnat

Makes 9 sandwiches

One of the things I love about French cuisine is its use of old bread and pastries. Bread for fondue is so stale it's practically rock hard. If it were any less stale, it would disintegrate in the hot melted cheese. Almond croissants are day-old croissants soaked in a simple syrup and baked to crispy perfection. And this sandwich uses day-old bread. Pan bagnat is a Provençal sandwich from Nice made with bread imbued with olive oil and filled with crudités and ingredients normally found in a salade Niçoise. The key here is that the bread must be stale enough to properly soak up all of the olive oil (in a pinch, you can dry the bread out in the oven; see Note). The longer the sandwich soaks, weighted down in the refrigerator, the better it will be.

Note To dry out bread that isn't stale enough, preheat the oven to 300°F. Place the loaf directly on a rack and toast for 15 minutes to remove some of the moisture. Remove from the oven and cool.

Eggs, large	3	
Garlic, minced	3 cloves	
Red wine vinegar	1 tablespoon	15 grams
Extra-virgin olive oil	7 tablespoons	98 grams
Anchovy fillets, minced	3	
Fine sea salt	to taste	
Freshly ground black pepper	to taste	
Sun-dried tomatoes, dry-pack	½ cup	55 grams
Spelt Ciabatta (page 247)	1 loaf	
Romaine lettuce	4 to 6 small leaves	
Tuna, good-quality, oil-packed	2 (5-ounce) cans, drained	
Oil-cured black olives, pitted	½ cup	90 grams

• In a small pot, combine the eggs with cold water to cover by 1 inch. Bring to a full boil, then turn off the heat. Let the eggs cook in the hot water for 10 minutes. While the eggs are in the hot water, fill a bowl with ice and water to make an ice bath. Use a slotted spoon to transfer the eggs to the ice bath and let them rest for about 10 minutes, until they are cool. Peel the eggs, rinsing them in the ice bath to remove any bits of shell. Dry the eggs with a kitchen towel and then cut into slices ¼ inch thick.

• In a small bowl, whisk together the garlic, vinegar, 3 tablespoons of the olive oil, the minced anchovies, and a little salt and pepper to taste. Set aside.

• Place the sun-dried tomatoes in another small bowl and cover with boiling water. Let soak for 5 minutes and then drain in a small fine-mesh sieve.

• Slice the ciabatta in half horizontally, making even top and bottom layers. Drizzle 2 tablespoons of the olive oil over the bottom half of the ciabatta and repeat, drizzling the remaining 2 tablespoons oil over the top half.

- Arrange the romaine leaves evenly over the bottom piece of the bread. Top with the tuna, then the black olives and sliced eggs. Top the eggs with the sun-dried tomatoes and drizzle the garlic vinaigrette over the tomatoes, letting it soak through the layers. Cover with the top ciabatta half.
- Wrap the sandwich tightly with plastic wrap and place in a zippered plastic bag. Put the sandwich on a large plate and weight it down with something heavy, like a cast-iron skillet. Refrigerate overnight, or for at least several hours, flipping it halfway through so that both pieces of bread get soaked.
- To serve, unwrap the sandwich and place it on a cutting board. Use a bread knife to slice it into nine squares.

Semolina Ciabatta

Makes two 500-gram ciabatta

I use both durum flour and coarse semolina, in addition to bread flour, to add chew, crunch, and flavor in this variation on the classic.

Equipment A 20 × 13½-inch baking stone, 18 × 13½-inch rectangular roasting pan lid, 12-inch oven peel

Poolish			Baker's %
Water (70°–75°F)	⅓ cup	78 grams	98
Instant yeast	¹⁄₁₆ teaspoon	0.15 gram	0.19
Bread flour	⅔ cup	80 grams	100
For the dough			
Water (70°–75°F)	1½ cups	353 grams	72
Durum flour	3 cups	360 grams	73
Coarse semolina	⅔ cup	93 grams	19
Bread flour	⅓ cup + more for dusting	40 grams	8
Poolish (above)	1 cup	158 grams	32
Instant yeast	½ teaspoon	1.5 grams	0.3
Fine sea salt	2 teaspoons	12 grams	2.4

Mix the poolish

• The evening before you plan to make the ciabatta (12 hours before you plan to mix the dough), pour the water into a 1-quart container (ideally one with a lid). Sprinkle the yeast on top of the water and sprinkle the bread flour on top of that. Mix with a spoon until no flour is visible, cover with the lid (or plastic wrap), and set the poolish aside at room temperature to ferment for 12 to 18 hours, until it passes the Float Test (page xxxi), checking it at 12 hours, though it could go as long as 6 additional hours. (If you find that it is taking too long, set it in a warmer place, such as near the stove.)

• If your poolish is ready before you are ready to use it, place it in the refrigerator. If using refrigerated poolish, bring your water to 80°F instead of 70°F when mixing the ciabatta dough.

Autolyse the dough

• In a stand mixer fitted with the dough hook, combine the water, durum flour, semolina, and bread flour. Mix on low speed for 2 to 3 minutes, until no flour is visible and very few lumps remain. Remove the bowl from the stand, but leave the dough hook in the bowl. Set the dough aside in a warm place (about 75°F) for 1 hour.

For more information on why we are resting the dough before mixing the poolish, salt, and yeast into the dough, see Autolyse (page 5).

Add the poolish, yeast, and salt to the dough

• Scoop the poolish out of its container and onto the top of the dough and place the yeast and salt on the top of the poolish. Return the bowl to the stand

and mix with the dough hook for about 2 minutes on low speed. Increase the speed to medium and mix for 5 minutes to develop the gluten.

Ferment the dough

• Remove the dough hook and wipe it clean with a wet hand. Cover the bowl with plastic or a linen kitchen towel and set the dough in a warm place (about 75°F) for 1 hour to ferment.

Stretch and fold the dough

• Uncover the bowl and use a wet hand to stretch and fold the top edge down two-thirds and stretch and fold the bottom edge to meet the top edge, so the dough is folded like a letter. Stretch and fold the sides inward in the same way. Re-cover the bowl and set aside for 1 hour to ferment.

Shape and proof the ciabatta

• Uncover the bowl. Heavily dust a work surface with flour. Use a plastic bowl scraper to scrape the dough onto the floured work surface. Dust the top of the dough with more flour. With a bench knife, cut the dough in half. Separate the two halves and gently coax each into an 8-inch square. Cover the two loaves with a lightweight kitchen towel and proof for 1 hour at room temperature, until they appear puffy around the edges and the sides do not spring back when pressed with a finger.

As the ciabatta proofs on the floured surface, it will absorb some of the flour. Using an ample amount of flour on the work surface prevents the ciabatta from sticking.

Bake the ciabatta

• About 30 minutes before the ciabatta is done proofing, arrange an oven rack in the center position with no oven racks above it. Place the baking stone on the center rack and place the rectangular roaster lid on the stone. Preheat the oven to 500°F.

• Place an oven peel on a flat work surface and lightly dust it with flour. Uncover the dough and use the bench knife to scoop under one of the pieces of dough. Use your free hand and bench knife to cradle the dough and flip it upside down, transferring it onto the edge of the peel. Re-cover the remaining piece of dough with the kitchen towel.

• Open the oven and remove the roaster pan lid from the oven. Place the edge of the peel toward the back of the stone, and with a series of quick jerks, shake the ciabatta off the peel and onto the stone. With oven mitts, place the roasting pan lid over the dough to cover it. Close the oven door.

• Bake the ciabatta for 15 minutes. Remove the roasting pan lid from the oven and reduce the oven temperature to 450°F. Bake the ciabatta for 5 to 10 minutes more, until it has a nicely burnished crust.

Cool the bread

• Slide the oven peel under the bread and place the bread on a cooling rack to cool. Repeat baking the second loaf the same way.

Pizza and Focaccia

You may be surprised to find a chapter on pizza (and focaccia) in a bread book. In many peoples' minds, pizza is separate and distinct from bread. Bread is a sliced loaf served at the beginning of the meal with butter or olive oil, and pizza is a meal. In my mind, they are both bread. They both require an understanding of mixing, fermentation, shaping, proofing, and baking. Pizza is a delicious flatbread with fun savory toppings.

When I worked at Roberta's as head baker, I was responsible for the bread program, which was separate from the pizza. I worked in the same space as the pizza team, watching them mix, shape, and retard their dough, as I mixed, shaped, and retarded my baguettes. We shared one large spiral mixer, taking turns mixing bread and pizza doughs. In fact, we shared nearly everything, including the pizza oven, which I used in conjunction with the bread oven to take advantage of the extra oven space.

The wood-fired oven at Roberta's was too hot to bake bread when the pizzas were being fired, but by morning, it had cooled down to roughly 500° to 600°F, which was a perfect temperature to bake loaves of sourdough bread.

In Naples, Italy, the birthplace of modern pizza, the pizza must conform to the standards set forth by the Associazione Verace Pizza Napoletana. The dough can contain only flour with a protein content between 11% and 13.5%, yeast, salt, and water. And the pizza must be baked in a 900°F oven for 60 to 90 seconds. These two requirements alone dictate much about how the pizza can be made. With such a hot oven temperature, the hydration of the dough needs to be low enough so that the pizza bakes in the required amount of time. This means that most Neapolitan pizza doughs have a hydration of about 60% (baker's percentage). Most home ovens don't get hotter than 500°F, which means it will take longer to bake the pizza. My pizza recipes reflect this by adding more water and some olive oil to keep the dough soft and hydrated during the longer bake time.

This chapter contains recipes for both yeasted and sourdough pizza dough that can be used interchangeably with one caveat: The sourdough pizza dough cannot be held indefinitely in the refrigerator because it becomes too acidic.

Master Recipe
Yeasted
Pizza Dough

Makes enough for 3 pizza biancas or 12-inch pizzas

I have made a lot of pizza at home, always tinkering with both the dough and the toppings. I've made straight pizza doughs—those without sourdough—and I've made a variety of sourdough pizzas, some with both a poolish and sourdough. The pizzas were all very good, but it wasn't until I did a pop-up with Joe Beddia, the owner of Pizzeria Beddia in Philadelphia, that my pizza dough skyrocketed into keeper territory. Joe added a small amount of olive oil to his dough, and I thought this was clever. Adding olive oil helps soften the dough so that it does not become cracker crisp while it's baking. This helps when you're baking pizza in a home oven at temperatures between 500° and 550°F. It also helps if you're baking pizza in a bread oven, like I did, because an electric bread oven also does not get super hot like a commercial pizza oven does.

I use about 10% spelt flour in my dough because spelt adds extensibility to the dough, which means it helps you stretch the dough out more easily. (For more detail about spelt flour, see Spelt Flour, page xvii.) I also like to autolyse my pizza dough. I combine the water and flours and let them rest alone without any interference from yeast, salt, or other ingredients. My autolyse time is long—2 to 3 hours. I know this is asking a lot, but please try it. Even a 1-hour autolyse is better than nothing. Still, if you are short on time, you can skip the autolyse and still have killer pizza dough with this recipe. One last note—I use rice flour on my oven peel to help the pizza shimmy into the oven. Rice flour is coarse (most rice flour, that is) like semolina, and its coarseness helps the pizza dough slide off the peel more quickly. You can substitute semolina or cornmeal if you have those on hand.

			Baker's %
Water (70°–75°F)	1⅔ cups	392 grams	69
Bread flour	4¼ cups + more for dusting	510 grams	89
Spelt flour	½ cup	60 grams	11
Water, warm (90°F)	1 tablespoon	15 grams	2.6
Instant yeast	½ teaspoon	1.5 grams	0.3
Extra-virgin olive oil	1½ tablespoons	24 grams	4.0
Fine sea salt	2½ teaspoons	15 grams	2.6
Nonstick cooking spray			

Autolyse the dough

· In a stand mixer fitted with the dough hook, combine the 70°–75°F water, the bread flour, and the spelt flour. Mix on low for 2 to 3 minutes until there are no visible dry patches of flour.
· Remove the bowl from the stand, but leave the dough hook in the bowl. Cover the bowl with plastic or a linen kitchen towel and place it in a warm place (about 75°F) for 2 to 3 hours to autolyse.

For more information on why we are resting the dough before mixing the yeast, olive oil, and salt into the dough, see Autolyse (page 5).

Add the yeast, olive oil, and salt to the dough

· Place 1 tablespoon (15 grams) warm water in a small bowl. Sprinkle the yeast onto the water and let it rest for 5 minutes. With a teaspoon, stir the yeast into the water to dissolve it. Uncover the bowl of dough and add the yeast mixture, olive oil, and salt. Mix on low speed for 3 to 5 minutes to incorporate the ingredients.

Ferment the dough

· Remove the dough hook and wipe it clean with a wet hand. Re-cover the bowl and set it aside for 30 minutes to ferment.

Make 2 stretch and folds and retard the dough

· Uncover the dough. With wet hands, scoop underneath the top edge of the dough, stretch it out, and fold it down two-thirds of the way toward the bottom edge. Stretch out and fold the bottom edge up to meet the top edge, as if you were folding a letter, pressing on the dough just enough to get it to stay in place. Do the same with the two sides, stretching and folding the right edge two-thirds of the way toward the left edge, and stretching and folding the left edge to meet the right edge. Then flip the dough upside down. This is your first fold. Re-cover the bowl and let the dough rest for 30 minutes.
· Repeat the stretching and folding a second time for the second fold. Re-cover the bowl and place it into the refrigerator to retard overnight or for a minimum of 8 hours.

Divide, preshape, and proof the dough

· Line a baking sheet with parchment paper and spray the paper with nonstick cooking spray.
· Lightly dust your work surface with flour. Using a plastic bowl scraper, scoop the dough onto the floured surface. Dust the top of the dough with flour and use a bench knife to divide it into 3 (325-gram) pieces.
· Put one piece of dough on the work surface in front of you. Dust your hands lightly with flour. Gently rest your palm on the dough and roll it into a tight round ball. Put the ball on the prepared baking sheet and repeat with the remaining dough, spacing them evenly on the baking sheet.
· Spray a sheet of plastic wrap with nonstick cooking spray and place it, sprayed-side down, to cover the baking sheet. Let the dough rise for 1½ to 2 hours, until a finger poked in the center of the dough holds its indentation.

Master Recipe
Sourdough Pizza Dough

Makes enough for 3 pizza biancas or 12-inch pizzas

I always dream of making (and eating!) naturally leavened (sourdough!) pizza. It is more toothsome, which appeals to me, and has a complex flavor. And like large sourdough loaves of bread, there is art and science in making sourdough pizza. Once I had my dream yeasted pizza dough recipe, I wondered what it would be like if I replaced the instant yeast with sourdough starter. Could this become my dream sourdough pizza? Could it be as simple as that? The short answer is yes, but with a few tricks. Anytime you add sourdough starter to a recipe, it makes the dough feel wetter, and the dough becomes more difficult to handle. That is why the autolyse of the water with the flours is so important. It really tightens things up. It helps the gluten formation kick-start without the interference of the yeast, salt, and other ingredients. So please don't skip the autolyse here. And yes, a longer autolyse here helps. Don't wait until the starter is too ripe. A young starter that just begins to pass the Float Test (yes, that again, see page xxxi) has a lot of energy, like a young athlete. Using a young starter will translate to your dough, and the pizza will have more oven spring. Lastly, this dough does best when used within 24 hours. You might be tempted to make one pizza and refrigerate the remaining rounds for later. If the dough sits for too long in the refrigerator it becomes too acidic.

You can use this recipe interchangeably with the Yeasted Pizza Dough (page 258), although this is my favorite for making Pizza Bianca (page 276), as it lets the flavors shine on their own.

Sourdough Starter			Baker's %
Water (70°–75°F)	2 tablespoons + 2 teaspoons	40 grams	100
Mother sourdough starter	1 tablespoon	25 grams	62.5
Bread flour	⅓ cup	40 grams	100
For the dough			
Water (70°–75°F)	1⅔ cups	392 grams	69
Bread flour	4¼ cups + more for dusting	510 grams	89
Spelt flour	½ cup	60 grams	11
Sourdough Starter (above)	½ cup + 2 tablespoons	105 grams	18
Extra-virgin olive oil	1½ tablespoons	24 grams	4.0
Fine sea salt	2½ teaspoons	15 grams	2.6
Nonstick cooking spray			

Mix the starter

• Mix the sourdough starter 2 to 3 hours before autolysing the water and flour. Put the water in a ½-quart container with a lid. Add 25 grams (1 tablespoon) of the ripened mother sourdough starter and all the flour and stir with a metal spoon to combine. Cover the container and set aside in a warm place (about 75°F) for 4 to 5 hours, or until it is ripe and passes the Float Test (page xxxi).

Autolyse the dough	• In a stand mixer fitted with the dough hook, combine the water, bread flour, and spelt flour. Mix on low speed for 2 to 3 minutes, until there are no visible dry patches of flour. Remove the bowl from the stand, but leave the dough hook in the bowl. Cover the bowl with plastic or a linen kitchen towel and place it in a warm place (about 75°F) for 2 to 3 hours to autolyse.
	For more information on why we are resting the dough before mixing the sourdough starter, olive oil, and salt into the dough, see Autolyse (page 5).
Add the sourdough starter to the dough	• As soon as the starter is ripe, add it to the dough, mixing on low speed for 3 to 5 minutes to incorporate it. Turn off the mixer, leave the dough hook in the bowl, re-cover the bowl, and let the dough rest for 30 minutes.
Mix the olive oil and salt into the dough	• Add the olive oil and the salt to the dough and mix on low speed for 3 to 5 minutes to incorporate.
Ferment the dough	• Remove the dough hook and wipe it clean with a wet hand. Re-cover the bowl and set it aside for 1 hour to ferment.
Make 2 stretch and folds and retard the dough	• Uncover the dough. With wet hands, scoop underneath the top edge of the dough, stretch it out, and fold it down two-thirds of the way toward the bottom edge. Stretch out and fold the bottom edge up to meet the top edge, as if you were folding a letter, pressing on the dough just enough to get it to stay in place. Do the same with the two sides, stretching and folding the right edge two-thirds of the way toward the left edge, and stretching and folding the left edge to meet the right edge. Then flip the dough upside down. This is your first fold. Re-cover the bowl and set the dough aside for 1 hour. • Repeat the stretching and folding a second time for a second fold. Re-cover the bowl and place the dough in the refrigerator to retard overnight or for a minimum of 12 hours.
Divide, preshape, and proof the dough	• Line a baking sheet with parchment paper and spray it with nonstick cooking spray. • Lightly dust your work surface with flour. Using a plastic dough scraper, scoop the dough onto the floured surface. Dust the top of the dough with flour and use a bench knife to divide it into 3 (360-gram) pieces. • Put one portion of dough on the work surface in front of you. Dust your hands lightly with flour. Gently rest your palm on the dough and roll it into a tight round ball. Put the ball on the prepared baking sheet and repeat with the remaining dough, spacing the balls evenly on the baking sheet. • Spray a sheet of plastic wrap with nonstick cooking spray and place it, sprayed-side down, over the baking sheet. Let the dough rise for 2 to 2½ hours, until a finger poked in the center of the dough leaves an indentation.

1　2　3

4　5　6

7　8　9

Master Class
Shaping and Baking Pizza

Preshape the pizza dough into balls	In breadmaking, preshaping dough helps to make the final dough shape nice and even. In pizza making, the dough should be preshaped into balls so that the pizzas can be shaped into rounds. I call for 325- to 360-gram pieces because that amount of dough will yield 12-inch pizzas. If you have a larger peel or baking stone, the dough can be divided into larger pieces. I like to use 450 grams of dough for a 16-inch pizza.
Proof the pizza dough	Like any dough, pizza dough should be proofed before baking. Choose a warm place, away from drafts, to let the dough proof. Sourdough dough takes longer to proof than yeasted dough. While the dough is proofing, organize the toppings and preheat the oven.
Prepare the pizza toppings in advance	The toppings for Pizza Rossa (page 268) and Pizza Margherita (page 271) do not require a lot of time to prepare. They can be prepared while the pizza is proofing. The tomatoes should be crushed, mozzarella cut, and finishing ingredients should be organized so that they are ready to go (pluck the basil leaves). The toppings for Best Clam Pizza (page 273), however, require more time and should be started before the dough balls begin to proof. I like to cook the clams and reduce the broth in the morning. I let the broth chill and then whip the cream while the dough balls are proofing.
Preheat the oven and baking stone	Arrange an oven rack in the center of the oven and place a baking stone on it. It is best to preheat the oven for 1 hour, which can be done while the dough is proofing.
Set up a pizza station to make workflow efficient	Place a small bowl of bench flour on the work surface where the pizza ball will be stretched. Place the toppings nearby. Have a ¼-cup or equivalent ladle ready to scoop out sauce. Portion any cheese in advance. Set the oven peel nearby. Set up a separate area for finishing and cutting the pizza once it comes out of the oven: You'll need a cutting board, pizza roller cutter, finishing cheese (and Microplane), and finishing olive oil.
Stretching the pizza dough	Dust an oven peel with rice flour and have it at the ready. Once the dough balls are proofed, use a bench knife to scoop under one ball and move it onto a flour-dusted work surface. Use ample flour so that the dough does not stick to your

hands or to the work surface. The dough can be stretched on the work surface until it stretches no more, but then it should be picked up and stretched with fists closed to get it to its final diameter. Work as quickly as possible when the dough is off the counter to avoid tears, placing the dough down on the counter as much as needed, and reflouring your hands. Once the round reaches 12 inches, place the peel on the counter next to the round and transfer the round to the peel before adding the toppings.

Top the pizza while it is on the peel

Rearrange the dough on the peel so that it is circular and then top the pizza. For tomato-sauced pizzas, the back of a 2- or 4-ounce ladle is perfect to spread the sauce. An offset spatula works best for the cream for the clam pie (page 273). If you top the pizza before it's on the peel, it's not the end of the world. Carefully move the pizza with toppings onto the peel and proceed.

Bake the pizza

Open the oven door and place the peel with pizza toward the back of the baking stone. Use quick jerking movements to shimmy the pizza off the peel. As soon as the pizza hits the baking stone and sticks to it, slow down and stretch the pizza out. Bake the pizza until the crust is a golden amber brown and the cheese, if you're using it, has just melted. The hotter the oven, the faster this will happen.

Finish the pizza

Adding toppings after the pizza comes out of the oven adds another dimension of flavor, particularly with aged cheese and olive oil. The aged cheese gets the heat from the pizza to release its complex flavor.

Tomato Sauce

Makes 1½ cups

My tomato sauce is straightforward: crushed whole peeled tomatoes with a little salt added. Quality tomatoes are what take a pizza from mediocre to superb. And canned tomatoes vary significantly in terms of ripeness and sweetness (versus acidity). My favorite brand of whole peeled tomatoes is Gustarosso, which uses San Marzano tomatoes grown in the volcanic soil south of Naples. These can be purchased online via gustiamo.com. My second favorite is Jersey Fresh, which uses crushed tomatoes from New Jersey. When I use Jersey Fresh, I just add a little salt and then I'm good to go.

Canned whole peeled tomatoes	1 (28-ounce) can
Fine sea salt	A few pinches to taste

- Place a fine-mesh sieve over a small bowl, pour the canned tomatoes in, and drain off the tomato juice. Discard the tomato juice or add to any pasta tomato sauce.
- Over a small bowl, crush the tomatoes by hand. If the tomatoes do not break down easily, place them in the bowl and use a small hand blender to break them up. (A food processor will work if you do not have an immersion blender.) Be aware that a hand blender can incorporate air, so be careful when using.
- Add salt to taste and refrigerate in a covered container until ready to use or for up to 3 days in the refrigerator and up to 1 month in the freezer.

Finishing Toppings

When a pizza comes out of the oven, additional toppings are added. These are ingredients that accentuate the pizza, but are not baked in the oven because doing so would destroy their flavor. Typical finishing toppings are aged cheese and extra-virgin olive oil.

Choose a finishing **extra-virgin olive oil** of the highest quality. It should be nuanced and aromatic. Do the same for the **aged cheese**. Choose a 24- to 36-month-old aged Parmesan or pecorino. Grating the cheese on top of a pizza straight out of the oven lets the cheese just begin to melt and brings out all its umami.

Other finishing toppings include torn **fresh basil** leaves and **fresh lemon juice** squeezed over the pizza.

Pizza Rossa

Makes one 12-inch pizza

For the better part of my life I did not like pizza rossa. I could not understand why anyone would want to omit the cheese from the pizza. It seemed wrong to me. Occasionally I would try a slice of pizza rossa and agree with my opinion. The pizza would remind me of overbaked tomato paste. I had an epiphany while eating at Starita in Naples. Pizza rossa is really about the tomatoes. Using good-quality tomatoes, good flaky salt, and good olive oil make one of the simplest pizzas one of the best. Simplicity, when the best ingredients are used, makes the best pizza. Here is my take on the pizza rossa from Starita. I add baby tomatoes on top of the tomato sauce for texture.

Equipment A 12-inch oven peel (or rimless cookie sheet) and a 20 x 13½-inch baking stone.

Yeasted Pizza Dough (page 258) or Sourdough Pizza Dough (page 260)	1 dough ball	325 grams
Tomato Sauce (page 265)	½ cup	130 grams
Baby tomatoes, halved	½ cup	85 grams
Flaky sea salt	to taste	
For shaping		
Bread flour	for dusting	
For baking		
Rice flour	for dusting the peel	
For finishing		
Extra-virgin olive oil	for drizzling	
Aged Parmesan cheese	for grating	

· About 30 minutes before you plan to bake the pizza, arrange an oven rack in the center position with no racks above it. Place a baking stone on the rack and preheat the oven to 500°F.

· Lightly dust a work surface with flour. Set the dough ball down and dust its top with flour. Flatten the ball with the palm of your hand. Then make an indentation in the center of the ball using your index and middle fingers. Continue to press down and stretch the indentation, spreading the pizza out as far as it will initially go, leaving a ½-inch perimeter around the edge of the dough untouched for the crust. While shaping, occasionally dust underneath the pizza with flour so it does not stick to the work surface.

· Once the pizza has stretched as far as it will go, flour your hands and pick it up. With your fists underneath the pizza, gently but quickly move them apart to stretch the dough, moving your fists underneath the pizza so that it moves in a counterclockwise direction. If the pizza begins to stick to your hands or becomes too thin in one area, put the pizza down on the work surface, flour your hands, and pick it up again to continue to stretch it out. Stretch the dough until the pizza is 12 inches across.

• Dust an oven peel (or rimless cookie sheet) with coarse rice flour. Scoop up underneath the pizza with both hands and transfer it to the peel. Reshape if needed.

• Spoon the tomato sauce evenly over the pizza dough, spreading it out with the back of the spoon until it reaches ½ inch from the edge. Evenly scatter the halved tomatoes over the sauce and sprinkle generously with flaky salt.

• Open the oven door and place the peel toward the back of the baking stone. With a series of quick jerks, shake the pizza off the peel and onto the stone. Bake the pizza for 10 to 12 minutes, until the crust has fully inflated and is a burnished brown.

• Scoop underneath the pizza with the peel and remove it from the oven. Transfer it to a cutting board. Drizzle with extra-virgin olive oil and use a Microplane to generously grate the Parmesan over the pizza. Slice as desired and serve.

Pizza Margherita

Makes one 12-inch pizza

Margherita pizza is all about the tomatoes and the cheese. That's why the quality of both is important. Mozzarella in Italy is more acidic and grainier than American fresh mozzarella, primarily because it's made with raw milk, which has more microbial diversity and loads of lactic acid bacteria. When I choose fresh mozzarella, I like a fresh-tasting, rich, creamy mouthfeel and look for a locally produced artisanal cheese made with the best milk.

Equipment A 12-inch oven peel (or rimless cookie sheet) and a 20 x 13½-inch baking stone

Yeasted Pizza Dough (page 258) or Sourdough Pizza Dough (page 260)	1 dough ball	325 grams
Tomato Sauce (page 265)	¼ cup	65 grams
Fresh mozzarella cheese, cut into 1-inch pieces	½ cup	80 grams
For shaping		
Bread flour	for dusting	
For baking		
Rice flour	for dusting the peel	
For finishing		
Extra-virgin olive oil	for drizzling	
Aged Parmesan cheese	for grating	
Fresh basil leaves	several	

· About 30 minutes before you plan to bake the pizza, arrange an oven rack in the center position with no racks above it. Place the baking stone on the rack. Preheat the oven to 500°F.

· Lightly dust a work surface with flour. Set the ball down and dust its top with flour. Flatten the ball with the palm of your hand. Then make an indentation in the center of the ball using your index and middle fingers. Continue to press down and stretch the indentation, spreading the pizza out as far as it will initially go, leaving a ½-inch perimeter around the edge of the dough untouched for the crust. While shaping, occasionally dust underneath the pizza with flour so it does not stick to the work surface.

· Once the pizza has stretched as far as it will go, flour your hands and pick it up. With your fists underneath the pizza, gently but quickly move them apart to stretch the dough, moving your fists underneath the pizza so that it moves in a counterclockwise direction. If the pizza begins to stick to your hands or becomes too thin in one area, put the pizza down on the work surface, flour your hands, and pick it up again to continue to stretch it out. Stretch the dough until the pizza is 12 inches across.

- Dust an oven peel (or rimless cookie sheet) with coarse rice flour. Scoop up underneath the pizza with both hands and transfer it to the peel. Reshape if needed.
- Spoon the tomato sauce evenly over the pizza dough, spreading it out with the back of the spoon until it reaches ½ inch from the edge. Evenly place the mozzarella cubes over the sauce.
- Open the oven door and place the peel toward the back of the baking stone. With a series of quick jerks, shake the pizza off the peel and onto the stone. Bake the pizza for 10 to 12 minutes, until the crust has fully inflated and is a burnished brown and the mozzarella is melted.
- Scoop underneath the pizza with the peel and remove it from the oven. Transfer it to a cutting board. Drizzle with extra-virgin olive oil and use a Microplane to generously grate the Parmesan over the pizza. Scatter the basil leaves over the pizza. Slice as desired and serve.

Best Clam Pizza

Makes one 12-inch pizza

This is my favorite pizza recipe. The trick to a good clam pie is to save the broth from the clams, which has so much flavor, and add it to the cream. As the cream whips, the clam broth is added in a slow stream, like making mayonnaise. The clam cream is spread on top of the pizza and bakes into a delicious topping!

Equipment A 12-inch oven peel (or rimless cookie sheet) and a 20 x 13½-inch baking stone

All-purpose flour	for dusting	
Yeasted Pizza Dough (page 258) or Sourdough Pizza Dough (page 260)	1 dough ball	325 grams
Clam cream (from Clams and Clam Cream; recipe follows)	½ cup	75 grams
Chopped clams (from Clams and Clam Cream; recipe follows)	scant ¼ cup	30 grams
Chile flakes	Small pinch	
Flaky sea salt	Generous pinch	
For shaping		
Bread flour	for dusting	
For baking		
Rice flour	for dusting the peel	
For finishing		
Extra-virgin olive oil	for drizzling	
Aged pecorino cheese	for grating	
Parsley, finely chopped	2 sprigs	
Lemon wedge	1	

· Prepare the clams and clam cream several hours before you plan to bake the pizza, giving the clam broth enough time to chill down before it is added to the whipped cream.

· About 30 minutes before you plan to bake the pizza, arrange an oven rack in the center position with no racks above it. Place the baking stone on the center rack and preheat the oven to 500°F.

· Lightly dust your work surface with flour. Set the ball of dough down and dust its top with flour. Flatten the ball with the palm of your hand. Then make an indentation in the center of the ball, using your index and middle fingers. Continue to press down and stretch the indentation, spreading the pizza out as far as it will initially go, leaving a ½-inch perimeter around the edge of the dough untouched for the crust. While shaping, occasionally dust underneath the pizza with flour so it does not stick to the work surface.

· Once the pizza has stretched as far as it will go, flour your hands and pick it up. With your fists underneath the pizza, gently but quickly move them apart to stretch the dough, moving your fists underneath the pizza so that it moves in a counterclockwise direction. If the pizza begins to stick to your hands or becomes too thin in one area, put the pizza down on the work surface, flour your hands, and pick it up again to continue to stretch it out. Stretch the dough until the pizza is 12 inches across.

- Dust an oven peel (or rimless cookie sheet) with coarse rice flour. Scoop up underneath the pizza with both hands and transfer it to the peel. Reshape if needed.
- Spoon the clam cream evenly over the pizza dough, spreading it out with the back of the spoon until it reaches ½ inch from the edge. Evenly scatter the chopped clams on top and sprinkle with chile flakes and flaky salt.
- Open the oven door and place the peel toward the back of the baking stone. With a series of quick jerks, shake the pizza off the peel and onto the stone. Bake the pizza for 10 to 12 minutes, until the crust rim has fully inflated and is a burnished brown.
- Scoop underneath the pizza with the peel and remove it from the oven. Transfer it to a cutting board. Drizzle with extra-virgin olive oil and use a Microplane to generously grate the pecorino over the pizza. Sprinkle with chopped parsley. Slice as desired and serve with a wedge of lemon.

Clams and Clam Cream

**Makes 3 cups cream and
½ pound chopped clams**

Littleneck clams	24	
Extra-virgin olive oil	2 tablespoons	28 grams
Shallot, minced	1 large	
Garlic, thinly sliced	5 cloves	
Parsley	8 sprigs	
White wine	¼ cup	60 grams
Heavy cream	1 cup	240 grams

· Place the clams in a large colander and rinse them under cold water to remove any sand and debris. Place the rinsed clams in a large bowl and cover with cold water. Let the clams sit in the cold water for 30 minutes to purge any sand. Transfer the clams to the colander and rinse again with cold water.

· In a large pot, heat the olive oil over medium heat until it is shimmering. Add the shallot and garlic and sweat, stirring frequently, for 5 minutes, or until they are translucent.

· Add the parsley, wine, and clams to the pot and stir. Cover the pot with a lid and steam the clams for 5 to 7 minutes, until they open. Remove from the heat. With a large slotted spoon, transfer the clams to a large bowl. Discard any that haven't opened. Set the clams aside to cool.

· Meanwhile, bring the remaining liquid to a boil over medium heat. Cook down the clam broth for about 10 minutes, or until it is syrupy and reduced to about ½ cup. Strain the broth through a small sieve and into a medium bowl. Refrigerate the broth to cool it completely.

· When the clams have cooled, remove the meat from the shells and roughly chop. Transfer to a small covered dish and refrigerate until ready to use.

· In a stand mixer fitted with the whisk, whip the heavy cream on medium-high speed until firm peaks form. With the mixer running, slowly stream the cold clam broth down the side of the bowl to combine it with the whipped cream. Cover the bowl with plastic wrap and refrigerate the clam cream until ready to use.

Pizza Bianca

Makes three 12-inch pizzas

Pizza bianca is pizza dough that has been stretched, traditionally to a length of 6 feet, and baked with only olive oil and salt. It is sliced crosswise to make sandwiches, the most iconic of which is simply filled with mortadella. When I worked as a baker at Sullivan Street Bakery in New York, the most daunting task was stretching and loading all 6 feet of the pizza bianca into the oven. This recipe is for three smaller, more approachable pizza biancas, perfect for home baking.

    Equipment A 12-inch oven peel (or rimless cookie sheet) and a 20 x 13½-inch baking stone

    Note For sandwiches, the pizza can be sliced in half horizontally and liberally filled with mortadella.

Sourdough Pizza Dough (page 260) or Yeasted Pizza Dough (page 258)	3 balls	325 grams each
For shaping		
Bread flour	for dusting	
For baking		
Rice flour	for dusting the peel	
Extra-virgin olive oil	6 tablespoons	84 grams
Flaky sea salt	for sprinkling	

- About 30 minutes before you plan to bake the pizzas, arrange an oven rack in the center position with no racks above it. Place a baking stone on the center rack. Preheat the oven to 500°F.
- Lightly dust your work surface with flour. Set one ball of dough down and dust its top with flour. Flatten the ball with the palm of your hand. Dust your fingertips and use them to poke dimples all over the dough. Drizzle about 1 tablespoon olive oil over the top of the dough, letting it fall into the dimples. Continue to dimple the dough all over to deflate the round and distribute the olive oil. With both hands, gently pick up the dough and stretch it out into a rectangle as far as it will stretch, about 12 inches long and 6 to 8 inches wide. Place it back onto the work surface. Drizzle the dough with 1 more tablespoon of olive oil and a generous sprinkling of flaky salt.
- Dust an oven peel with coarse rice flour. Scoop underneath the pizza bianca with both hands and transfer it to the peel. Rearrange and spread it out into a square. It will be a bit scrunched up on the peel, but you will stretch it out to a rectangle in the oven.
- Open the oven door and place the peel toward the back and left side of the baking stone. With a series of jerks, shake the pizza off the peel, stretching it into a rectangular shape as you pull out the peel.
- Bake the pizza for 10 to 12 minutes, until it is bubbled and golden brown. Remove it from the oven with the peel and transfer to a cooling rack.
- Continue to shape and bake the remaining pizzas in the same way.
- To serve, cut slices with a pair of kitchen scissors.

Pistachio Pesto with Burrata

Makes 1 cup pesto, serves 6 to 8

This pesto recipe has a sweet and tangy flavor profile. The sweetness comes from the golden raisins and is balanced by the freshly squeezed lemon juice. I love pairing this with a creamy burrata and dipping slices of pizza bianca into it.

Extra-virgin olive oil	⅓ cup + 1 tablespoon	90 grams
Garlic, thinly sliced	3 cloves	
Golden raisins	¼ cup	45 grams
Basil leaves, julienned	2 cups, lightly packed	60 grams
Lemon juice	1 tablespoon	15 grams
Fine sea salt	½ teaspoon	3 grams
Shelled pistachios, toasted	¼ cup	45 grams
Burrata	1 large ball	226 grams
Pizza Bianca (page 276)	1 pizza	

- In a small skillet, heat 1 tablespoon of the olive oil over medium-high heat. Add the garlic and cook for about 2 minutes, just to soften and lightly color the edges. Remove from the heat and scoop into a small bowl to cool.
- Place the raisins in a small bowl, cover with hot tap water, and set aside to soak for 10 minutes. Drain the raisins in a sieve.
- In a food processor, pulse the basil until the leaves are finely chopped but not pulverized. With the machine running, slowly drizzle in the remaining ⅓ cup olive oil. Add the lemon juice, salt, pistachios, cooled garlic, and any oil in the pan, and raisins and process until the pesto is cohesive, with small chunks of pistachios remaining.
- Refrigerate the pesto in a covered container until you're ready to use it or for up to 1 week.
- To serve, place the burrata in the center of a plate and tear open. Drizzle the pesto around the burrata and serve with pieces of pizza bianca.

Cumin, Turmeric, and Onion Sourdough Focaccia

Makes 1 focaccia

This focaccia recipe is a keeper. I add ground turmeric to the dough, and then I sweat onions with cumin seeds and fold those in as well. The onion filling is sweet and earthy and brings together the spices. I think this is a perfect bread to serve with eggs or a hearty stew.

Equipment A 13 x 18-inch baking sheet

			Baker's %
Sourdough Starter			
Water (70°–75°F)	2 tablespoons + 2 teaspoons	40 grams	100
Mother sourdough starter	1 tablespoon	25 grams	62.5
Bread flour	⅓ cup	40 grams	100
For the dough			
Water (70°–75°F)	1⅔ cups	392 grams	69
Bread flour	4¼ cups + more for dusting	510 grams	89
Spelt flour	½ cup	60 grams	11
Ground turmeric	1 tablespoon	8 grams	1.4
For the onion filling			
Yellow onions	2 medium	300 grams	
Extra-virgin olive oil	¼ cup	60 grams	
Fine sea salt	Big pinch		
Ground turmeric	1 tablespoon	8 grams	
Cumin seeds	3 tablespoons	24 grams	
Sourdough Starter (above)	½ cup + 2 tablespoons	105 grams	18
Fine sea salt	2½ teaspoons	15 grams	2.6
To finish			
Extra-virgin olive oil	3 tablespoons	45 grams	
Flaky sea salt	for sprinkling		

Mix the starter

▪ Mix the sourdough starter 4 to 5 hours before making the dough. Put the water in a 1-quart container with a lid. Add 25 grams (1 tablespoon) of the ripened mother sourdough starter to the container. Add the flour and stir with a metal spoon to combine. Cover the container and set aside in a warm place (about 75°F) for 4 to 5 hours, until it is ripe and passes the Float Test (page xxxi).

Autolyse the water, flours, and turmeric

▪ Put the water, bread flour, spelt flour, and turmeric in shallow 3- to 4-quart lidded container and stir with a metal spoon to combine. Cover the container and set it aside in a warm place (about 75°F) for about 1 hour to autolyse. While the dough is autolysing, make the onion filling.

For more information on why we are resting the dough before mixing the sourdough starter, salt, and onion filling into the dough, see Autolyse (page 5).

Make the onion filling

- Halve the onions root to tip. Cut crosswise into slices ⅛ inch thick.
- In a large skillet, heat the oil over medium heat. Add the onion slices and salt and cook without browning the onions for 5 minutes, stirring frequently. Add the turmeric and cumin seeds and continue to cook for 5 minutes more. Set the mixture aside for 30 minutes to cool in the pan to room temperature.

Add the sourdough starter to the dough

- As soon as the starter is ripe, add it to the dough, mixing it with your hand by scooping your hand under the dough and folding it into the center until the starter is thoroughly mixed in. Re-cover the container and set aside. Let the dough rest for 30 minutes.

Add the salt and onion filling to the dough

- Uncover the dough and mix the onion filling and the fine sea salt into it by scooping under the dough with a wet hand and folding it into the center until the dough is homogeneous. Re-cover the container and set aside. Let the dough rest for 1 hour.

Make 2 stretch and folds and retard the dough

- Uncover the dough. With wet hands, scoop underneath the top edge of the dough, stretch it out, and fold it down two-thirds of the way toward the bottom edge. Stretch out and fold the bottom edge up to meet the top edge, as if you were folding a letter, pressing on the dough just enough to get it to stay in place. Do the same with the two sides, stretching and folding the right edge two-thirds of the way toward the left edge, and stretching and folding the left edge to meet the right edge. Then flip the dough upside down. This is your first fold. Re-cover the container and set the dough aside for 1 hour.
- Repeat stretching and folding the dough a second time for a second fold. Re-cover and place the dough in the refrigerator to retard overnight or for a minimum of 12 hours.

Shape the focaccia

- Remove the dough from the refrigerator and let it rest, covered, at room temperature for 1 hour.
- Pour the 3 tablespoons olive oil onto the 13 x 18-inch baking sheet and spread it around with your fingers to completely coat the bottom and sides. Use a plastic bowl scraper to scrape the dough onto the baking sheet in a big lump. Dip your fingers in the olive oil on the baking sheet and use them to coat the top of the dough with the olive oil. Let the dough rest for about 20 minutes without disturbing it. (It does not need to be covered because the oil provides a protective barrier to prevent the surface of the dough from drying out.)
- Dip your hands in the oil on the baking sheet. Slide your hands under the lump of dough and gently stretch it out toward the sides of the baking sheet.

Press your fingertips into the surface of the dough to dimple it and stretch it evenly toward the sides of the baking sheet. When the dough starts to spring back, stop dimpling and stretching and let it rest for 20 minutes, then resume, dimpling and stretching the dough until it reaches the edges of the baking sheet. Set the dough aside in a warm place to proof for 45 minutes.

Assemble and bake the focaccia

- About 30 minutes before you plan to bake, arrange a rack in the center position and preheat the oven to 425°F.
- Place the focaccia on the center rack of the oven and bake for 30 to 35 minutes, until the surface and underside of the focaccia are golden grown (use an offset spatula to lift it up and peek), rotating the baking sheet front to back halfway through the baking time.
- Remove the focaccia from the oven. Using a large offset spatula, carefully slide it out of the baking sheet and onto a cooling rack. Once cool, cut into squares and serve.

Acknowledgments

When I began writing my first book, *A Good Bake*, I knew I wanted to follow it with a second book that included my bread recipes. When I proposed the idea to my editor, one of the things I said was "Bagels are bread, and all of my bread recipes should be in one place." Thank you, Lexy Bloom, for believing in this book. It was a difficult book for me to write, and the first book I've written without a cowriter. You believed in me and in my writing the entire time. And you were incredibly patient with me.

Thank you, Janis Donnaud. You also believed in me when I did not believe in myself. You listened to me. You were my advocate, and you were a tough cookie when I needed it.

Thank you, Tom Pold, for all of the editing work. I think you had a tough job, and I am grateful for all of your help. I also want to thank Carolynn Carreño, who cowrote *A Good Bake* with me. Your expertise and writing on my first book guided me in writing this one.

And thank you to the entire team at Knopf, from the meticulousness of the copy editing to the beautiful design—I am proud of this book.

Thank you to my photographer, Dana Gallagher. Your photographs gorgeously capture my bread. You are a perfectionist at your craft, and I loved working with you. Frances Boswell, I am in awe of your food styling. You made my bread look delicious, and you made the things that go with my bread look so delicious that I wanted to eat them all on the set. I came away from our sessions wanting to re-create all the foods that you cooked. Thank you. Ayesha Patel, not only were all of your props meticulous and beautiful, but you also led the way in creating the direction of the photos we shot. Thank you.

The recipes and knowledge within this book come from years of work and learning, and I want to thank all of those mentors and teachers along the way from whom I have learned. Jim Lahey, my knowledge of bread and fermentation blossomed while working at Sullivan Street Bakery under your tutelage. Nancy Silverton, your bread book taught me about sourdough. Dan Leader, you gave me my very first bakery job. It was a tough one, but one where I learned so much, and I am very appreciative. And thank you, Camron Kaiser, for all of your eager enthusiasm in testing recipes.

Index

C

Pumpkin Cinnamon Swirl Challah, 212–13

R

radishes, in Veggie Cream Cheese, 80, *81*

raisin(s):

    Cinnamon Bagels, 61–63

    Petits Pains de Seigle aux, 185–89, *187*

    Pumpernickel Bagels, 47–51, *49*

Red Onion Pickles, 110–11

Reinhart, Peter, 4

resting dough, 7

retarding dough, xxvi, 11

Rhubarb Strawberry Mountain Pies, 154–55

rice flours:

    brown rice, xvi

    for dusting bannetons and linen couche, 235

rising of dough:

    first. *See* fermentation

    second (proofing), 7, 11

Roast Beef Triple Deckers, 139–40

roasting pan lid, enamelware rectangular, xx

Roberta's, Brooklyn, xi, 32, 118, 202, 256

rolling out laminated dough, 166, 167

rolling pin, xxiv

rolls:

    Chapeau, 175–78, *176*

    Chocolate Brandied Cherry, 190–91

    Classic Parker House, 179–80

    Green Olive, 195–96, *197*

    Petits Pains de Seigle aux Raisins, 185–89, *187*

    Seeded Hoagie, *198,* 199–201

round loaves:

    baking in Dutch oven, xx

    Pain Ordinaire, *10,* 11–13

proofing in banneton, 7

    shaping, 6, *14–15*

Russian Dressing, 140

rye (flour), xvi

    Bagels, Marbled, 55–57

    for dusting bannetons and linen couche, 235

    for making sourdough starter from scratch, xxvi

    Marbled, *128,* 129–35

    Petits Pains de Seigle aux Raisins, 185–89, *187*

    Pullman, Caraway, 136–38

    Pumpernickel Raisin Bagels, 47–51, *49*

    Sprouted, Miche, 125–27

Rye (berries), Sprouted, Miche, 125–27

S

Sable, Togarashi-Cured, 76, *77*

Sadelle's, New York, xi, 26, 32, 94

salads:

    Chicken, Coronation, 221

    Coleslaw, 140

    Egg, My Favorite, 85

    Salmon, Baked, 84

    Whitefish, Smoked, *82, 83*

salami, in Italian Combo Sandwiches, 202–5, *203*

salmon:

    Baked, Salad, 84

    Beet-Cured, *78,* 79

    Gravlax, Dill and Black Pepper, *74,* 75

    gravlax, in The Works (bagel sandwich), 87

    Lox, Eggs, and Onion, 89

Salsa Ranchera, 104, *105,* 107

A NOTE ABOUT THE AUTHOR

MELISSA WELLER received a James Beard Award nomination for
Outstanding Baker in 2016. A French Culinary Institute graduate,
she trained at Babbo and Sullivan Street Bakery in New York City.
She was chef-partner at High Street on Hudson; the head baker at
Per Se, Bouchon Bakery, and Roberta's; an owner and founder of
Sadelle's; and the head baker at Walnut Street Café in Philadelphia.
Melissa graduated from Bucknell University with degrees in
international relations and chemical engineering and worked as an
engineer before switching her career to baking. She lives in Brooklyn.

A NOTE ABOUT THE TYPE

The text in this book was set in Miller, a transitional-style typeface designed by Matthew Carter (b. 1937) with assistance from Tobias Frere-Jones and Cyrus Highsmith of the Font Bureau. Modeled on the roman family of fonts popularized by Scottish type foundries in the nineteenth century, Miller is named for William Miller, founder of the Miller & Richard foundry of Edinburgh.

The Miller family of fonts has a large number of variants for use as text and display, as well as Greek characters based on the renowned handwriting of British classicist Richard Porson.

Composed by North Market Street Graphics
Lancaster, Pennsylvania

Printed and bound by C&C Offset
China

Designed by Pei Loi Koay and Anna B. Knighton